HARDBALL LOBBYING FOR NONPROFITS

HARDBALL LOBBYING FOR NONPROFITS
REAL ADVOCACY FOR NONPROFITS IN THE NEW CENTURY

Barry Hessenius

First published in 2007 by
PALGRAVE MACMILLAN™
175 Fifth Avenue, New York, N.Y. 10010 and
Houndmills, Basingstoke, Hampshire, England RG21 6XS.
Companies and representatives throughout the world.

PALGRAVE MACMILLAN is the global academic imprint of the Palgrave Macmillan
division of St. Martin's Press, LLC and of Palgrave Macmillan Ltd. Macmillan® is a
registered trademark in the United States, United Kingdom and other countries.palgrave
is a registered trademark in the European Union and other countries.

ISBN-10: 1-4039-8202-3
ISBN-13: 978-1-4039-8202-5

Library of Congress Cataloging-in-Publication Data

Hessenius, Barry.
    Hardball lobbying for nonprofits : real advocacy for nonprofits in the new century /
Barry Hessenius.
        p. cm.
    Includes index.
    ISBN 1-4039-8202-3 (alk.paper)
        1. Nonprofit organizations—United States. 2. Lobbying—United States.   I. Title. II.
Title: Hardball lobbying for nonprofits.

    HD2769.2.U6H45 2007
    338.7′4—dc22

                                                                                    2007060511

A catalogue record for this book is available from the British Library.

Design by Macmillan India Ltd.

First edition: June 2007

10 9 8 7 6 5 4 3 2 1

Transferred to Digital Printing 2012

This work is dedicated to all of those principled and compassionate people on the staffs and boards of directors of America's nonprofit organizations, as well as the volunteers of these organizations, in particular those in the arts and culture field, who have so selflessly and tirelessly given back to our country,

and

to those extraordinarily talented and visionary people at the nation's foundations, who have improved and enriched the lives of countless millions of Americans through their strategic thinking.

And wherever you are Mom and Dad, Warren, and Dexter, I think of you all still.

Contents

FOREWORD

Just because you don't take an interest in politics doesn't mean politics won't take an interest in you.

Pericles

This work is primarily a step-by-step tutorial on building, maintaining, and operating an effective nonprofit advocacy and/or lobbying effort. It gives details of how lobbying really works and explains various parts of the machinery of a lobbying effort heretofore not discussed in current advocacy manuals, including such topics as how to pay for it, how to motivate people, and how to organize the structure. Finally, it examines the background nuances that govern action on the nonprofit stage, and considers the role that nonprofit advocacy and lobbying might play and the impact a rethinking and retooling of a new approach to advocacy and lobbying might have in serving and protecting not only the nonprofit sector but democracy itself.

***

Lobbying has been corrupted by money and candidates' increasing need for money to get elected. According to the Center for Public Integrity, Washington D.C., in 2003/2004 federal elections, payments of nearly *two billion dollars* in fees to lobbyists were reported. It is difficult to discern the total contributions by interest groups or individuals to candidate campaigns motivated by the desire to gain access to decision makers or directly influence government decision making, but it is important to note that 96 percent of all people in America don't contribute anything to candidate campaigns, and less than 0.2 percent of the population gave over 86 percent of all political contributions.

The most flagrant abuses of the system make headlines every decade, but the resultant cries for reform have thus far failed to "fix" the process. Reform comes every so often, and there are changes and improvements, but the problem of how to reconcile the imposition of meaningful restrictions with protection of free speech makes it virtually impossible to completely overhaul the system as it exists.

It is not the purpose of this work to argue for reform or propose ways to implement it, but rather to suggest that until real reform is effected, if ever, nonprofits, if they want to have any chance of competing for access to decision makers and influence decision making, *need to play the game by the same rules that the private-sector special interests do.* The central goal of this book is to make the case for integrating the advocacy and/or lobbying function into the nonprofit organizational structure and for including it in the job description of all nonprofit leadership (as important as any other function of management, including fund-raising and program oversight); to argue that lobbying is a critically essential element of advocacy; and to put forward the proposition that support for, and involvement in, the election of specific candidates has become an indispensable cornerstone of successful lobbying.

Effective nonprofit advocacy efforts need full-time, dedicated staff. Nonprofits have the resources, ability, and capacity to build powerful coalitions that can raise substantial amounts of money to fund competitive and professional efforts—*if* they make the commitment. Nonprofit coalitions will need to create a 501c(4), a political action committee, and a 527 organization/fund in order to avail themselves of all of the lobbying tools used by the private sector (see chapter 4). It is time for nonprofits to shed the yoke of the past and to play "hardball" when and where necessary so as to compete with private-sector special interests in the attempt to influence governmental decision making as part of an overall strategy to protect and advance their missions.

This work is then an attempt to frame the nonprofit lobbying issues for the new millennium—a framework currently under construction by default and one likely to change many times in the coming decades. It is an argument for the nonprofit field to make wholesale changes in its basic approach to lobbying by including candidate support as an integral part of an overall strategy; it is a plea for nonprofits to embrace lobbying as a core management function. It is an updating and expansion of the application of the traditional tools, mechanisms, logistics, and rules of engagement, as it were, used by nonprofits to advocate and lobby. It assumes that forming coalitions of like-minded nonprofits and retention of full-time, dedicated staff are both prerequisites to building a successful effort; that advocacy cannot be a solely volunteer enterprise; and, that even a minimal apparatus will require raising funds to pay for adequately staffing the machinery. *This is not your father's advocacy book*—it is a plea to rethink, reinvent, and retool the nonprofit advocacy and/or lobby paradigm for the new century; to develop the capacity to play "hard ball" so that nonprofits will be regarded as serious players; and to embrace all aspects of lobbying as a means of exerting influence on government decision making.

Beyond this argument, this book is a detailed "how to" guide for effective advocacy and lobbying at any level——including organization, management, strategic planning, and the use of "nuts and bolts" tools to *make the case* for a given position and communicate with decision makers, the media, and the public.

ACKNOWLEDGMENTS

The author would like to thank and acknowledge the following people, without whose kind and gracious support, insights, suggestions, and valuable assistance, this book would not have been possible:

I am deeply in debt to Bruce Davis for his unwavering support, his unflinching friendship, and his insightful suggestions. I am similarly indebted to John Kriedler for the benefit of his extraordinary intellect and his continuing kindness toward me.

I owe a debt of gratitude to Paul Minicucci, Nina Ozlu, and Anthony Radich for their help with the editing of this work and their suggestions for changes. Paul, in particular, taught me much of what I know about government and lobbying. I am also in debt to Betty Plumb and Tim Wolfort, both of whom provided me with materials and comments.

I am particularly grateful to Moy Eng, the performing arts program officer for the William and Flora Hewlett Foundation, who continued to believe in me and what I was trying to do in the arts when I doubted myself. She became a friend, champion, and source of extraordinarily good advice and counsel. Cora Mirikitani, likewise, gave me the benefit of her sage and wise advice, and she too gave me the gift of believing in me. She has become a wonderful and true friend. Other members of the foundation community who have been generous to me with their insights and support include Nancy Glaze, Tom Peters, Bruce Sievers, Francis Phillips, John Killacky, and Harold Williams.

I am especially grateful to Congressman Adam Schiff, with whom I have had the pleasure and privilege of working extensively, as well as to the late Marco Firebaugh, former California State assemblyman and majority party leader. I am grateful to former California governor Gray Davis and the California Arts Council chairman Steven Fogel for giving me the opportunity to serve in state government.

I would like to thank Aaron Javsicas and the people at Palgrave Macmillan, my agent, Maureen Watts, and the incredibly thorough, patient, and skilled copyeditors at Macmillan India.

INTRODUCTION: THE VALUE OF NONPROFIT LOBBYING TO DEMOCRACY

There exists in human nature a paralytic dichotomy between our instinct for survival, for protecting ourselves and our territories—a basic "me first" human nature greed—and the loftier aspirations we have for the good of the whole, that deep yearning we have to be a part of something bigger than the smaller tribes (sometimes a tribe of one) to which we belong. We instinctively act and react to protect ourselves, while at the same time we form societies not only because we know we can benefit from cooperation, but because as pack animals we intuitively understand that there are both tangible and intangible benefits from belonging to a group. We cherish the rights of the individual; they are democracy's greatest strength. Yet we join together because the reward of the "sense" *and* reality of community is a highly prized benefit. The elusive balance between the two is what we strive to achieve.

This conflict manifests itself in many ways, including in our political system. We seem unable, at this point, to reconcile these two opposite forces into a workable, balanced, and fair protocol for conducting our political affairs and carrying on our governmental functions. Citizens, including corporate citizens, ought to have the right to make their case to government officials. The issue is how to ensure that access to those officials is open to all, irrespective of wealth or position, and that decisions are made on the merits of competing interests. In this context, the "for profit" sector justifies the bottom line as the only value for its investor base, and argues that anything that undermines its ability to maximize profit is harmful to the whole. Corporate America has, without apology, embraced the notion that any approach other than its own self-interest would be a breach of its fiduciary duty; that what is good for it *is* good for the whole, effectively burying its role as corporate *citizen* (and largely ignoring that shareholder value is the real bottom line, not profit). Other special- interest groups have adopted this rationale for defending their priorities as immune to any outside argument of a larger common good.

We are a pluralistic society, and interest groups, seeking to advance and protect themselves, behave exactly as they are expected to. The structure of representative government, elected by the people, was to be our system's built-in protection of the whole of us—fairly elected officeholders were to represent their constituent groups, free from any obligations to special interests. Unfortunately, money has corrupted the system and compromised both the fairness of the electoral process as well as the independence and impartiality of elected officials. Money has created an inequity of access to the decision-making process, with those that offer it having a disproportionate advantage in consideration of their needs. Support or opposition to legislation has become as much about political considerations as about the merits of the proposals.

The negative impact of special-interest money on how we elect people to public office as part of a larger strategy to influence how and what decisions government makes is not a potential threat but a reality. Promulgation of laws and regulations to curb the excesses of this abuse of the system and wrest power from the wealthy few, as the means to return democracy to the whole of the people, has thus far been a fool's paradise. Every reform has been fought tooth and nail to prevent its passage, and sidestepped and skirted after its adoption. Those charged with reform of the system include those who most benefit from the way it is currently organized. As the juggernaut that is our money-influenced process to elect officeholders rolls on despite attempts to stop it, some other systemic solution needs to be found.

Nonprofit corporations are by definition organized for the *public benefit*. They might have played a role in balancing the instinct for the self by being the counterpoint to special interests and advocating the larger "us," but, by and large, nonprofit advocacy has thus far been conspicuous by its absence. The instinct for survival by the individual—person or organization— overlapped the desire for the collective good long ago. Special-interest pluralism has devolved to a situation in which money rules the roost. The dirty little secret in democracy is not that the emperor is naked, as it were, but that *nudity* has become a fashion statement. It isn't enough that we haven't found a way to balance our love for the sanctity of individual freedom with the instincts we have to serve the pack, it's that John Kennedy's question—*"ask not what your country can do for you . . ."*—isn't even being seriously asked anymore.

In this context, the rationale behind IRS regulations seeking to limit nonprofit lobbying efforts because of the special tax status accorded to "public-benefit corporations" is exactly the opposite of what the policy should be. Lawmakers rely on lobbyists, as experts, to make known the complexities of various issues. The problem is that too often, there are no lobbyists on the other side of any issue, certainly not with equal resources, and thus there is a disparate presentation of information, with decision makers, who lack the time to thoroughly investigate all sides of every issue, getting a one-sided, jaundiced picture.

By advocating and lobbying for the benefits they confer, nonprofits will be advancing their mission, which is, by definition, to benefit the public. As "public" special-interest groups, with the same resources and power as private, special interests, nonprofits can provide a balancing counterpoint to the current dominance of the process by special, private-interest lobbying. A nonprofit sector commitment to advocacy and lobbying, including participation in the financing of the campaigns of those who seek public office, as a core function of nonprofit management, will help to further nonprofit agendas and protect and defend against both direct attacks and negative impacts brought about by their absence from decision-making tables; in the process, democracy may be served.

Nonprofits, lobbying for the public good, for the "whole" of society, should not only be allowed to lobby with virtually no restrictions (certainly no greater restrictions than those in the private sector), but, at the least, encouraged to do so. An argument *requiring* action in this arena as reasonable in exchange for special tax status isn't so far afoot. There must be a way to finance voices for the public so that the public voice can be heard. I would argue that 501c(3) public benefit corporations should, at least, be able to lobby to the same extent as private-sector interests, *and* that it is in democracy's best interest to continue to allow donations to the 501c(3) to be tax deductible. I would also argue that nonprofits should engage in all of the same advocacy and lobbying activities that private-sector interests engage in. Unfortunately, that is not the reality.

The range of nonprofit activity is as broad as society itself. The net effect of expanding nonprofit lobbying will be to empower a full range of people's advocates. The people who belong to numerous special-interest groups are the same people who contribute to nonprofits. While the selfishness of some will keep them from continuing to contribute if they perceive a threat to their self-interest, I would argue that there is a huge reservoir of people who yearn for a way to advance the "whole of us"; that this is a way to allow us to express both our self-interest and our need to support the whole, and in so doing protect the very democracy that allows us to be selfish. Under this theory, we don't need to create a new Common Cause; it isn't necessary to launch a new organization. Rather, if all existing nonprofits lobbied for themselves actively, the net result would be what the framers of all of the Common Cause type trial balloons envisioned.

When both sides are equally well funded, when candidates for office don't need the funds or blessing of any one organization or sector, when blocs of voters on both sides of an issue are organized, those previously holding the monopoly will be neutralized. There may well be geographical territories where a majority is on one side, but there will likely be territories where the other side is in the majority as well. It won't be a perfect balance, but any return of the pendulum toward the center will be a marked improvement.

I do not suggest this simple change will be the panacea for greed and fear in the political system. Certainly, nothing in the political system or the social fabric changes, except by the influence of an untold number of interdependent variables operating simultaneously in ways so complex to make them impossible to unravel. I am only suggesting that a radical change by nonprofits in their prioritization in the area of advocacy and lobbying, *and their participation in campaign financing,* might well be one of the more critical variables in a return to a balance in our political decision-making process. I am not arguing for broad, social agenda lobbying by nonprofits, whatever their political leanings, but for their lobbying for legislation, regulations, and their becoming involved in supporting and helping to finance candidate campaigns for elected office, as a way to further *their specific organizational missions.* In so doing, in the aggregate, they will constitute a counter force to private-sector lobbying.

I leave for others to predict the consequences of letting the current system of political decision making, compromised by a "pay to play" ethic that only a few can afford, continue to run rampant. If we haven't yet reached critical mass, it certainly won't be long now. And so we must consider any approach available to us.

The role the nonprofit sector might play as a force within the public-policy arena is potentially staggering—in terms of organization, mobilization of grassroots citizen armies, fund-raising, lobbying activities, and changing media coverage of the political process. According to the IRS and 2000 census data, there are over two million nonprofits, employing five to ten million people and involving another ten million directly as board members and volunteers; an industry with an army of expert fund-raisers that generates over $150 billion in annual contributions alone, exclusive of churches, and not counting other revenue streams. Those two million nonprofits are really just two million small businesses, for nonprofits have the same problems and bring the same advantages to communities as do any other small business. The percentage of people in the United States who give something to nonprofits is a robust 70 (according to the American Association of Fundraising)—a clear majority of people who understand in some measure the need for the greater good. The nonprofit sector has the potential to change the entire political decision-making process and representative government, *if* it wakes up from its long and deep slumber. And it will benefit both itself and the whole of the public in so doing.

SUMMARY

Nonprofits are the voices of the whole of us. It is, I would argue, time to empower those voices so that they may be heard over the shouting and the din of private-sector interests that have for too long monopolized the stage; it is time to use the private sector's own tools to advance a bigger agenda, and perhaps, in the process, begin to change the very priorities of society. All of us are, every day, faced with the conundrum of what is good for our private lives and what is good for the whole of us, and there is no question that we compartmentalize each so that we don't have to address the conflict between the two. The most obvious example of that conflict is our investment in corporations whose obsession is the bottom line, while they sometimes engage in activities and practices that hurt us—as individuals and as members of the whole. The time has come, perhaps, to at least engage in the dialogue about where and how to balance self-interest and the welfare of the whole. Giving greater voice to the nonprofit sector, or more accurately, expanding the means and increasing the tools to communicate with that voice, may be one way to begin to resolve this conflict that lies at the heart of the health of the republic.

This is not a casebook—presenting models to be replicated, analyzing what went right and what went wrong for specific organizations or specific campaigns in the past. It is also not specifically a primer for the individual 501c(3) nonprofit organization, but rather aimed at "fields" of nonprofits. There are many books and online guides that offer the 501c(3) persuasive arguments why they should advocate and even lobby, what is and isn't permissible, and the basic approach such advocacy and lobbying involves. Many of these resources also touch on how nonprofits can form coalitions and work together, and encourage them to do so. This is an attempt to move the marker two or three steps forward—to engage in a deeper examination and discussion of the "how to" aspects of lobbying and the related ancillary subjects such as how to finance, manage, and motivate the operation, often ignored in other works on the subject. Finally, it is an argument for nonprofits to make lobbying, including candidate support, a core function of their operations.

CHAPTER 1

FRAMING THE CONTEXT FOR A NEW APPROACH

We must do the things we think we cannot do.

Eleanor Roosevelt

The topic of nonprofit advocacy is unwieldy and complex. Indeed, the very term "advocacy" has different meanings depending on who is defining the term, or to whom and which activities it is being applied.

To advocate is *to plead the cause of something; to support it.* To lobby is *to attempt to influence or sway (as a public official—elected or otherwise) toward a desired action, particularly as related to specific legislation.* Dissemination of information and efforts to educate and inform public officials and the public or media are advocacy efforts, but not lobbying, *as long as they are not accompanied by a request for specific support or opposition to specific legislation.*

NONPROFIT ADVOCACY VERSUS LOBBYING

Pleading their cause is part of the raison d'etre of most nonprofits. Increasingly, nonprofit advocacy is related to the attempt to influence the decision making of elected officials. While advocacy encompasses activities (e.g., educational materials) only indirectly related to influencing government decision making, lobbying seeks to directly impact an authorizing environment's decision making. Advocacy is more of a generic term, while lobbying has a legal definition and legal and/or tax consequences. The distinction is important primarily because nonprofits may advocate without limitation but may lobby only within prescribed limitations and rules and regulations. Lobbying is but one form of advocacy.

Generically, advocacy has become a catchall term to describe the myriad forms of activity included in the attempt to rally support and leverage influence. There are multiple types of nonprofits and layers of advocacy goals and strategies. There are industry nonprofits, whose purpose is to lobby for private-sector objectives including, as often as not, pure profit motives, under the guise of impartiality; ad hoc lobbying efforts borne out of the need to support or defeat certain legislation or ballot initiatives; citizen lobbying group nonprofits formed solely for the purpose of advancing a political or social agenda; charitable nonprofits, religious based and otherwise, that address the societal needs of underserved populations, some of which have adopted governmental policy relationships as part of their service to their declared clients; traditional nonprofits in dozens of fields, from arts and culture to those concerned with the environment; health-centered nonprofits; and nonprofits focused on human rights and social justice. Of these, there are a few large national nonprofits with substantial political clout and presence—not only in Washington, D.C., but also in state capitols across the country; there are also successful grassroots efforts, and there are anemic coalitions of nonprofits with no more than a modicum of advocacy or lobbying activity at any level. The silent majority of traditional nonprofits are not involved in real advocacy and/or lobbying at all.

Lobbying is defined within the rules and regulations of the IRS delineations of nonprofit status based on permissible and prohibited activities. Thus, within the twenty-one-plus categories of nonprofit organizations as formed by the IRS, trade unions, associations, and 501c(4) nonprofit organizations are permitted almost unfettered issue-oriented (but not candidate-oriented) "lobbying" activity, but are denied tax-deduction status for contributions made to them. On the other hand, 501c(3) nonprofit lobby activities are prescribed and regulated (again, no candidate support), but donations to them are tax deductible. Reliance solely on the IRS classification to paint a clear picture of the advocacy and/or lobbying efforts of the nation's nonprofit sector is not wholly adequate when compared with the actual political aggressiveness of a given organization or field of nonprofits. Coalitions of like-minded nonprofits, formed specifically to represent the advocacy and political objectives of a field, are a growing trend that may skew the raw IRS classification numbers and obfuscate the real picture of who is doing what.

Indeed, the data suggest that very few nonprofits lobby in the strict sense of the word, and the total expenditure in this area of those that do is a relatively tiny percentage of their budgets. According to a paper by Jeff Krehely for the Urban Institute, "Less than 1.5% of all nonprofits filing IRS 960 forms are engaged in lobbying, and those groups spent less than 1.7% of their budgets on the activity. Of those that did report lobbying expenses, those situated in just eight states accounted for over 40% of all lobbying activity, and 60% of all funds spent. Forty-three percent of all expenditures for lobbying by nonprofits were spent by organizations in the health or related fields."

Of course, not all nonprofits report all activities that might be classified as lobbying. Many efforts of nonprofits to inform the public, educate lawmakers, and otherwise explain and expand on what they do and the positive impact they have are legitimately excluded from the lobbying classification, even though they are the foundational groundwork for real *lobbying*. Doubtless, other informal, ad hoc activity by *individuals* within nonprofit structures is lobbying in the strictest sense, but goes unreported. And some lobbying activity simply isn't officially reported.

Any system of quantifying complex activity is fraught with variations that skew the data, and cooperative ventures is no exception. Still, it is clear that by and large traditional nonprofit organizations and coalitions of sectors within various fields in the nonprofit world are not yet involved in any meaningful way in lobbying relative to legislation or in the campaigns of specific candidates for public office, compared with the private sector. As yet, nonprofits are simply not part of the spectrum.

If you do the same thing you always have, you are likely to get the same results you have always gotten . . .

Although nonprofits have stepped up advocacy and lobbying, there is little indication of any profound change in their approach, which is to just "make the case" for their cause or position. There is also little indication of any refocus of energies on strategies and use of "insider hardball tactics"—for example, use of professional lobbyists or candidate financial support and endorsement. Among nonprofits, there is some indication of increased activity in the area of mobilizing grassroots public support as a tool to influence decision makers, but even in this safer approach (seemingly an asset with great potential for nonprofits), most traditional nonprofit sectors are virtually invisible. What advocacy exists is much the same as it has always been—part educational, part plea.

Nonprofits make a critical mistake when they erroneously assume that if they can just convincingly make their case, if they can provide enough credible evidence as to their value, they will win the day. This approach ignores the political reality that governmental decisions are about choices, and that for political reasons, the choices that are made are not always, and perhaps not even usually, based on who makes the best case. Even grassroots efforts that seek to exert public pressure on elected officials ignore, to some extent, political reality. For the most part, decisions are made as a balance between competing interests, with no "right" or "wrong" position, and almost always in consideration of the *political* realities impacting the chances for election or reelection.

Certainly, nonprofits should endeavor to make the best case they can and generate as much public pressure as possible. Exerting influence is about the rightness of one's position, the arguments in favor of the benefits involved; but it is also about power—money, sheer numbers of people, public opinion, reputation, and image. Being a victorious lobbyist often has nothing to do with making a good case or even generating groundswells of opinion; rather it has everything to do with being powerful. Nonprofits need to embrace a comprehensive advocacy strategy that uses *all* of the tools available to maximize their leverage on impacting decision making. There is no reason whatsoever why nonprofits cannot be effective power brokers and, therefore, lobbyists. It is, at this point, a matter of conscious choice, and once the choice is made, the commitment to the realization of building the mechanisms necessary.

Much of nonprofit advocacy and lobbying is *reactive*—in response to some threat or crisis (legislation with negative impact, drastic reduction in funding)—and the machinery that runs the response has lain dormant and must be created anew. While sometimes the rallying cry yields a relatively massive response, and sometimes that effort is successful, often it fails. Such a "crisis" mode approach is inefficient and lacks the benefits and advantages of ongoing efforts and the relationships and knowledge bases that are the fruit of such continuing enterprises. It is, at best, a risky crapshoot, and can hardly be termed "strategic."

Nonprofit organizations are accorded special tax and other governmental status precisely because as "public-benefit corporations," their reason for existence is to benefit the wider public. Corporations, nonprofit or profit, are regarded by the law as citizens. As such, they are living entities with rights and duties. "For profit" corporations have long taken advantage of the benefits of the way the law treats them. Nonprofits have not. "For profits" boldly assert their rights. Nonprofits tiptoe quietly lest they spur regulation and scrutiny. Many nonprofits, the recipients of government grants, feel awkward lobbying public officials lest they put those grants at risk. They refuse to recognize that their inaction as lobbyists puts those grants at even greater risk.

Nonprofits, consciously or not, have tried to operate above, or at least outside, the political arena in their attempt to influence governmental decision making. This is because of nonprofits' conception of what they should do to further their objectives as stated in their mission statements, and the historical and practical reason of scarce resources—lack of time, money, expertise, experience, and history. Faced with habitual scarcity in these resources (to even advance their primary mission goals), advocacy and/or lobbying has never gotten off the back burner, if indeed the pot was ever on the stove.

Even in the areas where nonprofits recognize and accept that a more engaged advocacy effort, one including lobbying, is to their advantage, there still remains a reluctance to fund the effort at the level necessary to be competitive. Whether teacher unions, industry trade groups, or groups such as the National Rifle Association (NRA), successful interest groups are willing to dig into their own pockets to pay the costs of representing their own interests. Most nonprofits seem unwilling, or unable, to make this type of commitment, and until that fact changes, they will be unable to avail themselves of the same tools and options open to those that do, resulting in their diminished access to, and influence in, the political realm.

The net effect of this behavior has been to silence nonprofits, hamstring their efforts at wielding influence in governmental matters, and put them at the lower rungs of the ladder in terms of protection and support. Advocacy and lobbying still aren't considered a management function for the nonprofit world.

Nonprofits understand that there are certain management and fiduciary responsibilities attendant to their existence, and they have accepted program management and fundraising as essential. They have yet to embrace advocacy and/or lobbying as an equally important part of the job description and realize that lobbying might be critical to realizing their goals and objectives. One thing nonprofit leaders have in common with politicians is that they are being forced to spend increasingly more of their time on fundraising. For nonprofits, courting foundations, corporations, and individual contributors is the same thing as "dialing for dollars" is for officeholders. If they want to increase their influence on legislation and the governmental decision-making process, nonprofits need to add advocacy fund-raising to their already crowded priority list; it is unavoidable.

Few things are more easily dismissed by elected officials than short-term transitory advocacy efforts by groups that will be long gone by the next election. Players tend to respect other players, not sideline sitters or those they perceive as dilettantes. The investment of sufficient capital to equip a nonprofit with expert staffers and consultants buys not only consistency but also experience and knowledge of the way things are done in political situations. Indeed, employment of savvy former staffers and insiders increases the ease with which advocacy and lobbying can be pursued. The major difference between those that effectively wield political power and those that do not is the former's participation in support for specific candidates for office—support more often than not manifested in financial contributions.

Expansion of the advocacy apparatus will take time, but the necessary timeline required is irrelevant to the reality and the choice. If it takes fifty years and the non-profit starts tomorrow, then next year it will take forty-nine years. If it waits, it will still take fifty years from whenever it does start. I am advocating that nonprofits become competent, successful advocates within the system as best they can, including lobbying and candidate electioneering, and to do so as soon as possible.

INTERNAL HESITANCY—WHY NONPROFITS HAVE BEEN RELUCTANT TO LOBBY

Perhaps the failure by traditional nonprofits to recognize advocacy and/or lobbying as a function and appreciate its benefits to their "businesses" is due to the fact that many nonprofits don't even conceive of themselves as businesses. Nonprofits may have unwittingly internalized the wider societal view of nonprofits as amateurish in comparison with the more serious "for profits." Nonprofits suffer under the stigma that they are run either by well-meaning people who couldn't cut it in the real world, or by people who are retired or otherwise no longer involved in the corridors of real power; that they are inadequate to the task, that running a real business is a challenge beyond their ken. This view is more widely held within the business community than nonprofits care to admit.

Nonprofits need to combat the idea that being "nonprofit" means that they don't operate as responsible financial institutions—they need to emphasize that they provide jobs, generate economic activity (that generates tax income), and are important to any number of industries (e.g., the arts are important to the tourism industry). Nonprofits are no less important or relevant to local economies than are other businesses. Taken together, they are a critical economic engine, the absence of which would cause havoc within the national economy. Elected officials should know this, but most don't recognize it. The public doesn't realize this. This needs to change, and while orchestrating changes in public attitudes is a time-consuming prospect, it must start somewhere.

There also remains a legacy of nonprofits viewing lobbying as unseemly, compromising their very lofty missions and purposes; a holdover belief that nonprofits, dependent for their funding on philanthropy, shouldn't cross the line where "real" businesses operate lest they alienate those that feed them. Nonprofits are still too understaffed, too preoccupied with the programs, projects, and services created to discharge their primary purposes, to pick up yet another function. Because they are the outgrowth of philanthropy in this country—and philanthropy was initially considered the province of the wealthy, almost a "hobby," a volunteer activity—nonprofits early on identified themselves as constrained by certain assumptions as to what was proper activity and what wasn't. Because philanthropy was the province of women, and women were not accorded access to the halls of commerce and government, this gender bias may have colored what was acceptable behavior. Whatever the reasons, times have changed, and nonprofits must squarely face the *lobbying* issue today and decide if, and how, candidate support should and can be a part of their overall advocacy efforts.

This is not to suggest that nonprofits have no record of success in the advocacy and/or lobbying arena, or that there have been no changes in approach. There are scores of examples of effective nonprofit lobbying, of victorious nonprofit campaigns, many accomplished on shoestring budgets, with minimal resources available in comparison to more traditional private-sector lobbying efforts. But in most nonprofit organizations a divide continues to exist between factions that see advocacy as essential to the organization's health and success and those that see lobbying as outside the purview of the organization's charter and mission, and nonprofits may be muted and marginalized because of these conflicts.

Another factor that may have implications for a nonprofit's decision to advocate/lobby or not is a fear of alienating one segment of its constituency. Organizations with large, diverse core constituent or member bases may have such a wide-ranging spectrum of viewpoints that consensus on most advocacy strategies involving political stances is difficult, if not impossible, to achieve. And as raising money to support advocacy and/or lobbying efforts must be separated in the case of political action committees (PACs) and 527 organizations, nonprofits may see such efforts as in direct competition with their efforts to raise funds from largely the same sources for their operational and program functions.

Where government funding is important to the nonprofit there may be factions within each organization that believe flying under the radar is the best course, so as not to trigger IRS scrutiny and jeopardize their tax-exempt status. Adoption of such a strategy obviates the need for any active advocacy effort. There is no empirical evidence to suggest that this fear is borne out in reality. And in the general sense, if the nonprofit is silent and inactive, it presents little incentive to decision makers not to favor others that are active when choices have to be made. The "choice" isn't usually between something "good" and something "bad"—it is between things that are all relatively "good" or "bad"; it is about the allocation of limited resources and competing needs. In politics, the "squeaky wheel" does get the grease.

For many nonprofits the question of whether to lobby at all is asked and answered with little, if any, serious thought. Indeed, the answer may just be an unspoken assumption that "we don't have time for that," or "that's beyond what we do." Many nonprofits have never spent any time or resources on any kind of advocacy. In the pantheon of political activity, the nonprofit sector lobbying presence is hard to quantify because it is so infrequent and scattered.

> It is the duty of every citizen according to his best capacities to give validity to his convictions in political affairs.
>
> Albert Einstein

The thesis of this book is that changes in the political process, competition for increasingly scarce resources, and the way in which people are elected and reelected to public office have resulted in many of the old rules, approaches, and protocols of advocacy as recommended to, and practiced by, nonprofits, being no longer workable, no longer efficacious, and no longer sound strategy when applied as the sum total of advocacy efforts, and that a new set of assumptions and strategies are now required. As there are loopholes and ways around efforts to limit the role of money in the attempt to influence decision makers, and as long as the private sector avails itself of the opportunities for legitimate financing of lobbying, nonprofits' failure to be participants in the system, as constituted, will further erode their ability to discharge their missions and lessen the public valuation of the benefit nonprofits bring society. As a policy issue, that nonprofits are not competitive lobbyists and advocates within the whole of the political system has the consequence that not only are myriad individual organizations rendered second class and relatively powerless, negatively impacting the value they might have brought, but society as a whole is the loser because of this unequal playing field.

The clients, constituencies, and audiences of nonprofit organizations may encompass nearly all of society. There is the potential to raise funds to professionalize lobbying efforts and to contribute meaningfully to candidate campaigns (by creating new structures that will permit such activity), and there is the potential to organize vast armies of grassroots supporters—whatever the mission or cause of the organization or coalition. The nonprofit field remains vivisectionist in its organization, "isolationist", without awareness of its potential power base, and reluctant or incapable of exerting the influence that it surely could were the sleeping giant ever to wake up.

Nonprofits simply cannot afford to ignore government, even if such action were possible. Failure to sit at and exert proportionate influence at decision-making tables threatens to possibly imperil the very existence of nonprofits in the long term. Because of the increased cost of getting elected to office at every level, nonprofit advocacy and lobbying, which exists without a mechanism for direct involvement in candidate campaigns, is increasingly one dimensional, limited, and ineffective.

DIVIDED WE FALL

Because of the size and complexity that is government today, and the scope of resources necessary to play the lobbying game, virtually all interest groups seeking to influence decision makers must build sustainable coalitions of similarly situated individual organizations in pursuit of like-minded goals. Certainly, single, independent nonprofit organizations will find it easier (and less taxing on their resources) to shoulder their proportionate share of involvement with many others rather than go it alone. But before they can commit themselves to a coalition, they must first make the commitment to advocacy and lobbying internally. Nonprofit advocacy coalitions will work only if substantially all organizations in a given field participate.

There are legal requirements and organizational structures that must be created in order to lobby and participate in candidate support, and traditional 501c(3) nonprofits need to affiliate with others in order to justify the time and expense of strict compliance with all the rules and regulations involved; it is exponentially more difficult, and success more problematic, to engage in the exercise as distinct, separate organizational entities. Nonprofits have substantial experience in this area, having formed workable coalitions for a wide variety of other purposes in the past, and mastering the logistics should not be a major hurdle for them. The cornerstone of building coalitions is trust, and that may be one of the primary barriers facing nonprofits.

NO MORE MR. NICE GUY

Nonprofits have traditionally played "softball," and they now need to graduate to playing "hardball" if they want to succeed. Nonprofits can no longer afford the *genteel* approach that has reduced them in large part to acting like Oliver Twist with their hands gripping their little bowl, begging, *"Please sir, may I have some more."* Nonprofits must compete with all other sectors in the influence arena precisely because of the impact decision making can, and does, have on their success in discharging their very mission statements. The only way to do that competitively and effectively is to play by the rules of the game as they exist. Only a fool enters the boxing arena with one hand tied behind his back, and that is precisely the state of affairs in which the nonprofit lobbying effort currently finds itself. It is time to take off the "kid" gloves and go bare knuckle, toe-to-toe with the big boys. I am not suggesting that nonprofits abandon the protocols of courtesy and respect, nor am I suggesting that they adopt illegal, unethical, or questionable tactics, but simply that they reward those decision makers that support them, and punish those that oppose them, as best they can, within the system, which is precisely what the for-profit sector has done for a long time. This strategy is adopted not for personal reasons or on the basis of party preference, but for protecting self-interest—this is, after all, *just business.*

In short, nonprofits need to stop tiptoeing around the lobbying game and get serious. They need to dig into their own pockets as the beginning of funding competitive advocacy and/or lobbying efforts. They need to be polite, but not necessarily meek. They need to be courteous, but should make demands. They need to figure out how to mobilize their memberships to action on a consistent basis. They need to be active in the election process, build personal relationships with elected and appointed officials over time, occasionally exercise their power in supporting one candidate over another, and put the credibility of their power potential on the line. It is tricky to engage in the process of supporting candidates in their election/reelection bids, monetarily and otherwise, and still maintain nonpartisanship—to be both friend and potential enemy to an elected official is a thin line to walk. But that is the game. In a democracy, if your representatives don't *represent* you, your alternative is to vote them out of office. Doing exactly that—or at least making every concerted attempt to do so—is essential for democracy to work.

Money invested in candidate campaigns or in any lobbying activity will not, by itself, ensure that decision makers will side with the one spending the money and doing the lobbying. It isn't that simple. The cause needs to be attractive, of benefit to people; there need to be persuasive arguments in the nonprofit's favor and credible evidence to support its claims; and there should be some identifiable public and media support. Unfortunately, all of that, by itself, isn't enough to ensure that decision makers will side with the just cause. The truth is that leveraging influence with government decision makers is the result of complex factors, exigent circumstances, and human relationships that continually change. But, as discussed in the next chapter, money has become indispensable in the process of leveraging influence.

Nonprofits must expand their advocacy and/or lobbying strategies to include the full range of optional tools. If you have but one arrow in your quiver, and you miss your mark, you go home hungry. That's not a very smart strategy. Ten arrows in your quiver give you a better chance of succeeding, particularly if you have very skilled archers using those arrows; and your odds are even better if you have organized your people to beat the bushes to drive the prey to a desired location. The problem is there aren't enough deer in the political forest to feed everyone, and if you don't hunt at all, or have only that one arrow, few skills in using it, and no other plan to increase your chances of bringing home a meal . . . you're in trouble. Maybe you won't even miss a meal or two now, but someday you might starve. Many nonprofits are starving, whether or not they're lucid enough to acknowledge it.

CHAPTER 2

TOWARD A NEW PARADIGM FOR NONPROFIT ADVOCACY/LOBBYING

One of the penalties for refusing to participate in politics is that you end up governed by your inferiors

Plato

MAKING THE CASE FOR 'REAL WORLD' NONPROFIT LOBBYING

The political process in the United States is fluid, dynamic, ever changing, and evolving. Power changes with the swing of the electoral pendulum, public opinion moves constantly, priorities change, and there is a never-ending ebb and flow of players. Substantive discussion of issues is increasingly replaced by sound bites and attack ads that do little to advance solutions to the real problems that face us. But for a dozen big issues, everything else is ignored or put on the back burner. Television is the election media of choice, and it is expensive. Those sectors that can help candidates garner the spotlight of media coverage and raise and disburse campaign money wield more influence.

OPERATIONAL STATUS

The primary focus of political parties has always been the election of candidates, but times have changed. Faced now with a vast array of issues that impact their lives, individuals have reshuffled their priorities, precipitating both a shift of alliances and priorities and a diminution of loyalty to previously powerful groups, and a trend toward individual independence in voting patterns and attitudes. The political machines that once dominated the landscape of big cities across the country are now gone. Historically, special interests concentrated their activities on trying to influence legislators *after* they were elected. PACs changed that situation and moved special-interest activity into the electoral arena, forever altering the dynamics and relationship between the two.

At the same time, the expansion of television as the single dominant media colossus of daily life, coupled with the hectic pace of modern living, has left people less time for careful consideration of issues and has given rise to sound bites as the core election strategy—the thirty-second spot as the means to victory. Today, candidates who cannot afford television time run the risk of being marginalized, or worse, eliminated from serious consideration at the outset. Unable to deliver blocs of voters, strategies turned to raising funds to buy media time, and this in turn has revolutionized American politics, access to lawmakers, policy, and the way legislation is conceived, drafted, and passed or defeated. Campaign fundraising is now a 24/7/365 job.

Out of this unfortunate reality has come an increasing partisanship of issues. Those providing funding for candidates naturally tend to gravitate to those who share their ideological orientation and platforms on specific issues. The result has been dogmatic posturing and less compromise, conciliation, and independence of thought and action. While the American public seemingly moves toward the middle, our political representation has been moving away from the philosophical center.

Coupled with this development is the reality of increasing demand for government support and attention from a growing number of interest areas, while at the same time limited resources have made it impossible for government to address the needs and wants of all sectors. As a people we simply cannot afford to address all the societal needs that justly cry out for support. Moreover, differing interests are in diametric opposition to each other. The tax burden weighs heavily on our citizenry and there is a limit to what can be levied. The very fact of our limitations has spurred the competing forces to increase their attempts to leverage influence in an effort to claim an inside track.

Campaigns are now professionally run by paid staffs with an emphasis on marketing functions—from polling and focus groups (to determine what stance to take), to public relations and media manipulation. Stances taken by candidates on issues of wide interest to the public are now less clear because they are continually subject to "spin" by the campaign machine operatives. Despite outcries and criticism, campaigns are now less about issues and more about the negative qualities of opponents, because such strategies have proven reliably successful. Runners-up can never afford to take the high road, and the front-runner has learned to respond in kind or risk defeat. The public universally rails against this sullying of the election process, but ascribes blame to every elected official *except* the ones representing them. Pork legislation is a cancer on the body politic, but a feather in the cap for the elected official when talking to local constituents. Increasingly, voters make their decision on the basis of the candidate's image, likeability, and stance on "values" as opposed to positions on specific issues. Creating the right "image" is expensive.

Candidates are sold like detergent, and everyone knows that if the message is repeated often enough, if the brand is established, if the creativity in delivering the message is high, enough people can be sold on a specific candidate (or against an opponent) to virtually guarantee success. To be sure, it isn't yet as simple as owning elected officials (although in more and more cases such an argument is persuasive), but rather providing the means to victory affords the provider access, and that access is but the first step in an overall strategy to influence how government impacts the provider.

Laws originally designed to restrict special interests from using funds to exert unfair influence on candidate elections have been largely circumvented by redirecting funds into expenditures in support of issues rather than candidates, even though in practice these issue advertisements were nothing more than thinly veiled endorsements of specific candidates, or, as often as not, directed in opposition to a candidate who had the "wrong" position on an issue. Issue advocacy became the new label for supporting one candidate over another because of his or her stance on the "issue." Political parties became particularly adroit at this sleight of hand in the 1990s.

> Opportunity is missed by most people because it is dressed in overalls and looks like work.
>
> Thomas Edison

For too long, nonprofits have refused to enter the political fray, as they lack either the wherewithal or the motivation to operate on the political stage—to consciously and strategically manipulate the media, move the public, and raise and disburse, within the political matrix, the level of funds necessary to compete with other interest groups plying the system. Nonprofits are, by and large, small business enterprises, with a disproportionate percentage of all nonprofit organizations qualifying as mom-and-pop operations with less than five employees. Most nonprofit leadership is understaffed, overworked, and underpaid. They lack the time, the skill sets, the networking options, and certainly the funds to even participate in a larger interest-group advocacy effort, or at least that is how they perceive their circumstances. Increasingly, their job is as fundraiser, and it is difficult to raise funds for multiple purposes. Finally, lobbying simply isn't historically a part of the nonprofit organizational responsibility mindset; rather it is eschewed as beyond the scope of the nonprofit profile.

Even in the many sectors of the nonprofit field that recognize and accept the responsibility of advocacy and lobbying as part of their job description, there is reluctance to join similarly situated organizations within their field to marshal the resources to mount a united front. Nonprofits have been slow to apply the collaborative approach to the advocacy function. It is only where contributions to a political action arm are mandatory (e.g., teacher's unions) that nonprofits have had success in the political arena in the past two decades. But they represent a small fraction of the total nonprofits operating in the United States.

Moreover, for decades, advocacy etiquette for nonprofits has proscribed their conduct and essentially forced them to behave like "beggars." Nonprofits suffer from an institutional belief that advocacy and/or lobbying is either illegal, improper, or not the province of the average nonprofit organization. They believe that the IRS prohibits them from any kind of advocacy or lobbying work. Some nonprofits believe that to "stir the pot" can only bring negative results, and prefer to "fly under the radar." To the extent that old canard has fallen in recent years, most nonprofits still embrace rules that require them to subscribe to an antiquated value system whereby their conduct within the lobbying arena is ever refined, polite, and essentially nonconfrontational. They make the crucial mistake of assuming that the value of their work and the benefit of their results are sufficient to sway elected officials to their positions. They erroneously assume that if they can get their message heard, the battle is won. Unfortunately, the political system doesn't work that way anymore (assuming it ever did). It is to the politician's advantage to perpetuate this conduct on the part of nonprofits; an active, mobilized, demanding nonprofit sector will only make their jobs more difficult.

IN-YOUR-FACE ADVOCACY

State Senator Shiela Kuehl, Democrat of California, previous president pro tem of the state Senate, and keen, astute observer of the political scene, advised nonprofit arts leaders at a public hearing in Los Angeles in October 2003 to "get in the faces of legislators more, even to the point of being rude. Why? Because it works, that's why." It isn't often that a powerful elected official is so candid and honest in her counsel, but Kuehl's advice reflects the political truth growing more obvious and apparent every day—those that push and play hardball (again, within rules and protocols to be sure) are today more successful than those who don't. Period. *In-your-face advocacy* is not about confrontation or ultimatums except by inference; it is a resolute demand for action and attention; it states unequivocally that there is a highly committed and active group of people in an elected officials' district for whom an issue is paramount, and that this group intends to do whatever it takes to have its issue(s) addressed and resolved. By implication it says these people will not go away quietly, that they are organized and financed, and that they will vote and support only those candidates who support them. It is a declaration more than a warning; it is impersonal—just business.

The net result of shying away from advocacy, let alone "lobbying," of failing to organize and deploy the muscle associated with numbers and money, of refusing to play *hardball,* and of not raising sufficient funds to lobby on the same level as private-sector special interests is that nonprofits have ever-decreasing power and prestige within the ranks of elected officials. To be blunt, nonprofits are regarded as unable to either help or hurt an elected official, as without any real power or influence, as nonplayers in the political scheme, and therefore as ineffectual, inconsequential, and irrelevant. Not that many elected officials do not agree with the objectives of nonprofits when proposed, not that they don't appreciate the value involved, not that they don't at least "mouth" support for the unassailable goals of the nonprofits. But when confronted with difficult "choices," the nonprofit, more often than not, brings nothing else to the table that would help to balance the power, money, and muscle other sectors wield, and so finds itself on the short end of the stick. Elected officials and other decision makers can, and do, ignore them. The nonprofits simply aren't taken seriously, and as a consequence their purposes are marginalized, and that is a tragedy for society.

THE POLITICAL THREAT

Politics in the United States ranges from periods of relative calm, wherein the electorate is by and large on the same page, to periods of marked strife and enmity—cycles of economic boon and lean times. The United States is currently an increasingly divided nation, with huge philosophical chasms and sectors with aggressive agendas that threaten their opponents. Nonprofits are engaged in activity that segments of both the right and left consider threatening and even inappropriate. Indeed, state sanctioning of "public-benefit corporations" via special tax status is seen by some as philosophically inconsistent with the proper role of government. While such a sentiment may be unfathomable to the majority, the pendulum swings, and nonprofits' failure to be prepared to defend themselves on the political stage may be fatal if the political divide widens and deepens. The United States is seen as the country of choice for those wishing to emigrate from their own lands, and estimates project an increase in the country's population to over four hundred million by the year 2050, which would increase demand for perhaps ever scarcer governmental services. Will the nonprofit universe see its government funding sources shrink even further? One purpose of having lobbying machinery is self-defense. Nonprofits need to take a long view of how they can best protect themselves, and such a view includes assessment of enemy strategies and objectives.

It is enormously difficult to predict political sentiment in the very short run, and virtually impossible to chart it for the future. Underestimating threats has been the undoing of many a population.

If nonprofits (which are in fact "public-benefit" corporations) are to change this situation and increase their political power, clout, and the effectiveness of their efforts to move elected officials to certain specific positions, then there will need to be a sea change in the way they perceive their role in lobbying, the way and extent to which they fund lobbying, and the way they conduct their lobbying efforts. Specifically, nonprofits (the whole of the organization, including board, staff, constituents, and stakeholders) must first accept and embrace the concept that advocacy and lobbying are a primary function of their leadership and organizational structures; they must make a commitment to devote the requisite time, energy, and money to that effort, including raising campaign funds, and they must alter their approach and conduct and play a competitive form of political hardball with the private sector. Only then will there be any chance of nonprofits' needs being addressed through the public/government apparatus. Failure to alter their approach and behavior toward advocacy and/or lobbying is likely to result in ever-decreasing public support and sympathy, and that could very well mean, for an enormous percentage of all nonprofits, a whole new systemic restructuring of the way they have financed their work and delivered their product. It could also threaten their existence as presently constituted.

Most people believe that the purpose of a corporation is to make a profit for the shareholders, but that isn't exactly correct. The real duty of a corporation is to enhance shareholder value. Making a profit will usually accomplish that objective, but not always, and the two are not the same thing. Investment in personnel, production improvements, strategic positioning within a market, retooling, and other actions may actually reduce current profit, but, in the long run, enhance shareholder value. Net profit is short-term gain. Shareholder value is long-term worth. Nonprofits have a similar purpose—to enhance *public* value. The niche populations, no matter how large or how small, that the nonprofit seeks to benefit, are clients of the organization, not the shareholders. Nor are the staff or volunteers who work for the nonprofit shareholders—they are employees. The public is the shareholder of the nonprofit. Like for profit corporations, there may be times when investment in aspects of the nonprofit (in this case in advocacy), will, in the long term, enhance public value, even if at the short-term expense of client and constituent benefits through the nonprofit's programs and services. Appreciation of this distinction is critical for nonprofits.

RULES FOR LOBBYING

Rule 1: The lobbying function must be embraced and internalized by the nonprofit organization as a core function.
Corollary: Lobbying must be continuous and ongoing—24/7/365.

Rule 2: The lobbying effort must be fully funded—there must be dedicated, full-time staff.

CHAPTER 3

THE DECISION-MAKING PROCESS

An honest politician is one who, when he is bought, will stay bought.

Simon Cameron

THE ROLE OF MONEY IN THE PROCESS

It's been said that the real business of elected officials is *getting elected*. Getting elected to public office is expensive. The higher the office, the more expensive the campaign. The need to raise ever-increasing amounts of money requires elected officials and those seeking office for the first time to spend more and more time on campaign fund-raising activities. Money is needed to wage media advertising campaigns and to employ legions of professionals to guide and manage the effort (Dow Jones reported that in the 2004 U.S. presidential elections, six hundred million dollars was spent by President Bush, Senator Kerry, their political parties, and allied groups on advertising alone). Most of the key positions within a campaign are now occupied by professionals, not volunteers. Campaigns are no longer run by "pols" in cigar-smoke-filled backrooms, but by pollsters and marketing gurus; speechwriters hammering out position papers have been replaced by glib-talking, media-savvy spin doctors.

While the trend in election campaigns has been to focus on "sound bites," not issues, contributions to campaigns continue to be driven by specific issues. Major contributors understand that their funds will be used to create and project the right image and send the right "message"; candidates understand that these major contributions are made because the contributors have been assured that the candidate favors a specific position on certain issues. In an attempt to placate all sides and alienate no one, candidates try to carve out stances that are simultaneously bold and vague. Politicians are adept at appearing to support all positions while really making no commitment at all. And though they work hard to create the illusion of clear differences between their positions and those of their opponents, the difference between candidates is often, in truth, one of subtle nuance, not substance. Electioneering is increasingly about image, not issues. Thus, office seekers, needing to raise money to pay for media buys, court the interests that can (and will) support them, and the issues raised by these interests aren't always the big topics that campaign rhetoric focuses on during elections. The public isn't interested in, and the media does not cover, the complexities of most issues and legislative responses to those issues because they are, by and large, boring. This leaves special interests free to operate without watchdog scrutiny.

Over the past two decades there has been a redrawing of district boundaries on both the national and state levels, which has resulted in a situation where most districts are now heavily either Democratic or Republican. This redistricting has made pandering to the edges of the pendulum swing productive, and candidates looking for ever more funds are increasingly courting the core faithful of their party and taking increasingly dogmatic positions, with less and less movement toward the center. Yet despite the redrawing of districts, even incumbents in safe districts feel compelled to raise ever-greater amounts of money. Why? The answer lies in a combination of factors: first, candidates have an underlying fear that voters can be fickle, and that if they don't spend money, they might lose, even if the odds are heavily against that scenario (and the 2006 congressional election was a confirmation that, from time to time, incumbency is no guarantee of reelection); second, candidates raise money to build war chests they can use to help other candidates that will increase their power base within their parties; and third, at least historically, to build up the funds they might use for personal purposes on retirement.

Where does this money come from? In isolated cases, the candidates themselves may have the required wealth and the willingness to spend it on their own campaigns. But the vast majority of candidates need to raise that money. While all candidates seek small contributions from the "average Joe or Jane Citizen," traditionally this funding stream hasn't been large enough to cover the costs of even a minimal effort, as reported by the Center for Responsive Politics, Washington D.C. Moreover, soliciting and receiving small contributions take time and resources and are therefore inefficient as well as unreliable sources at the launch of a campaign. It remains to be seen whether or not the Internet fund-raising success that began with the 2004 Howard Dean presidential campaign will filter to lower levels that historically don't attract the attention and interest of the larger races. But while public interest in elections rises and falls, the availability of special-interest money is a constant.

Much of the funding for campaigns comes from special interests, either groups or individuals, most of it with the clearly understood, yet unspoken assurance of the quid pro quo of, at the least, *access* to the victorious candidate (with the possible exception of presidential races, where a portion of all donations are from individuals who do not expect anything in return, but support the candidate's position on major issues). Once embraced, it is difficult to break the bonds of this system. Politicians who kid themselves that their independence remains uncompromised are in a state of denial. In an ironic bastardization of Marshall McLuhan's famous dictum, "The medium is the message," the most clearly understood "message" in politics, in favor of those who want to leverage influence to their advantage, is the medium of the campaign contribution. The medium is money, and the message is unmistakable; it speaks loudly, clearly, and is universally understood.

Attempts to reform the system and curb the role of money have sought to limit the influence of wealth by confining participation to individuals rather than businesses. Subsequent reforms have sought to achieve an equal playing field by preventing wealthy individuals from exercising a disproportionate influence. And still further reform seeks to plug the loopholes that puncture the "dam" like a sieve, allowing parties, candidates, business, and every other sector that is willing to raise and spend money to break the rules and use money to maximize their influence on successful candidates. McCain/Feingold (U.S. senators who jointly authored a bill to limit campaign contributions in federal elections) simply clarifies the rules and attempts to equalize the playing field somewhat; it makes no real attempt to remove or reduce the influence of money on the system.

The "hard" money (contributions from individuals) and "soft" money (contributions from organizations—corporations and labor unions) distinction belies the underlying problem of money compromising the principle of equality of access. Today, nobody believes that there is equal access to the political bounty that comes from elected public officials who are dependent on, and obligated to, the finance machines on which their holding public office is based. The successful interest groups, whatever their orientation or classification, are the ones that have adapted to the contemporary changes in how candidates are elected and how access is obtained—they have become big contributors to campaign war chests. Everyone seems to wish it were otherwise, but it isn't, and as long as money plays a major role, everyone is obligated to play the game as the current rules dictate or accept that their influence will likely be less.

All of this doesn't necessarily mean that elected officials are dishonest, that "fat cats" have them in their pockets, and that the system is corrupt beyond redemption (yet anyway). Nor does it mean that contributing to the campaign coffers of powerful decision makers guarantees that interest groups will get what they want. But it does increase access, sympathy, and the willingness of decision makers to *try* to address interest groups' needs, and that is a huge advantage. Introducing specific legislation to benefit a specific interest group is but the most blatant means of favoring a contributor; there are many other ways to help. A clause in the tax code exempting a certain industry, government funding of a project via a "pork" bill (member-request legislation), or a regulatory benefit tacked onto legislation as an amendment or rider are all ways to help an interest group to achieve its goal, short of specific legislation addressing its issue.

While I join others in decrying the situation, my purpose is to identify the system *as it really is*, and propose ways by which nonprofits can succeed within that system—for as long as it exists—with the hope that in so doing nonprofits will impact the one-sidedness of the system and restore the balance between special interests and the interests representing the whole of the populace.

This much seems true: those who help in the election or reelection of officials have a different type of relationship with those officials than do the rest of us.

We can bemoan this trend, but it is increasingly clear that sectors that did not support elected officials when they were candidates are at a distinct disadvantage in terms of real access to these officials and in having their needs prioritized and addressed. Both the private sector and the union or organized interest group sector have known this for a long time and operate within this reality. The nonprofit sector, by and large, does not.

INSIDER GAME—GOOD OLD BOYS' NETWORK

Legislative bodies don't operate in a vacuum—all sorts of outside forces exert pressure on their decision making. Professional lobbyists play a particular role in the process. Special-interest groups hire professional lobbyists for a variety of reasons, predominantly because lobbyists have the time, expertise, experience, resources, and skills to manage the general and specific advocacy interests of a given client. Most importantly, lobbyists have existent relationships with legislators and other elected officials. Indeed, their ranks are swelled by former legislators, staff members, and other elected and appointed officials. They know the game, the rules of the game, and the election processes and pressures. As former elected officials, many can claim expertise and experience in specific areas. They also are good sounding boards for the sentiment of voting interests. And because they are former elected officials or staffers, they can help wade through the minutiae of details and help formulate arguments for or against a given piece of legislation; they can help draft legislation that will pass the muster of the courts, all of which is a boon to overworked, and often novice, legislative staffs Far and away, their most valuable purpose, and tool, is that they disburse campaign contributions. They attend the endless round of fund-raisers—at $1,000, $5,000, $10,000, and more a plate—discussing campaign finances and their client's needs. They can, and do, tap additional contributors during election years, and are knowledgeable in how to funnel legal contributions through various mechanisms to support candidates. Budgets allow them to carry their messages and make their arguments in ways that others cannot. Because they are in contact with elected officials throughout the year, and because they are thoroughly familiar with, and often previously involved in, party politics, they spend "time" with elected officials on numerous levels. They know staff people because they interact with them regularly—professionally and socially. Indeed, some staff people may owe their jobs to lobbyists. There is a *relationship* between the lobbying community and elected officials. In short lobbyists wield power and influence. They control money, sometimes indirectly, media reaction, and even inner party politics that govern careers and futures. They are an institutional cornerstone of politics in the United States, and interests that cannot afford their help are handicapped compared with those that can. Unfortunately for nonprofits, they don't come cheap.

After candidates take office, the relationship between the "donors," through their lobbyists, and the recipient officeholder continues unabated; it is a solicitation dance that often barely skirts even the appearance of an arm's-length relationship between funder and electee. The same lobbyists who channel money into campaigns squire candidates around the world on fact-finding junkets that include exotic vacation locales; introductions are made and networks formed around the tacitly understood dictum of potential future campaign contributions. The courtship provides the beneficiaries with perks of all kinds that are questionable, if not illegal. Thus the relationship born out of this system grows over time, having a profound—if often difficult to precisely define and characterize—impact on the government's entire decision-making process.

And though there have been recent attempts to curb abuses and limit perks for legislators, all evidence points to this courtship growing and expanding and becoming even more woven into the fabric of the institutions to which it belongs. As it manifests itself in unique individual relationships, the courtship is ever more difficult to pinpoint, yet ever more entrenched. That attempts to regulate and reform it are resisted and thwarted is testimony to its resilience. It has metastasized throughout the body politic and now lies so deep within the layers of customs of how political business is done that it is dangerously close to consuming its host. It would be naïve to think that ways around regulations won't be found, that it is even possible to clean up the situation once and for all—occasional public and media outcries notwithstanding.

By and large, elected officials are underpaid in comparison with what they could earn in the private sector. Most officials are wealthy individuals before they go into politics; others are not. It is unreasonable to expect elected officeholders not to seek the benefits and luxuries that money can buy. We all want a little taste of the good life, and lawmakers are no different. When exposed to the trappings of wealth, it is then understandable how some less-affluent decision makers are at least subliminally influenced by indirect benefits conferred on them simply by virtue of working with lobbyists representing deep-pocket clients. We ought to pay those charged with running our government at least as much as, if not more than, we pay those charged with managing our money, but we don't. We unrealistically expect the rewards of serving the public as adequate compensation for good people forgoing the benefits of serving private interests. This makes no sense. The public and the media scrutinize lawmaker pay with a large magnifying glass but let pass without a glance certain boondoggle government-financed programs that cost hundreds of times more. We are too often *penny wise and pound foolish*.

A pluralistic society is built on the very premise of divergent groups lobbying to have their voice heard, and in our system, the expression of that voice is constitutionally protected free speech. Yet, in practice, special-interest lobbying has become a cancer that threatens to silence all but the wealthy and powerful—the antithesis of democratic precepts.

Many interest areas in the private sector employ lobbyists and law firms not to gain access to government to advance a pro-agenda or garner special treatment, but rather to keep government from making decisions that negatively impact them. Many would prefer to just be left alone. Indeed, there is a whole wing of conservative politics that coalesces around the goal of minimizing governmental interference in the lives of citizens, including corporate citizens. Contributions are made to elect to office people who share this view. These interests employ lobbyists to keep government from impacting them. On the other side are those who engage in the lobbying game to obtain government action that favors their position, even if at the expense of another sector of society, or society as a whole. Many social causes that ostensibly benefit the whole community call for the implementation of regulations that restrict in some way what some section of the business community is doing.

It is in this environment that government decisions are made—decisions as to whom and what to tax, and where to spend the revenue; whom to regulate, how and when; whom to subsidize and support and whom not to. Legislative and administrative decisions are made not just by elected officials but by appointed heads of departments and agencies, within the framework of policy dictated by those who are elected. Many of these decisions involve making choices between conflicting interests within society that require prioritization. Almost all government action, or the omission of action, benefits some segment at the expense of another. If one lobbying interest can claim victory, it is usually at the expense of another. In making these difficult choices, the effect of the choice on society is lost in the spotlight on which side of an issue has won, and which side has lost. That society might also be a winner, or loser, is but a minor part of the equation, and this is ultimately injurious to democracy; it has most certainly been injurious to the missions of nonprofits.

> Politics, n. Strife of interests masquerading as a contest of principles.
>
> Ambrose Bierce

Interest groups in the United States range across the broadest of spectrums—in the private sector every type of business interest has some collaborative mechanism representing it. Larger corporations can afford to hire and finance governmental affairs departments that focus solely on their own specific interests, though even the multinational corporations affiliate through industry associations. In the quasi-public sector, unions, trade associations, and groups of people rallying around a specific concern such as the environment are often equally represented. The upper echelons of many businesses and associations of interests contribute to parties or candidates, and are even friends with elected officials, some relationships going back over time. But the thousands of interest areas that have not managed to band together or that lack, for whatever reason, the financial wherewithal to afford professional advocacy and/or lobbying efforts manage governmental affairs in whatever way they can. Their efforts are, more often than not, minimal, putting them at a clearly competitive disadvantage to those that can, and do, employ professional approaches.

There can be little doubt that contributions to candidates' campaign coffers afford donors increased access to elected officials and perhaps increase the likelihood of their priorities and agendas finding sympathy with the recipients of these contributions. While some campaigns may generate contributions from individuals who feel a philosophical alignment with the views and positions of the candidate, either generally or on some specific issue, there is little evidence that contributions made by organizations of whatever stripe are altruistic, principle based, or anything other than an attempt to curry favor with the official and advance their own agenda. The "pay to play" phenomenon may have very obvious and bold manifestations, or may be a covert tactic that is virtually impossible to trace, but there is widespread acknowledgment that it is now part of the system.

Within every legislative body there are unwritten rules and protocols, evolved over time, that govern the interaction of the members and players in that milieu. The multiple layers of nuance about how things really get done are learned only by experience, by "paying one's dues" over time. Lobbyists and those that interact within these ecosystems on a daily basis have an advantage over those that have only tangential relationships with them in that they have become part of that ecosystem, are familiar with its workings, and are comfortable in its surroundings. Involvement in election campaigns allows lobbyists familiarity with the individuals they are lobbying on a level unavailable to outsiders, thus improving their personal relationships with and ease of access to these persons as well as their ability to influence them.

It's simply common sense that if elected officials must spend more and more time fund-raising in order to get reelected, they will be spending more of their time with those people who are providing the needed additional funds, and they will feel, at the very least, more obligated to be open and considerate of these contributors' stated needs and advice. This creates a bond between the elected official and the contributors—seemingly artificial or contrived, perhaps, but nonetheless real. There are only twenty-four hours in the day, and the more time one spends within smaller circles of people, the more those people will constitute one's network, and networks play a critical role in influencing decision making. Money not only buys access to an elected official's limited window of available time, it also helps to forge the symbiotic relationship and interdependence on which networks rely.

It isn't as though there is a defined, stated quid pro quo involved in giving money to a candidate; rather it is access and time spent together that result in a subtle influence. The force at work is the human characteristic of wanting, if possible, to help one's *perceived* friends and those with whom one is in philosophic agreement. Increasingly, those that enjoy that situational relationship are more likely to succeed in swaying opinion, in getting people to one side or the other of an issue. Nonprofits largely do *not* have that advantage, have moved little, if at all, toward creating that advantage, and stand to fall farther behind in the influence they exert as a result.

PERSONAL ENRICHMENT

There has been another, darker side to the phenomenon. Rather than contributions being initiated by the interest group, with the elected official remaining neutral in the initiation of the process, the official initiates the process by soliciting contributions to "campaign" war chests—not directly, but indirectly, by the introduction of legislation or otherwise that will negatively impact a specific interest group or area. The result is that the affected group will seek to defeat the threatening government action by making contributions to the lawmakers behind the action or to others in the same voting chamber who can defeat the legislation's passage, adoption, or implementation. While this practice is seldom discussed, and because the practice is very difficult if not impossible to prove, it remains largely off of any radar screen. In the author's estimation, it does happen. Although this practice certainly compromises some of the basic and popular premises of democracy, it is just the more odious and blatant side of the same coin. The practice is more widespread in some jurisdictions than others, embraced by many, eschewed by others.

There has heretofore been a dearth of laws governing the use of campaign funds after an elected official leaves office, and in many instances lawmakers have been able to legally appropriate those funds to almost any personal use, including their own retirement accounts (the McCain/Feingold legislation prohibits any personal use of funds raised for federal campaign purposes, but it is unclear whether it governs state officeholders). That such an option exists provides a powerful incentive to some to engage in practices that are patently offensive. Indeed, there is evidence that elected officials continue to raise substantial funds during their final year in office, when it would seem apparent, on its face, that there is no one else to benefit from such fund-raising except the officeholder, after retirement. The practice is hardly confined to legislators, but is adopted by many executive branch elected officials, who wield large patronage power. Some appointments are virtually for sale. Many ambassadorships are awarded to large contributors to a presidential campaign. According to an article in the German magazine Spiegel in June 2005: "Despite legislation enacted in 1980, under which campaign contributions may not be used as a factor in the selection of new ambassadors, U.S. presidents, including George W. Bush, have never felt particularly bound by the law. According to the most recent count, thirty of the Republican Party's biggest donors have been rewarded with posts in sun-drenched island nations such as Mauritius and the Bahamas or in prestigious European capitals."

PAY TO PLAY

Given the current data available, it is difficult to discern the extent to which the "pay to play" system rewards or punishes those involved and whether it directly impacts government action or inaction. But there is little argument that the system exists, and that it is growing, despite the fact that many of the players on both sides would ideally have it otherwise. There are many ways the group that donates money to a candidate's campaign might benefit beyond the "for" or "against" vote on a specific legislation. A sympathetic and grateful committee chair, who controls what legislation is heard, may exercise options to help the supporting group. This is one example of other, less apparent, ways to help a constituent. Member request legislation (popularly known as "pork" legislation) singles out specific interests for reward.

What is apparent is that sectors that are not part of this system, whichever side they may be on and whatever their objectives or motives, are not as likely to succeed as those who play the game. This is not to say they can't succeed without playing the game, or that they never do, but that the odds are not in their favor; and as politics has become a game of "odds," it is better to have the odds in the nonprofit's favor. Nonprofits, by and large, fall into the category of not being players—they are either unwilling or incapable of using money to advance their missions, and this has handicapped their ability to win the victories they need.

While the chumminess of the relationship between lobbyists and elected officials might lead some to conclude that the whole system is corrupt beyond salvation and that the government is for sale, the fact is that most elected officials try to separate those relationships from their votes on legislation. There is still life left in the democratic body politic, though how much is questionable. The truth is that despite direct campaign contributions and long-standing relationships, not every vote goes as a lobbyist and his or her client might hope, whether they seek to get a bill passed or defeated. While money, increasingly, is the grease that lubricates the machines trying to exert sway over legislatures and government agencies, it isn't true that all, or even most, legislation and agency action is bought and sold. But even in the best-case scenario, the other side of that truth is that those contributions and those relationships at least allow the contributors greater opportunities to make the case for their interests and present their arguments, give pause to the legislator who must vote against their interests, and very often—when the choice is not difficult, when media scrutiny might be minimal, when the issue isn't black or white—produce the desired vote and support where they otherwise might not. That is a huge advantage, one that may not be available to the same extent, if at all, to those that do not operate on this level. Nonprofits, by and large, find themselves in the latter category, and they have suffered because of this.

For the elected officials, the way the "game" of financing campaigns has evolved gives them few options not to "play"; and once play is initiated, it is hard to stop or to violate the "rules." Success becomes addictive, and, after a while, comfortable. While politicians decry this "game," they certainly have the power to pass the reforms that would change the rules, but they haven't done that. The reasons for this include the need to prepare for retirement—many officeholders opt to move over to the lucrative and familiar lobbying side of the fence; pressure put on them by former colleagues and close ties; ambition and a fear of not being able to raise funds from other sources, which are necessary to ensure they can wage competitive campaigns; and, the fact that the game has become part of their culture. Nobody wants to be first in pushing for change. I suspect many lawmakers also believe that ugly as the system is, it isn't really corrupt and *their votes* are not bought or sold—an arguable "can't see the forest for the trees" position. Whatever the reasons, reform legislation seems to pass only when public scrutiny compels the votes, but then final passage is of a watered-down version with less bite to it. Rules of engagement may change, the game does not. The tempo barely skips a beat as ways around limitations are found and adopted.

Rule 3: The lobbying strategy must include participation in candidate campaigns as a key plank.

LIFE OF AN ELECTED OFFICIAL

Government is too big and too important to be left to politicians.
                                                        Chester Bowles

As life becomes more complex, as demands increase and resources shrink, the life of an elected official also becomes more complex. At virtually every level, the volume of needs, demands, ideas, and projects and ways for government to become involved or stay away have increased, and it is our elected and appointed decision makers who must deal with these concerns. As officials often spend much of their time between the site where government conducts its business and the district where their constituents live, travel is extensive. There are countless daily committee and subcommittee meetings, hearings, caucuses, and staff meetings. There is an endless schedule of special events, lunches, and dinners to attend, and a nonstop array of fund-raising events at which to make an appearance—both for the benefit of the elected official and for his or her brethren. More bills are introduced every year, and the issues they seek to address are more complex and have an increasing impact on other areas of society. Media scrutiny is greater. All of this is in addition to the requirements of campaigning. There is the revolving door of lobbyists and constituent groups that want time to plead the case for their specific interest and an endless parade of interests that want the legislator to vote this way or that. It is virtually impossible to keep up with all the documentation and background materials that arrive in huge stacks on a daily basis, let alone the media coverage in the home district. It is little wonder that elected officials can spend very little time absorbing the materials nonprofits provide them to make the case for their public value. Even their staff cannot keep pace with the rise in the demands on their time and the onslaught of ever-growing evidentiary materials to consider. In addition to all of this, lawmakers and other elected officials are increasingly vilified and excoriated, put under ever more microscopic scrutiny (their private lives perceived as a public domain), second-guessed even when they are trying to do their best, and generally paid less than comparable private-sector positions.

For these reasons, those that want to sway elected officials should understand that these officials will rely on people they know well and with whom they have a relationship—people who, if not exactly their friends, are at least respected and valued, if not wholly trusted.

Why people seek office is a mystery to some, given the negatives associated with such a career choice. The reason is doubtless a complex mix of wanting to be in public service, for all the right and wrong reasons, and the heady intoxication of power and prestige. Someone once said that politicians are just people who are too ugly to be movie stars but crave the public spotlight. Whatever the reasons, most elected officials want to do the right thing—of course, the right thing is very subjective and difficult to define. Politicians are human beings, with the best instincts and all the foibles and weaknesses of any of us. You can't influence them unless you can relate to them.

When all is said and done, the typical elected official has a set of unspoken criteria that guide his or her decision-making processes. Most elected officials have a set of values that influence whether or not they think a given vote, one way or the other, is a good or bad thing and whether it is of benefit or not to their constituents, and indirectly, to themselves. However, these values are a luxury that may not be always available to elected officials.

In making their final determinations, elected officials must consider their party position, what their leadership wants, and the cost of bucking the party position (support for a piece of legislation particularly important to them; campaign support; a committee assignment; future consideration; reputation?). They must think about whether or not a vote in favor or opposition will lessen or increase the chances that a bill important to them will be supported or opposed by those on one side or the other of the bill at hand. They must consider how their vote will play with their constituents, how the hometown media will treat their vote, and how much opposition to any potential vote exists, who benefits, and who gets hurt. They must think about the position, if any, of their major contributors. They must consider the political reality of whether the bill in question has any chance of passing. They must also consider their future ambitions for higher office, their careers, and the impact of what they do on their families. And finally, where legislation involves the expenditure of public funds, they must always consider that funding one program may mean there will be no money for another, and so everything becomes a priority.

Most elected officials are people of conscience who believe their votes are for the public good, who care about who they represent, and who try hard to represent their constituents and their interests. But it is naïve to think that they always vote according to their consciences; that compromises aren't foisted on them; that they can buck the system, their party, or outside pressures; and that they always vote with their best instincts. Moreover, their vote is often not a choice between what is good or bad; it is about prioritizing limited resources and balancing competing interests, about choosing one good over another good or one bad as less onerous than another one.

First-time elected officials invariably come to their posts optimistic and idealistic, determined to make a difference and change the system; the system more often than not changes them. There is a maxim in politics, "Go along, to get along," and lawmakers quickly learn that governing involves trade-offs. Most career politicians leave office somewhat resigned to a system that ultimately required them to play by some of the same rules they had sought to change in the first place. They leave a little more cynical, a little less optimistic, and a little more realistic. That isn't to say that in making difficult choices they necessarily "sold-out"—loyalty to certain standards simply isn't always possible, and politics is the art of compromise and the possible. The best ones can say to themselves that they did what they could do; accomplished some big, but mostly small, victories; changed things slowly; and made a difference on some level. Their choices, are, of course, made in the context of their own ambitions, needs, and values. In politics, self-interest is the guiding principle to which all subscribe—that is not an indictment, but rather further evidence that there are real people involved in this process.

Politicians break ranks with their party when adherence to a party plank would generate criticism in the home district. Gun control is the right position in California but the wrong position in Wisconsin, where there is a tradition of hunting and gun ownership, where induction into the adult activity of hunting is passed on from father to son. Politicians are, if nothing else, practical people. Few risk supporting action that could alienate significant voter support. In democracy's favor is the fact that politicians will vote according to their "self" interest—and their self interest is in recognizing constituent priorities. Unfortunately, there are but a handful of big-ticket issues that generate strong constituent opinion; most issues are complex and subtle, and absent from public radar screens. Politicians have become blinded to the intertwined nature of governing decisions, and they assuage their own consciences by rationalizing specific votes. Perhaps it is unrealistic to expect those we elect to office to be saints; like all "real" people, there are those who are noble, and those who are jerks. Elected officials, as much as any segment of society, wrestle with the instinct for self-preservation and the desire to serve the whole of society on a daily basis.

There are two ways a nonprofit can get the attention of elected officials—it can either *help* them or *hurt* them. It can help them by supporting them, garnering them positive media, rallying groups or blocs of voters on their behalf, or raising, and committing, substantial funds to their campaigns for election or reelection. The nonprofit can hurt them by not making any of those efforts, or by doing so on behalf of their competitors.

The second force elected officials respond to is their individual (personal) and their party's perceptions of what government ought to do and what government needs to do. Given the plethora of societal needs that government ought to address and the increasingly scarce resources available to address those needs, most of the causes and efforts of nonprofit groups are falling ever further down the list of priorities. While most nonprofits have an excellent "product" (i.e., the cause they espouse is of "benefit" to society), in the real world of the new millennium, this product's importance may be eclipsed by the real and perceived problems highlighted by the private sector and other well-heeled, special-interest groups, which are geared to molding public opinion, working the media, and raising substantial campaign contributions. Proving that (and even quantifying how) the nonprofit is beneficial to society via evidence, no matter how credible, may often no longer be enough to secure the desired elected-official stance. Even an orchestrated public outcry and media focus are not always necessarily enough to extract a positive response from elected officials, unless that outcry and media focus can be demonstrably converted into political action—votes and campaign-finance contributions.

Experience and circumstances form any politician's priorities. An official may have lost a loved one to a drunk driver; a daughter may have had her life transformed by the ballet; a relative's land may have been polluted by chemical toxic waste. Negative events might make the legislator want to prevent others from being similarly harmed. Virtually all elected officials have their own personal pet cause, and if a given nonprofit field in a given place is fortunate enough to have its mission dovetail with a well-placed politician's personal agenda, then all can be right with the world—for that group, in that place and at that time. The cold reality is that very few nonprofits find themselves in this coveted position. For all the rest, they must, like any private-sector interest, competitively work the system to their advantage to produce the desired results. This means they must be political—they must exert influence and hold the power to help or hurt the politician; they must lobby, and lobby as effectively as paid professional lobbyists, which means raising and disbursing campaigns funds, at least to a minimal level. It also means relating to the official on a personal level—getting to know the individual and, ideally, forming a bond or friendship that can transcend the process. It means contact—contact that will remain constant over time, breeding familiarity.

Elected officials will support the nonprofit's position because:

- **They want to:** The nonprofit may secure support owing to personal relationships and ties, and a belief in the group's value. The more officials relate to the nonprofit personally, the more receptive they are likely to be to the organization's needs and cause.

- **They perceive that it is in their interest; they think they have to:** The more power the nonprofit can wield on behalf of the organization, the more incentive for the official to support it irrespective of its relationship. Sometimes legislators will trade their vote on one issue for support from colleagues for a bill important to them. Sometimes a vote comes during a crisis period, when, under intense media/public scrutiny, voting at odds with the overwhelming majority of both parties would create a public-relations nightmare, and thus the elected official votes with the herd. Sometimes a vote is dictated by the party, and the costs of voting contrary to the party position are too high. There are numerous situations in which a lawmaker's vote is influenced by pressure from other quarters. And they go along, to get along—because that's how it's done. If the nonprofit has a personal relationship and wields political clout, there is a greater likelihood that the lawmaker will think that supporting your position and cause is the right thing to do. That's just human nature.
- **They think it is the right thing to do:** The stronger case the nonprofit can make for its organizational needs, cause, and positions, the greater the likelihood that an official can justify supporting it. If officials believe in the nonprofit's position and cause, they will try to find a way to support it if they can.

It may not matter what their reasoning is for taking the nonprofit's side, but it is obviously beneficial if they support the group's position for all three of the above reasons. Effective lobbying strives for this "triple" score—in large part because everything is always in flux, so none of these reasons can be relied on absolutely. To a large extent, lobbying is about hedging one's bets and covering one's contingencies; as in a war, it is prudent to cover all one's flanks. The nonprofit should make sure it never succumbs to the false assumption that all it needs do is have "right" on its side, because that isn't how the system works. Being in the right is often the least of the reasons why the nonprofit succeeds.

SUMMARY

There exists a "pay to play" system in American politics that has a profound impact on access to, and the ability to influence, the decision-making process. Those who "pay" have an advantage over those who do not.

HOW GOVERNMENT (REALLY) WORKS: PROCESS AND PROTOCOL

Government in the United States is essentially a two-party system, divided into Executive, Legislative and Judicial branches at the federal, state, county, and city levels. We are also a pluralistic nation—there are many divergent interests, with overlapping purposes, all competing for influence that would advance their agendas and purposes and protect their constituents.

Government intersects with the citizenry and its various component interest groups at two important junctures: (1) it enacts laws, rules, and regulations allowing, prohibiting, promoting, supporting, and otherwise affecting and impacting what people and organizations must, can, and cannot do; and (2) it exacts payment in the form of taxes, fees, and other charges or in expenditure support and payment from the government coffers in the form of entitlements, grants, subsidies, operating expenses, contracts, and other support.

Basic civics classes teach the theory of how government theoretically operates. It is important to also understand how it *really* works in practice. The two are rarely the same. The following discussion is generally applicable to both the federal and state government apparatus.

THE EXECUTIVE BRANCH

The Executive Branch (president, governor, mayor, and the bureaucracies that they head) is often involved in proposing legislation, and, more often than not, submits the budget for spending. The Legislative Branch also proposes legislation and processes and approves all the proposals and the submitted spending plan. The Executive implements laws and enforces regulations, and while it does not "make law" per se, it interprets laws by selective enforcement and by promulgating rules and procedures incidental to the implementation of statutes. It also approves or vetoes legislation and the final spending plan submitted by the Legislature. The Executive has the power of appointment, and in many cases this power over patronage is considerable, as it is in the case of judicial appointments. The courts' involvement is to interpret the laws and the rules under which the other two branches operate, but only when a dispute arises and parties seek the courts' judgment. The Judicial Branch and its role are not within the purview of this work, although lawsuits are increasingly a tool in many advocacy and/or lobbying strategies.

The Executive Branch houses the numerous agencies and departments that implement, oversee, and enforce much of the legislation legislatures pass—what is commonly referred to as the "bureaucracy"—the vast majority of which are not appointees but "civil servants." When government agencies are charged with the implementation and enforcement of legislation, the Executive establishes the rules, protocols, procedures, and regulations that govern this work. These enactments have a tremendous influence on the impact of legislation; they are the "teeth" of compliance, and can expand or weaken the effect legislation may have. While generally overlooked as a lobbying strategy (at least by nonprofits), lobbying Executive Branch agencies during the drafting of the rules for compliance can have a significant effect on the scope and extent of the legislation's impact.

Whatever action a nonprofit seeks from the government—legislation, the repeal of legislation, favorable rulings in interpretation of statutes, or money (remember that all government expenditures require authorizing legislation)—success is easier to achieve legislatively *if* the Executive Branch is supportive. There are several reasons: (1) the Executive commands a bigger "bully pulpit" and is perceived within our system as the focal representative of *all* the people; (2) if the Executive is supportive, the Legislative Branch probably need not worry about a veto; if the Executive opposes the legislation, the specter of the veto looms large; (3) the Executive holds a great deal of power (appointments, veto, budgetary process, bully pulpit, etc.) and the Legislative Branch needs to cooperate with the Executive; and (4) the Executive is a power player within the two-party system and, in particular, the "big *kahuna*" (big gun) of fund-raising. As a consequence, effective lobbying always includes strategies to win Executive support.

The larger the political jurisdiction (small town, big city, state, nation), the greater the likelihood of the Executive bureaucracy being larger, and thus the more insulated and less accessible the chief of the Executive is likely to be. In state and federal governments, one nominally deals with departments, agencies, and other branches. The finance and budget departments are the controlling agencies governing proposed allocation of funds, and control over the purse strings at any stage of the process equals power. Moreover, in a world where favors beget favors, no one has more power to grant or deny favors than the Executive Branch—both within the operation of government and on the campaign trail. It is harder to say no to an Executive request than to others.

Executives who win can claim public mandates. Charismatic leaders and those blessed with the gift of being able to communicate with the public wield power, around which seasoned political players tread lightly. Executive popularity can, and is, translated into political capital that has significant value. Backing by "the people," or the perception of such backing, is potentially intimidating and "currency" worth having.

As the introduction and expansion of "term limits" (in some states) has reduced the power of legislators who were previously able to make lifelong careers out of public office, so too the "lame duck" status of the chief executives during their last term reduces their power, particularly in the final stages of their occupancy of office. Nothing in politics is less relevant than someone who will soon be out of power.

In some jurisdictions, the Executive has what is called a line-item veto within the budget, which means that once the Legislature passes a budget and sends it to the Executive for final approval, the Executive can veto a single proposed expenditure (the line item) without having to veto the entire budget. This gives extraordinary additional power to the Executive Branch to control the purse strings.

One of Machiavelli's first maxims is that the Prince is judged by those he surrounds himself with, and there is truth in that observation still. A chief executive's key appointments will impact how he or she is perceived, and how legislators will react to him or her. Each inner-circle appointment is important, for those individuals will carry out the chief executive's agenda. If they are perceived as knowledgeable, well-connected, experienced, and astute players of the political game, they will be more effective on the chief executive's behalf. Appointments may be made on the basis of the appointee's contacts and ability to "sell" the chief executive's agenda to a given sector.

THE LEGISLATIVE BRANCH

On the Legislative side, at the state and federal levels, we are a bicameral system with two chambers—more often than not a "House" or "Assembly," and a "Senate," with each seat in the former theoretically representing a proportionate share of the territory's population, and in the latter, seats allocated to a geographical territory itself in an equitable number so as to provide all jurisdictions (e.g., rural areas) representation (irrespective of their populations). In practice, the redrawing of districts (usually every decade) has skewed the theory behind equitable representation.

Legislators are, except for infrequent exceptions, members of one of the two major political parties, and as such, subject to the pressures of their party to toe the party line. Most legislators heed, to a large extent, their party line, because they need the party to stay in office. The party controls much of the fund-raising activities necessary to pay for campaigns, it has control of many endorsements, it can at least play a role in soliciting, if not always in delivering, blocs of voters, and can provide often-needed organization to an election campaign. It can also withhold any or all of these perks.

It is worth noting that on the national level, and in many states, there is a highly entrenched level of competition—and even distrust and enmity—between the two branches of the legislature. An old political story sums it up best: After a particularly close vote on a piece of important legislation, a junior senator from the Republican side of the aisle was in the inner office of one of his party's long-time leaders in the Senate. The junior senator chimed into the conversation that he was gratified that they had beat their enemy on this one; that the Democrats had come up short. The conversation grew quiet, and the senior senator looked at him as though he were a schoolboy. Then he said, patiently:

The Democrats aren't the enemy, son. The House is the enemy.

Unless you are an insider, it is impossible to understand and fully appreciate a distinct and relatively isolated world that has for a long time refined its customs and procedures. Politics and government is an insular world, and except for those who walk the corridors of the capitols as principals, everyone else is an outsider—no matter how much you interact with that world. Legislatures are very small worlds, like private clubs, and prefer to operate quietly to the extent they can. Lobbyists are the brokers between these two spheres; they are part of this world—their clients are not.

Not so long ago, new legislators, in both houses, were expected to spend their first terms learning the ropes, maintaining low profiles, and not rocking the boat. While term limits and changing times have eroded to some extent the period of apprenticeship for freshmen legislators in the jurisdictions where such limits operate, there is still a long-standing code of conduct as to "paying ones dues," and bucking the system makes it harder to play the system to one's advantage. In Congress, freshmen legislators have shown a tendency toward greater independence and appear less willing to follow the tradition of apprenticeship. Newly elected legislators seem to have an increasing sense of urgency and a burning desire to get something done. Still, those mavericks that refuse to "go along" risk having their agendas ignored by their party leadership; and worse, they may have to forgo "choice" committee assignments, preferred office space, the luxury of additional staffing, support for their legislative priorities, campaign contributions, and more for their independence.

THE LEGISLATIVE PROCESS

Any given bill is usually introduced by one or more single members of one of the chambers. The same or similarly worded bills introduced in each chamber are referred to a committee that has been given jurisdiction over the subject matter of the proposed legislation, and then further referred to a subcommittee. The bill must pass through the subcommittee and the full committee before it goes to a final vote in each chamber. This gives enormous power to the chairs of these committees and subcommittees, who can often kill legislation by procedural means, pass it quickly as a consent item, or influence its chances of passage in other ways. As American politics centers on the budget process, chairs of committees that directly consider budgetary matters are especially powerful.

When both chambers have passed the bill, it goes to the Executive. When the wording of the legislation as approved by the two chambers is different from each other (or, in budgets matters, where the appropriation is different in the two chambers), the bill is forwarded to a special conference committee composed of a small, select number of members of each of the two chambers, which then resolves any disputes before sending the matter back for a final vote. These conference committees are thus very powerful, and appointments to them are highly coveted.

Often, if there is no strong opposition, a single member of the majority of any given committee or subcommittee is all that is needed to at least advance a piece of legislation or line item in the budget, and for this reason it is important to identify at least one friendly member on these committees and enlist the member's support early on. Although only one committed member is not enough for passage from the committee, other members of the same party will often go along with another member's wishes if pushed, and, if enough members are supportive, this can ensure passage. Thus, it is in the nonprofit's interests to identify and cultivate an "angel" on each relevant subcommittee that has jurisdiction over any given piece of legislation as early in the process as possible.

Note that the system described above is applicable to most states and the federal government. City councils and county boards of supervisors as well as boards and commissions of other departments and agencies may have less, or different kinds of, hierarchical systems and a less complex procedure for considering, passing, or rejecting legislation.

Because of the Executive's power, bills that otherwise might pass or might be defeated end up with an opposite effect when the Executive chooses to use its power to gain passage or ensure defeat. Both the Executive and Legislative branches lobby each other—publicly and privately. The Executive often has more resources to trade for the votes it wants.

It should also be noted that some legislation and some issues are of much greater concern to the whole of the legislature than are others. Some legislation is basically drafted to deal with a narrow, specific issue, and some is simply the "pet project" of a given legislator. Politics is characterized by trade-offs—legislators will support legislation important to one lawmaker in exchange for support from that lawmaker for a bill important to them. While any quid pro quo for votes might be unacceptable on its face, it happens all the time and it is part of the grease that lubricates the system and allows it to function. The party leadership is concerned with "major" legislation and will work the "trade-off" mechanism to ensure enough votes for passage or defeat. The Executive Branch has considerable power in this area to trade its support for votes. Both parties have increasingly sought to hold their members to the party line, more for political reasons than support or opposition to a given piece of legislation.

Legislation is, more often than not, amended prior to its passage, and frequently, amendments benefit a narrow interest group. This device of amendments receives little media attention and accomplishes the same desired result as passage or defeat of specific legislation—for example, exemptions from regulations in legislation may be as valuable as defeat of the bill to the interest that sought to kill the legislation. The volume of legislation introduced in any given session is enormous, and only a tiny fraction is ever under the scrutiny of the public microscope.

In some cases a lawmaker's vote might be different if the vote is likely to receive a great deal of media coverage. Votes then can be strictly for "appearances" sake, and that is an indication that not every issue is one of principle, or even one on which people have a strong feeling one way or the other. It is also indicative of the fact that lawmakers cast votes based on their perception of how voters in their district side, wholly apart from what they might personally believe is the right side to be on. This may be good in that it validates that lawmakers vote as their constituents want, it may also mean they vote as "some" of their constituents may want, or it may be a sign that they vote according to their consciences some of the time, but not all of the time. It is one more indication that voting decisions are based on a multitude of considerations, some having to do with the issue, some not. Politics does indeed make strange bedfellows.

Finally, at the state level, there is often a quasi-official super committee composed of the leadership of each party and the Executive that meet to try to resolve disputes as well as stalemates and disagreements over the proposed budget.

LAWMAKING

Bills are introduced, sent to committees, and taken up by the full chamber, which passes or rejects them. They are then forwarded to the Executive for passage and approval on a timeline that starts with the legislative session and continues up to the end of the fiscal year. Fiscal years differ from one government entity to another; some extend from July 1 to June 30, that of the federal government is from October 1 to September 30, and still others coincide with the calendar year or with elections and installment of new victors. Most legislative bodies meet in session each year, some only once every other year. Awareness of the timeline deadlines is necessary to manage the advocacy process. Often, committee meeting dates are changed, many at the last moment, then rescheduled, making personal appearances before the committees difficult for those living outside the capitol district. Items and bills taken up before committees are often tabled, and the vote is postponed. The budget process generally goes on during the entire session, simultaneously with other legislation. Sometimes, to meet deadlines, there is considerable action toward the end of a legislative session, when there can be a flurry of compromises and votes, often late into the night and thus under less public scrutiny. For all these reasons, a presence in the site of the government bodies is essential for nonprofits, and another reason to hire a professional lobbying firm.

As discussed elsewhere in this book, votes on issues and budget allocations are very often along party lines as the trend toward partisanship continues. Thus, the majority party has a distinct advantage in any given legislative chamber, as it normally controls the committees and subcommittees. But a well-disciplined and united minority can have power too, and in instances where a two-thirds vote is necessary, there can be a tyranny of a cohesive minority that can exact concessions and compromises because it controls enough votes to thwart the necessary majority vote (in California, for example, the budget requires a two-thirds vote to pass).

Finally, the media and the public, when they are focused on specific legislation, can impact how a vote goes. The media alone may be insufficient for an impact, often because the media does not speak with a single voice. But there are countless situations in which the media can critically influence legislator positions, such as in close elections, in smaller jurisdictions, and particularly in situations where it puts officeholders on the defensive by portraying a given stance as fiscally irresponsible or demonstrative of favoritism—two images no politician wants to paint. Overwhelming public consensus in support of or opposition to legislation is rare, but politicians are adroit at discerning which side of a given issue the public in their district is likely to support, and often, public sentiment that fairly evenly divides the nation is very close on a national basis and is much more one-sided in a given district.

THE BUDGET PROCESS

The budget process is normally the centerpiece of each legislative session around which legislation is introduced. Money is power. Laws mean nothing if the money to implement and enforce them is not appropriated. The ability of the bureaucracy to enforce compliance with statutory mandates is dependent on Congress appropriating sufficient funds to carry out the obligation of that enforcement. Legislative powers of Congress that have been eroded in favor of the Executive over time are often resurrected by the power for appropriation. Executive branches that have the line-item veto power have considerably greater power over legislative branches.

In each jurisdiction, the funding process has a history and legacy, codified rules, regulations and procedures, and informal protocols. It is also governed by forces that are seemingly beyond anyone's control and have evolved over time—once a program is funded, an interest group committed to its continuation comes into being and grows, making it harder to defund it at a future point. General economic conditions, which are now determined in part by global influences, also govern the funding process. Competition for scarce government funds is extraordinarily fierce.

Often, bills that require continued funding or the expenditure of new funds must also be heard by a separate appropriations committee before they are sent for a vote of the full chamber. It doesn't matter what laws are passed—if they don't have an appropriation of funds in the budget to implement and enforce them, they may be of little effect. Thus the appropriations committee and its process are critically important, and legislation that can't be killed can be made impotent by deliberately omitting to secure appropriation for its implementation. As the budget process is an annual procedure, lobbying over appropriations is an ongoing reality.

As available funds are finite and as the total available funds are never enough to fund everything, the various departments and agencies within the Executive lobby the legislature in favor of their budget requests. There is measurable distrust, suspicion, and enmity between various sectors of the Executive, and individual departments are usually very territorial. Not only do they lobby the legislature for preferential treatment, they also lobby their bosses within the Executive Branch for support for their agendas.

For passage of a current year's budget, approval is first through the budget subcommittees, and then through the full committee within each chamber. Often, funding for a given program or department differs from chamber to chamber, as it may be reduced or augmented by the funding proposed by the Executive Branch. When this happens, and the amounts are different in the "House" and "Senate" versions, the item goes to a special conference committee to resolve the differences, which gives the committee (and the staffers of the members of the committee) extra power.

While most legislation requires a simple majority vote (50 percent plus one), appropriation of funds sometimes requires a higher plurality of as much as a two-thirds vote, and this situation can give increased power to the minority party. Most bodies require a two-thirds vote to override an Executive veto of legislation, but currently only three states require a greater-than-majority vote for budget approval, and in these jurisdictions, the minority parties have increased power as they can prevent the budget's passage. Securing passage of the budget in almost all jurisdictions usually requires compromise and a strategy involving "courting the middle" so as to secure the largest number of votes possible.

The Senate and the House have different self-perceptions, and they view each other with a certain arm's-length distrust and suspicion. The Senate has always thought of itself as a "superior" body. Because the House and the Assembly chamber are larger bodies, representing smaller constituent bases, they tend to be more polarized than the Senate, where larger districts force legislators to consider the wider impact of their decisions. This results in a situation where it is usually the Senate that first passes the budget, which is yet another indication of the significant differences between the two chambers, the factors that influence the conduct of their business, and the ways in which they conduct their affairs.

LEGISLATIVE LEADERSHIP

It is important to note that not all elected officials have equal power. As a two-party system, the majority party is virtually always more powerful. Not only does it constitute a majority within its respective chamber, but it usually controls the election of the chamber's leadership (the House Speaker and the Senate majority leaders). This leadership, in turn, usually controls the appointment of the committee and subcommittee chairs and the membership composition of the committees. Moreover, it also dons the party leadership "hat" in the chamber and imposes discipline so as to keep the vote predictable and unified. The leadership is also usually at the top in fund-raising efforts, commands more media attention, and has greater access to the Executive power and greater success at amassing a war chest beyond its own needs. It therefore has considerably more power and clout than the average member. Leadership is often determined by seniority, by party politics, and even by the size of campaign war chests, which can be used to help elect or defeat party candidates who are too independent and rebellious to toe the party line.

It is important for the nonprofit to pay extra attention to develop strategies to win over as much of the leadership in each chamber as is reasonably possible, and standard approaches such as letter-writing campaigns more often than not include targeting the leadership. Having the leadership on its side can make all the difference in the world to the nonprofit's chances of success, as it can fast-track its legislation, assuage the feelings of members who are opposed to it, and broker deals and compromises that allow the group's legislation to move forward (or help to defeat legislation it deems not in its best interest). It is therefore exceedingly important for the nonprofit to cultivate personal relationships with the leadership over time.

The Way It Really Is—"Go Along, to Get Along"

Most legislation is passed with relative ease either by an overwhelmingly bipartisan vote, or on strict party lines with the majority prevailing. It is only on a very few controversial or otherwise newsworthy bills that the vote is close or ever in doubt. When the cameras are off, the tradition of politics pushes for compromises and trade-offs, because these are what have always made the system work. Power is almost never so concentrated that it can be exercised without either giving something up or getting something in return, and this is true from the White House and governor's mansions to every city hall in the country. Power is about building a bank of chits—giving some to get some, and calling them in when necessary. While philosophical beliefs are deeply held, they are trumped more often than is realized by those who know when to go along, to get along. Adherence to dogmatic positions with an intransigence that is too rigid simply means that you are likely, as a politician, to get very little accomplished, ever. You do favors for people to get favors in return. Yet today, there are increasing signs of an erosion of the civility that was so long a cornerstone of conduct in the environment of legislatures. Compromise seems out of favor, and this can only increase the political aspect of decision making.

The story of how Lyndon Johnson supposedly secured Southern Democratic support for the ticket in the 1960 presidential race is perhaps the most famous anecdotal homage to the power of playing the game:

> Weeks after John F. Kennedy was nominated by the Democrats and he had selected Lyndon Johnson for the second spot, the major Democratic politicians of the south had still not rallied to endorse and throw the weight of their support to the ticket. LBJ invited hundreds of them to his ranch in Texas for a BAR B Q, and after a long afternoon of food and drink, he assembled all of them and, so the story goes, said to them: "Now I know many of you boys are having a hard time getting behind me and Mr. Kennedy in this race. And I know that's because many of you just aren't completely comfortable with Mr. Kennedy being from up there in Mass-a-chu-setts, and his being a Catholic and all, and I understand that. And I would never tell you to ignore your consciences, let alone the voters back home. But I did want to tell you what is going to happen if you don't help us, and do it real soon. We're going to lose this election is

what will happen. And after that, well, I will go back to the Senate, where I will be the most powerful man in Washington DC. And Mr. Kennedy, he will go back to the Senate too, and he will be very, very powerful too—because this election is going to be close. And ya-all should know this: if you think any of you are going to get any of your little ol' bills through our little ol' Senate, you better think again."

There was widespread Democratic leadership support in the south when JFK and LBJ won the 1960 Presidential election that November.

PARTISANSHIP

One final development in the political process needs to be noted: the unfortunate growth of partisanship and entrenchment of positions. Several factors have contributed to this dangerous trend. First, the redrawing of district boundaries has, over the past several decades, become increasingly partisan, with the result that more and more districts are drawn so as to favor one party or another. This has meant that the incumbents in such districts are largely secure in their reelection bids, most of which are, in reality, uncontested races after the primary. The effect is that without legitimate contests, candidates increasingly cater to one end or the other of the political spectrum; the middle ground, compromise—a movement toward the center of mainstream America—is disappearing in favor of core bases.

Second, term limits, where in effect, are changing the historical role of seniority and thus control over committees and control of the leadership. Term limits have also resulted in a disruption of the "gentleman's agreement" as to conduct within various chambers across the country; increased partisanship and acrimony have begotten polarization that has compromised the tradition of civil behavior. Moreover, term limits have put pressure on officeholders to move agendas at a greater pace.

Third, there has been an intangible change in the assumption that an elected official should represent the entire constituency and not partisan agendas and loyalties essential to election or reelection.

Fourth, certain issues that use to have bipartisan support or opposition have now become aligned with one party or the other, and as such, support or opposition has become rigidified according to party affiliation, wholly apart from the merits or demerits intrinsic to the issue.

Taken together, there is increased pressure for officeholders to conform to party positions and to become dogmatic and inflexible in their stances. As nonprofit concerns, issues, and needs are often perceived as outside the core elements that all politicians agree are the province of government to one extent or another, it is harder to rally bipartisan support for these concerns. Nonprofits have an increasingly harder time protecting their interests as the ethic of representing majority interests has been compromised.

That said, experience tells us that most elected officials still want to do the right thing. But exactly what the right thing is remains, as always, open to interpretation. As in any lobbying effort, the challenge is to convince someone that your way is the right way. At the same time the process is highly competitive; you are trying to put forth your case, and others are trying to do the same thing. Often the combatants are on diametrically opposite sides of a given issue. If you want to succeed, you need access, an open mind on the part of whomever you are trying to sway, evidence to support your position, proof that large numbers of an elected official's constituent group agree with you, information as to why a particular lawmaker is or is not predisposed to support you, and more than just a little bit of luck. You must be organized, focused, resolute, and persistent.

SIZING UP THE MEMBERSHIP

According to the Democracy Center, there are five main categories of legislators to think about in terms of lobbying strategy, each requiring its own special approach:

- **Champions:** All interest groups need at least a few lawmakers dedicated to being tireless, committed advocates for their cause. What they can do for the nonprofit is make the case to their colleagues, help develop a strong "inside" strategy, and be visible public spokespeople. What they need is useful information and visible support outside the Capitol.
- **Allies:** Another group of legislators will be on the nonprofit's side but can be pushed to do more—to speak up in party caucuses or on the floor, or otherwise express their support in strong terms.
- **Fence-sitters:** Some legislators will be uncommitted on specific issues and potentially able to vote either way. They are the nonprofit's key targets, and lobbying strategy is about putting together the right mix of "inside" persuasion and "outside" pressure to sway them the group's way.
- **Mellow opponents:** Another group of legislators will clearly vote against the nonprofit but will not be inclined to be active opponents on the issue. The key is to keep them from becoming more active and lobby them enough to give them pause, but not so much as to make them angry.
- **Hard-core opponents:** Finally, there are those lawmakers who are leading the nonprofit's opposition. What is important here is to isolate them, to highlight the extremes of their positions, rhetoric, and alliances, and to give other lawmakers pause about joining them. Stakeholder support is important in demonstrating widespread community support for the nonprofit's position as a strategy to isolate its hard-core opposition.

In addition, I believe the nonprofit needs to try to find at least one *guardian angel* among its champions—someone totally committed to its cause and willing to take it on and go to the mat, someone willing to lead the effort and offer compromises and trade-offs to get legislation passed, who will stand up for the group's cause publicly as a priority, and expend valuable personal political capital on its behalf. In many situations, the nonprofit will have but one or two champions, and in some instances, none. It needs at least one champion, and preferably, a guardian angel. The best guardian angel (in the legislature) is the majority party leader of one or the other chamber—either the Speaker or the Senate president pro tem (the minority party counterpart may be a good backup). The next best guardian angel is the chair of the committee, or subcommittee, hearing the bill. Of course, the chief executive makes an excellent guardian angel. The nonprofit may not be able to get a guardian angel, but if it can, this will help immeasurably in moving its cause along. Allies need to be converted—if not to champion status, then at least to *highly supportive* status. Similarly, fence-sitters need to be pushed to become supporters who might not necessarily be vocal, or even active, but who will be committed when it is time to vote. Mellow opponents need to be neutralized, and the strategy to convert them to fence-sitter status is to determine why they oppose the nonprofit's position. What is their rationale? Is it based on principles or on practical considerations? Do they really understand the nonprofit's issue, or do they have a false impression? If the latter, give them reasons why their opposition is counterproductive. There are several ways to do this: (1) show them that large numbers of voters in their district want the legislation passed; (2) get editorial support from the local newspapers; (3) beat the drums for media coverage; and (4) identify people close to the legislator and have them lobby for your position. It doesn't hurt if the nonprofit's PAC has contributed to their campaign.

Hard-core opponents are a major problem, particularly those whose opposition is based on ideology, and isolating them is no easy task. They need to be lobbied by their own party so as to reach an accommodation with them whereby they won't make the nonprofit's issue a priority to defeat. The nonprofit's goal when it is dealing with these people is to make its issue bipartisan. They may vote against the nonprofit and even raise obstacles to its success, but in the final analysis they won't make the group's defeat their *priority*. The nonprofit wants to make sure it is not their number one concern.

If the nonprofit has angels, champions, staunch supporters, mellow opponents, and not too many fence sitters, it can enlist the help of those who support it to persuade the group's hard-core opponents not to actively seek the defeat of its interests. Still, there will be situations in which the nonprofit may find itself the target of hard-core opponents, and the group must defeat these persons by keeping the votes on its side.

LEGISLATOR STAFF

Because the schedule of a legislator (and of many agency and department heads) is so hectic and the volume of materials presented to legislators in favor of or in opposition to an issue is so heavy, staff have an increasingly important role to play. Legislators rely on their staff to brief them on issues, interpret legislative language, and advise them on constituent matters. Staff also play the role of schedulers and gatekeepers, and access to the legislator is often "through" staff members. The nonprofit should not underestimate the influence key staff members may have on the elected official and the role they may play in determining whether the official supports its position or not. The best approach for the nonprofit when dealing with staff or anyone else is to treat everyone as it would treat the "number one" person—with respect, courtesy, and some deference (but as an equal), and it should always include them in the mix where possible.

While it is important to be resolute and determined, friendly people beget openness, receptivity, and courtesy and tend to win favors. Much of political success for the nonprofit lies in people doing it favors. If the group wants favors, it needs to do favors in return. This may not always be easy, as the personalities and competencies of staff members are different—but they should be courted in the same way as their bosses are. Staffers are one step removed from the "firing line," as it were, and thus have the luxury of being more open to all sides of an issue. Convincing staffers of the nonprofit's value may be easier than convincing the officeholder, and those staffers may then be able to change their boss' mind or be of help to the cause in other ways. Paying attention to these relationships is important.

Because the sheer volume of work in Washington, in state capitols, and in city halls has become so large, staffers are increasingly wielding power. They are often the ones actually drafting the bills and are frequently the ones charged with making the initial, and sometimes also the final, compromise allocations of funds to line items on behalf of their bosses on appropriations committees. It is not uncommon for key staffers to be more familiar with the issues and the details than those they work for. Some key staffers have been at the center of the fray, as it were, longer than their employers, and while some are there only for a short time, they may end up occupying positions of power. Remember, staffers may themselves have their own ambitions, including running for office, somewhere down the line. As advocacy is an ongoing enterprise, cementing relationships with lowly staffers now may ensure that somewhere in the future, the nonprofit's interests have a friend who is in a position to help them. It is impossible to take advantage of this kind of long-term thinking if the nonprofit doesn't have a substantial advocacy machine in place, over time.

In jurisdictions with term limits, there is far greater turnover in officeholders and their staffs. Some staff members follow an official from one post to another; some stay in the same position as their bosses transition in and out of their current office to newer, elected positions; still others are in position no longer (and often for less time) than the elected official they serve; and some go on to run for office themselves while others become lobbyists. While some staffers are longtime residents of the Capitol, others are fresh from the district that a legislator represents.

Key legislative staff positions include

- **Chief of staff:** the elected official's executive in charge and the person who supervises the rest of the staff. Getting to know the chiefs of staff personally and developing a relationship with them can be of enormous help in making the nonprofit's case to the elected officials. The nonprofit should invite Chiefs of Staff to lunch or an event associated with its organization. The group should court them and woo them in the same way as it would their boss. *It has to invest the time to get to know them personally.* And it should remember, some of these staff members may end up being elected to an office themselves one day. Chiefs of staff of leadership and committee chairs are usually *very* busy, but they are approachable. The nonprofit should schedule a meeting.
- **Legislative assistant:** the staff member charged with oversight and tracking of the legislation introduced during a session. Their primary focus is probably on the bills that their boss has introduced personally and is trying to get passed. They may provide advice and counsel on legislation that a nonprofit might propose and play a role in drafting its language. They are key persons good to know.

- **Scheduler:** usually the staff member charged with keeping the official's schedule and making appointments. Obviously if the nonprofit wants, or needs, access to the official, knowing this person can be helpful.
- **Field representative:** full-time staffers who run the district offices of State and federal legislators and are residents of the district. Since meetings in the district are logistically easier for the nonprofit to attend, and since officials look to their field staff to keep them up-to-date on local concerns, it is good for the group to know the field representatives. They may also be more accessible to local constituents and easier to court and lobby.

LEGISLATIVE COMMITTEES

Committees play an important role in the legislative process. There are too many bills to consider and too much business to transact for the whole chamber to deal with, and therefore work must be broken down and assigned to committees to process. Standing committees are permanent bodies that are part of the chamber's structure for handling business—from the budget to education and from government operations to judicial matters. Each chamber has standing committees that control certain procedural matters, such as the rules committee, ways and means committee, and the appropriations committee. These committees can be very powerful because they can determine whether or not a bill even gets heard and whether there is any funding for it, irrespective of whether or not it is passed. Many standing committees also have subcommittees to divide the workload. There are all kinds of ad hoc, select, joint, and special committees that can be permanent or semipermanent, or of limited term, and they generally deal with specific areas—for example, the economy, clean air and water, and transportation. Some of these committees have enormous workloads and are essential to the legislative process; others are figurehead and "image" committees with fewer substantive functions. For the most part, the standing committees have the power to vote on whether or not to move a bill forward, and the power to conduct investigations as opposed to merely gathering information.

Committee chairs exercise enormous power over committees by determining whether bills will be heard and when; evidence that will or won't be considered; who will testify and when, and who won't; when votes will be taken, if at all; and other matters that can impact a bill's chances of survival. Chairs may also hold patronage power in determining who will be hired to fill committee staff positions. A perk of power for such chairs may be hiring additional staff for the committee who will work in the chairs' own offices. Often these additional staffers work on a range of jobs for the chair, beyond just the work of the committee, thus giving the chair additional staffing resources. The larger one's staff the greater one's prestige and power.

Chairs thus have many things to "trade" with legislators who want the committee or subcommittee to move their bill(s) forward. In systems where the seniority system is in place and there is a dominant party, some legislators in safe districts are in power for decades, their power growing enormous over time. Their opposition can be fatal to any piece of legislation save for instances where they would stand virtually all alone were they to obstruct a bill's passage.

At the state and federal levels (and to a lesser extent at the city or county level), committees and subcommittees often also have staff support, including

- **Chief consultant:** Usually posted to the office of the chair of the committee, the chief consultant oversees the work of the committee for the chair. The nonprofit should note that the chief consultant often wears several hats and may simultaneously work in more than one area.
- **Chief minority consultant:** The minority party is often accorded the courtesy of having a consultant assigned to the committee via the ranking minority member.
- **Counsel:** Some committees may have their own legal counsel on staff; others may have access to the office of the legislative counsel. The draft wording of a piece of legislation is often under the purview of the counsel.
- **Other staff:** Depending on the size and importance of the committee, there may be one or more other staffers who organize hearings, conduct research, and perform other tasks.

The same rules of engagement apply to the staff of committees and subcommittees as apply to the staff of elected officials. The nonprofit should get to know them personally—the better the relationship the easier to enlist their aid in pushing its agenda. They can be enormously helpful in providing the group access and information, now and in the future. Again, remember that many of these people will also have long-term personal ambitions (and that is why politics is a long-term game and why relationships are so critical).

HEARINGS

While virtually all visible committee work is conducted in sessions open to the public, and there is often testimony before committees as part of the process of gathering information and data in the analysis of legislation prior to the committee vote, decision making is most often not so visible and is done in private. The open meetings are normally attended by government/administration and interest-group representatives so as to be on the public record; they are usually not of any interest to the media unless they have, as their subject matter, some issue of particular public interest. As they are of little interest to the media, they are really just pro forma events in the legislators' minds.

Most interests that have a stake in a given bill will have met with key committee members and staff prior to these hearings, but testimony will be given "for the record." As time is limited in these hearings, testimony is also limited, and thus submission of written testimony allows interested parties to present more detailed and comprehensive information. Often the committee vote, if not postponed or delayed, will be pro forma and previously known to everyone, but occasionally there are surprises. These committees also hold public hearings in voter districts periodically—both to solicit public input and as a grandstanding device.

INDEPENDENT OFFICES

In many legislatures, there are theoretically independent offices (though they are financed by and part of the legislature or the administration) that provide impartial analysis of legislation and make recommendations to the committees and chambers. One important area in which these offices operate is in budget oversight, where the office makes independent recommendations on approving, reducing, augmenting, or eliminating a line item in the budget on the basis of overall fiscal policies.

These offices and their recommendations are often ignored if the members of the committee want to advance or defeat the budget item for their own reasons (often political). Conversely, the recommendations (if negative) can provide a convenient cover for legislators who want to oppose a budget item or reduce allocation. There are other offices that provide a similar function with respect to other areas. These offices usually hold meetings with the departments and agencies that may be dealing with the subject matter of their recommendations, but generally they are not open to public lobbying. However, as they are permanent arms of government, it would be naïve to think that there is no interchange between them and the lobbying arm, or that no influence on them is ever exerted. Like special commissions with blue-ribbon appointees, created from time to time to study an issue, they are embraced when they suit a politician's purposes, and ignored when they don't. Much of their legitimate function has become nothing more than a "show" for appearance's sake, yet the "show" may be important to a given lawmaker, and one should therefore never treat cavalierly what might be yet another avenue to develop a relationship.

PARTY CAUCUSES

At the state and federal levels, each party tries to promote a unified front and control the voting patterns of its membership. Party caucuses meet periodically as a means for the leadership to set forth the "party" position and maintain discipline. This is one of the reasons why much lobbying effort is directed at the party leadership, and why the parties and special-interest lobbies have the relationship they do.

There are also special caucuses composed of legislators belonging to identified groups. Special caucuses may be formed along the lines of ethnicity (the Black Caucus, the Latino Caucus), interest areas (the arts caucus, the environmental caucus), length of membership in the body (the "freshman" legislator class caucus), geography (urban vs. rural interests), and other categories. These caucuses try to build bloc-voter support for their specific agendas, which are usually designed to advance the interest of a specific group. In some ways it is harder to lobby the caucuses, in other ways it is easier—depending on what the nonprofit is seeking from them. If the nonprofit can make the case—that what it wants benefits the caucus and advances the caucus' agenda—the caucus' support may be easier to secure, and this may be either a powerful endorsement or of face value only.

NURTURING THE RELATIONSHIP

The importance of developing solid *relationships* with decision makers, elected or otherwise, cannot be overemphasized. The more the relationship can transcend the issues that affect the nonprofit, the more personal it can become, and the more trust may be built between people and between an official and an organization. Therefore, it is advisable for the nonprofit to interact with the elected official on levels wholly apart and separate from both politics in general, and the issues of the nonprofit in particular. If the group interacts with officials only when it needs them and only about specific issues that impact the group, then it will always be perceived as having an agenda and nothing more. Whereas if the group communicates on a range of topics and issues and interacts socially and otherwise with the official (and acts as a financial contributor, and not just someone making constant demands and continually asking for some kind of support), it is likely to be perceived in an entirely different light and treated as a "friend" of the official, and not as a group to be held at arm's length. The best lobbyists might just be those who have been closest to the official over the longest period of time and who have been supporters from the earliest days. Those are the people the politician trusts. And remember that politicians have learned to be highly suspicious. Any lobbying strategy should seek to first identify any people involved with the nonprofit/coalition who already have relationships with the lawmaker. Even brief acquaintances have the advantage of some history on which to build and expand.

APPOINTED DECISION MAKERS

The Executive Branch of government is where what is commonly referred to as the "bureaucracy" is housed—that semipermanent collection of departments and agencies that manage the ongoing functions of government and implement and enforce statutes, rules, and regulations. Normally the chief elected officeholder (president, governor, mayor) has at least some power of patronage, that is, the power to appoint the heads and other senior-management leadership of these departments and agencies. These political appointees come in with the election of the executive leader and leave with his or her exit. They are, more often than not, people who were involved in the election of the chief and also in party politics, were major contributors to the campaign, or are people the newly elected chief felt otherwise obliged to reward with the appointment. Qualification for office, although it is not ignored, is thus not necessarily the most important criterion, and the appointment process is not always based on merit.

These senior appointed leaders generally adopt the overriding agenda of the executive officeholder who appointed them. Many of them serve at the pleasure of the executive officeholder and thus can be removed if their chief feels that they are not following his or her lead, agenda, or wishes. Many appointees are former legislative functionaries or holders of other offices. Their obligation is to support the appointing person or to resign from office. Most of the time, appointees follow the custom of taking the lead from the chief executive, but sometimes a maverick will follow an independent agenda. This bucking of the system may or may not be tolerated.

Because government is a large apparatus, many appointees have wide latitude in how they run their departments or agencies. Although they may receive broad and general guidelines from the chief executive, they have the power, within statutory prescriptions, to change policy, approaches, rules, regulations, and other ways their department or agency functions. Often a chief executive's agenda is not specific, and the mandate for the department head is rather to implement a "philosophy," thus giving the appointee considerable latitude in how to do that. These appointees are often given the power to make appointments to lower positions within their departments or agencies, which gives them more control, and, indirectly increases the chief executive's power. Their broad decision-making authority makes them the target of considerable lobbying efforts. They walk the thin line of loyalty to their superior's agenda and the demands of those over whom they have authority, all within the boundaries of statutes, customs, and their own viewpoints and priorities.

Many departments are large and cumbersome, and thus work slowly. Some interests want these departments and agencies to move slowly, if at all, whereas competing interests want them to expedite their decision making. The appointed head may or may not be able to change the way the employees that ostensibly report to him or her do business. Each agency and department within a bureaucracy has its own entrenched "culture, and it is difficult, if not sometimes impossible, to buck the established bureaucratic protocols and processes.

As most department and agency non-executive employees are civil servants, they are not subject to changes in administration, nor are they necessarily intimidated by the appointees, who are their superiors but, in truth, have little power over them. On the other hand, in some situations, even if the appointees have little direct power over the employees, they can exercise a great deal of indirect power that will affect the working environment. Most of the appointed heads wield considerable power though the nature of this power is different in each situation.

In the federal, state, and some large city jurisdictions, departments and agencies may be very large, with layers of bureaucracy, and thus access to the appointed head may not be easy. Sometimes it may be necessary to work with someone lower on the hierarchical rung, but one should try to deal with people at the appointed level as they are more likely to have greater decision-making authority and are more likely to be subject to the politics of the situation. Even in large bureaucracies, one should begin by approaching the highest-level appointee.

Highly visible department or agency head appointees may find themselves in the unenviable position of scapegoats for the elected chief executive should a situation arise that would prove politically embarrassing to the executive; more than a few such appointees have been sacrificed on this altar.

Lobbying these appointed decision makers is a game slightly different from lobbying legislators:

First, as they are obligated to follow the dictates of the chief executive's agenda and to carry out and implement the elected chief executive's priorities, those who seek changes in this agenda or the way it is being implemented are really lobbying the appointees to get them to lobby the chief executive. While lobbying the chief executive directly to seek a change in the priorities or the course of action would seem the most logical course of action, accessibility may be a problem. Therefore, seeking the help of the executive's appointees may make more sense.

Thus, it is essential for the nonprofit to tailor its positions, if possible, to fit into the overall agenda of the chief executive. If the nonprofit can make the argument that support for its position promotes a priority of the administration, it may have an easier time getting department support.

Second, there is a tendency for appointed department and agency heads to engage in lobbying within the Executive Branch. Once appointed, department and agency heads tend to become the spokespeople for their department; they tend to develop a loyalty to the agency they head, seek to protect it, and work to enhance its importance within the overall government structure. They become, in effect, lobbyists in their sphere of influence. One way to increase their effectiveness as lobbyists is to rally the powerful constituent groups over which their department may have oversight or control and mold them for a lobbying effort to impact how the boss (the chief executive) views the department. Thus a symbiotic relationship develops between those who govern and those who are governed. Many of those who are governed are powerful people (perhaps more powerful than the appointed department or agency head) and they may become major players in the lobbying game, by employing lobbying firms and by contributing to the campaigns of candidates. Many appointees come from the field that the department oversees or have long-standing relationships with the constituencies that come under their oversight as a department or agency head. These relationships and their level of expertise and experience may have been a primary qualification for their appointment in the first place.

Thus, putting together an alliance of organizations operating within the area over which the department has authority and individuals with prestige and power in that field, in support of the nonprofit position, may increase the chances that the appointed department head will be supportive.

Third, departments and agencies are generally governed by rules, regulations, laws, and procedures created by the Legislative Branch, and therefore the latitude accorded to the appointed bureaucrats to make decisions may be severely or slightly limited. Custom and the history of the way the department or agency conducts its affairs may also impact its decision-making authority. Public scrutiny, the level of media focus on their activities, and the number and nature of competing interests in the arenas over which they have oversight also impact the appointee's decision-making processes.

Thus, nonprofits should know what laws, statutes, and customs govern the decision-making authority and processes of the department or agency they are trying to influence. They should use the legislature's ultimate power over the department or agency to exploit its relationship with key people in the legislature.

Anyone who wishes to influence decisions that are made at the executive department/agency level will need to bear in mind these contextual influences on their lobbying efforts. Knowledge of these contexts and the nuances of how they apply is learned over time, and this is yet another reason why people hire professional lobbyists to help them navigate this complex system. Once again, relationships with key people in key positions, makes lobbying those people easier. Over time, the world of elected and appointed government officials is really small; the players move from position to position—from the legislative side to the administrative side—and back again. For this reason, it is wise to never burn bridges in this world; you never know whether the person who is "out" of power now might not be back "in" power soon.

APPOINTED BOARDS AND COMMISSIONS

Some areas are governed by regulatory boards or commissions, the members of which may be appointed. Often, appointments to these boards are not at the pleasure of the appointing executive, but are for specified terms, and thus the appointees are less constrained by obligations to follow the appointing executive's agenda. Generally these oversight bodies are less subject to lobbying efforts, as decision making is by committee and hearings, and deliberations are, more often than not, public, placing the process under greater scrutiny. Still, they generally make decisions by votes, and if the area the nonprofit is concerned with is subject to control by a board or commission, getting to know the members and staff and developing relationships with them help make the nonprofit more informed, better educated, and more knowledgeable about the members' decision-making process. All of this is of value in trying to make the case for the nonprofit's position and influence the decision-making process. The rules applicable to lobbying for the appointment of specific people are not as stringent as those for lobbying for or against candidates for elected office. The rules governing lobbying of the boards or commissions themselves may fall under proscriptions similar to those applicable to general lobbying.

ELECTED BOARDS AND COMMISSIONS

Some governing bodies, such as school boards, are composed of elected members who serve specific terms. While these bodies operate under protocols and procedures different from those of true legislative bodies, many of the same rules apply to efforts to influence their decisions. They generally have staff and standing committees, hold public meetings and hearings, and have a voting procedure. Some of their elected members are affiliated with political parties, and sometimes run as nonpartisan independents. But each of them runs on platforms and takes positions on issues, and they can be approached and lobbied in the same way other elected officials can. Rules for supporting elected members of boards and commissions are generally the same as those for supporting other elected officials.

CHAPTER 4

ADVOCACY, LOBBYING, AND THE LAW

> The law, in its majestic equality, forbids the rich as well as the poor to sleep under bridges, to beg in the streets, and to steal bread.
>
> Anatole France

INTRODUCTION

This chapter is meant to provide the reader with a general overview of the current legal framework for nonprofit lobbying, and what a coalition of nonprofits would need to do, as a hardball lobbyist, to avail itself of all the tools to influence decision making by public officials. It's not meant to be relied on as definitive legal advice, and as this area of the law is in a state of flux, nonprofits—both individual organizations, and coalitions of organizations—should seek both legal counsel and accounting advice within their jurisdictions to ensure that they are in complete compliance with the existing state and federal statutes, laws, and applicable governing rules and regulations. The specifics of all the rules and regulations may seem so complex that it's impossible to decipher all the details, but this is why nonprofits hire lawyers and accountants, and in reality, compliance isn't that complex at all. In fact, it's relatively simple to achieve. Nonprofits shouldn't use the apparent complexity as an excuse to not become effective lobbyists. The playing field will forever be unequal if nonprofits don't use the same structures that the private sector uses for lobbying.

Confusion over what lobbying activities are permitted for nonprofits seems to persist. Nonprofits seem reluctant, almost afraid, to lobby. And often, the mistaken belief that they can't lobby or that lobbying will jeopardize their tax-exempt status, is used as an excuse for ignoring advocacy altogether. The truth is that nonprofits *can* engage in advocacy *and* lobbying—they can support or oppose specific legislation, and even support candidates for public office *provided* they create the structures required by law and adhere to the rules and regulations governing each.

For a nonprofit coalition to avail itself of the full range of options to lobby, it needs to create four legal entities. A coalition composed of nonprofit organizations under the Internal Revenue Code Section 501c(3) needs to create the following relevant structures;

- a new 501c(3) organization that will represent the coalition;
- a 501c(4) organization;
- a PAC; and
- a 527 organization/fund.

The differences in each of these structures have to do with the

- tax consequences to the organizations and to their donors;
- varying reporting requirements;
- permissible lobbying areas and activities;
- ceiling amounts on permissible donations/contributions;
- ceiling amounts on permissible spending; and
- restrictions as to the permissible use of funds.

The categories used in determining the regulation of lobbying are as follows:

- where the funds come from to finance the activity
  - a distinction is made between "hard" money, contributed by individuals, and "soft" money, contributed by organizations or corporations.
- whether the activity engaged in is classified as advocacy or lobbying or candidate support.

Regulations of activities govern the following:

- the nonprofit's tax-exempt status;
- whether or not a donation or contribution will be tax deductible for the donor or contributor;
- the ceiling limits on the amount an individual, organization, or corporation may contribute to any given solicitation for funds (depending on the use of those funds);
- the imposition of a tax on income used for prohibited expenditures by the nonprofit; and
- the obligation to make certain declarations as to the categorization of the activity and to report certain information, including the donor source of income and where and how the money was spent.

The IRS defines lobbying as *any attempt to influence legislation* (whether at the federal, state, county, or city level), and also distinguishes between *direct* lobbying (attempting to influence legislators on proposed legislation) and *grassroots* lobbying (attempting to persuade the public to influence legislators on proposed legislation). The law distinguishes between lobbying in support of specific *legislation* and that in support of specific *candidates*.

Here's the short version of how it works:

- A coalition of 501c(3) nonprofits in a given sector, with a common advocacy agenda, bands together and forms a new 501c(3) organization, the purpose of which is to advocate, educate, and lobby on behalf of the coalition members. This new organization is like any other 501c(3). It can advocate and educate elected officials, the public, the media, and its own membership on policy matters, the only restriction being how much of its budget it can spend on direct lobbying. As long as this new organization follows the rules and regulations for lobbying, all contributions to it are tax deductible for the donor, and the organization itself is tax exempt.

  The linchpin of this work is that nonprofits need to band together to form coalitions to be effective in their lobbying efforts. For the vast majority of individual nonprofit organizations (which should also engage in advocacy and educate and lobby decision makers on an ongoing basis), all they would likely ever need is to make the 501(h) exemption election. Establishing the 501c(4), the PAC, and the 527 fund are for larger coalitions.

- The new 501c(3) then forms a new 501c(4) organization. There is no tax on the income of the new 501c(4) entity; however, contributions to it are *not* tax deductible for the donor. The new 501c(4) organization is not restricted on how much of its budget can be spent on lobbying to influence specific legislation. Like the 501c(3), it can't endorse or otherwise support individual candidates for office.

- The new 501c(4) then creates a PAC, which can be little more than a segregated "fund." The 501c(4) can solicit donations to its PAC from its members, but those contributions are *not* tax deductible for the donor. The 501c(4) can't accept contributions from corporations, including nonprofits. The new PAC created by the 501c(4) can't be funded by the parent 501c(3) organization, but there can be overlapping governance of the two entities.

- Finally, the last option is for the new 501c(4) to create a second "fund"—a 527 fund that will allow it to solicit funds from a wide pool of people, and support or oppose both issues meaning the 527 fund can use money raised to lobby in support or opposition to any given issue, and/or to support candidates for office by such things as taking out advertisements urging people to vote for a specific candidate, provided there is no connection or coordination between the candidate's election campaign and the 527 fund administrators; the 527 fund monies cannot be given to a candidate, but can be spent to promote his or her election and, indirectly, candidates for public office, so long as there is no connection or coordination between the 527 fund and its expenditures and the campaign organization of the candidates who are being supported.

This seems, on its face, so confusing as to discourage many nonprofits from engaging in any lobbying or electioneering activity. But forgoing participation that is permitted, even if compliance with all the rules is time-consuming, is a mistake. It really isn't as complex as it seems, and nonprofits can comply with the rules and regulations as easily as the private sector. The strategy for nonprofits ought to be to avail themselves of the same opportunities to influence governmental action that are available to private-sector interests so they can effectively compete in the arena to leverage influence on the decisions made by government, to no greater, or lesser, extent. The erroneous belief that lobbying, PACs, and the like are not permitted for nonprofits continues to negatively impact the sector's exercise of the tremendous political power that it might wield to serve its missions.

In this chapter, I am purposely not drilling down to all the minutiae of every regulation, because I want the reader to just grasp the overall concept of the structural framework of how it's done. Leave the detail work to lawyers and accountants—it really isn't that complex and shouldn't be expensive to construct. There are a number of websites that help to explain current laws, rules, and regulations as to what lobbying activity nonprofits may and may not engage in. They include www.npaction.org (nonprofit action) and www.clpi.org (Center for Lobbying in the Public Interest).

501C(3) LOBBYING

There are essentially two categories of lobbying permitted to 501c(3) nonprofits by the IRS rules, depending on whether or not a nonprofit makes a simple election.

Prior to 1976, the IRS prohibited 501c(3) organizations from engaging in anything more than "insubstantial lobbying." While the IRS never defined exactly what would constitute more than "insubstantial," it was generally agreed that about 5 percent of an operational budget and the time of employees and officers would be a general cut-off point. Post-1976, nonprofits that "elected" to be governed by the 1976 rules fall under specific guidelines delineating how much time and money they can spend on lobbying. In 1990, Congress clarified these guidelines.

Thus, nonprofits today fall under two situations. If they elect to be governed by the 1976 rules, as amended in 1990, they must complete a 501(h) election form (Form 5768, a simple one-page form, which, once filed, is retroactive to the beginning of the year it was filed, and remains in effect unless cancelled by the nonprofit). While some nonprofits continue to cling to the old wives' tale that making such election will "red flag" the organization and subject it to IRS audits and closer scrutiny, the exact opposite is the truth. There is no evidence whatsoever that nonprofits making the 501(h) election suffer any negative consequences as a result. In fact, nonprofits that do *not* make the election continue to be subject to the vague "insubstantial" test, and their lobbying activities are arguably therefore much more subject to interpretation. All nonprofits are required to report expenditures on lobbying efforts each year. There is simply no good reason for any nonprofit *not* to make the annual 501(h) election, even if they don't intend to engage in lobbying of any kind. Yet, an overwhelmingly vast majority of all nonprofits never make the election. This fact is at the heart of their decreasing and declining political power at all levels of government. Adherence to this kind of thinking portends dire consequences for the health of nonprofits in the United States.

If a 501c(3) elects to take the 501(h) exemption, it's governed by the following rules. The *total* lobbying expenditure limits under the 501(h) election are

- 20 percent of the first $500,000 of exempt purpose expenditures, plus
- 15 percent of the next $500,000 of exempt purpose expenditures, plus
- 10 percent of the next $500,000 of exempt purpose expenditures, plus
- 5 percent of the remaining exempt purpose expenditures up to a total cap of $1 million.

(Exempt purpose expenditures are all payments made in a year, except those on investment management unrelated businesses, and certain fund-raising expenses. Thus, exempt expenditures include, for the typical 501c(3), the lion's share of its budget.)

Under the 501(h) election, the IRS distinguishes between direct and grassroots lobbying. *Direct lobbying* is when nonprofits state their position on specific legislation to legislators or other government employees who participate in the formulation of legislation, or urge their members to do so. In order to count as direct lobbying it must refer to specific legislation and express a view on it. A call to "protect the environment" is not direct lobbying as it does not refer to specific legislation.

Grassroots lobbying is when nonprofits state their position on specific legislation to the general public *and* ask them to contact legislators or other government employees who participate in the formulation of legislation. If they do not include a call to action in their communication to the general public, it isn't lobbying. Thus, informing the public about a specific bill, but not stating a position for or against, is not grassroots lobbying. Coalitions should exercise caution in the wording of their communications to avoid the inference that action is being urged if they want to categorize the activity as direct, and not grassroots, lobbying. (They should note that the only reason for making such a distinction is to meet the ceiling restriction of 25 percent total expenditures allowed for grassroots lobbying.) Urging their own members to lobby counts as *direct lobbying,* not *grassroots lobbying.*

The distinction between direct and grassroots lobbying is important under the 501(h) election because the 1976 Lobby Law specifies different expenditure limits for grassroots and direct lobbying activity. The expenditure on grassroots lobbying should be only one-fourth of that on direct lobbying. For example, if an organization's annual permissible lobbying expenditures are $100,000, it can spend only $25,000 on grassroots lobbying; it can spend the remaining $75,000 on direct lobbying. It can, of course, spend the full $100,000 on direct lobbying.

The benefits of taking the 501(h) election include

- restriction-free lobbying activities that do not require expenditures, such as unreimbursed activities conducted by bona fide volunteers;
- clear definitions of various kinds of lobbying communications, enabling electing charities to control whether they are lobbying or not;
- higher lobbying dollar limits and fewer items that count toward the exhaustion of those limits;

- less likelihood of losing tax exemption, because the IRS may only revoke exempt status from electing organizations that exceed their lobbying limits by at least 50 percent averaged over a four-year period;
- exemption from personal penalty for individual managers of an electing charity that exceeds its lobbying expenditure limits.

All 501(c)(3) organizations (except churches, an association of churches, and integrated auxiliaries) must report lobbying expenditures to the IRS. For nonprofits that do not elect to be governed by the 1976 Lobby Law, the IRS requires detailed descriptions of a wide range of activities related to lobbying. For organizations that take the 501(h) election, the only requirement is to report how much was spent on lobbying, and how much of that total amount for the year was spent on grassroots lobbying. (There are different and additional reporting requirements for the 501c(4), the PAC, and the 527 organization/fund structures.) There may be a great deal of nonprofit lobbying going on that isn't being reported, and the custom of the IRS excusing or overlooking this failure may be changing to one of stricter compliance. Note that the reason for increasing the regulation of, and the imposition of additional requirements on, activities by nonprofits is the increase in nonprofit lobbying and electioneering. As long as nonprofits were largely absent from these arenas there was no need to impose greater regulations.

Not all activity, even though it may impact an elected official's vote, is actually lobbying. There are five activity categories that are excluded from the term "influencing legislation." They are the following:

- **Self-defense:** communication on any legislation that would affect an organization's existence, powers and duties, tax-exempt status, or deductibility of contributions.
- **Technical advice:** providing technical advice to a governmental body in response to a written communication.
- **Nonpartisan analysis or research:** studying community problems and their potential solutions is considered nonpartisan if it's "an independent and objective exposition of a particular subject matter . . . [which] may advocate a particular position or viewpoint so long as there is a sufficiently full and fair exposition of pertinent facts to enable the public or an individual to form an independent opinion or conclusion."
- **Examinations and discussions of broad social, economic, and similar problems:** communication with the organization's own members with respect to legislation that is of direct interest to them is not lobbying, so long as the discussion does not address the merits of a specific legislative proposal and contains no call for action.
- **Regulatory and administrative issues:** communication with governmental officials or employees on nonlegislative (i.e., administrative) matters such as rule-making is exempt.

Moreover, an effort to educate and inform elected officials and the general public about the general value and benefit of a nonprofit's programs, services, mission, projects, and so on, as long as it does not relate directly to, or urge specific action on, any given piece of legislation, is not lobbying. Thus, keeping an elected official apprised of what the organization is doing or informing officials and the public about the positive results and benefit to society of a given program or programs, is not lobbying—as long as the effort is not connected to urging specific action on specific legislation, and nonprofits can engage in this type of education and information dissemination without limitation. Specifically, nonprofits may inform their own membership of a given piece of legislation and include their position in support or opposition as long as it doesn't urge the membership to lobby one way or the other. *All* nonprofits should constantly be engaged in this type of education and information dissemination.

And finally, lobbying is deemed to have occurred only when there is an expenditure of funds by the nonprofit on an activity. Therefore, if there is no money spent, the activity isn't lobbying subject to the rules and limitations. If an organization's volunteers lobby on its behalf, and there is no expenditure by it assisting or facilitating that lobbying, there is no lobbying by the organization. On the other hand, if, for example, the organization provides training to those volunteers, any expenditure on this program would be a lobbying expense.

501C(4) LOBBYING

Nonprofit corporations under 501c(4) may engage in any lobbying activity to influence specific legislation without any of the above restrictions; however, the ban on supporting, in any way, specific individual candidates for office still applies to them. The 501c(4) entity pays no income tax, but contributions to it are *not* tax deductible for the donor. The 501c(3) may effectively control the actions of the 501c(4) (all that is required is that the 501c(4) be separately incorporated, and that accurate books and records reflect that no tax-exempt contributions to the 501c(3) were used to fund the lobbying activities of the 501c(4) (including its proportionate share of overhead, such as rent, travel, phones, personnel, and so on). The two organizations may have identical boards of directors and may share staff and office space, and the 501c(3) may pay for some of the overhead costs of the 501c(4). There are restrictions on who may be solicited to contribute funds to the 501c(4).

POLITICAL ACTION COMMITTEES

Political action committees are allowed to support, endorse, and make contributions to the campaigns of candidates for office, which is prohibited for both 501c(3) and 501c(4) organizations. But the 501-c-(3) and the 501-c-(4) can create a PAC, which can be nothing more than a separate "fund" set up by a 501c organization. The committee can't solicit or accept funds from a corporation (including nonprofit corporations) or a union general fund, and thus a PAC created by a 501c(3) or 501c(4) nonprofit can't operate with funds from the parent nonprofit's general budget. It could appeal to its members to contribute funds to its PAC, but those contributions won't be tax deductible for the donor. There are limitations on how much individuals can contribute to a PAC, and limitations on how much a PAC can contribute to a given candidate and on the total that can be given to all candidates. Accurate books and records of where the money came from must be maintained.

Political action committees can be "connected" (raising funds exclusively from within the ranks of their "parent" organization or organizations), or "unconnected" (raising funds from supporters among the general public if the PAC is not the creation of a parent 501c(3) or not otherwise directly affiliated with an existing organization or group). There are also "leadership PACs," which are also unconnected to any parent group, created most often by politicians to expand their power by having a pool of funds to distribute to their fellow candidates of the same party. Apart from PACs there is individual support (by both single people and an individual group) whereby money is spent to influence voters to elect one candidate in preference to another, but is not given directly to the candidate's campaign and has no connection to it. As long as there is this separation, no limits apply to the amount the "individual" can spend—the only requirement is a reporting one. Organizing multiple "individual" contributions (called "bundling") can be by a PAC or by invisible forces.

The McCain/Feingold reform law seeks to plug loopholes in the federal election campaign laws and clarify limits on how much money can be contributed, by whom, when, and for what purpose. Most of these limitations have relatively little impact on nonprofits because nonprofits will likely depend on much smaller individual contributions than the levels McCain/Feingold sets. If a PAC lobbies for or against legislation, or beyond the limits set for candidate support, there may be tax consequences of expenditures over the ceiling amount, and for this reason, lobbying regarding specific legislation should be left to the 501c(4), and care should be taken in segregation of accounts and accurate record-keeping as to expenditures and source of income.

To the extent PACs have a sullied public reputation and the image of being devices employed by "fat cats" working behind the scenes to manipulate the system to their own advantage, and because the impact of their statutorily limited contributions has waned due to inflation (lessening the purchasing power of the maximum contribution), they may be out of favor. The action may have shifted somewhat to other devices such as the 527 organization or individual "bundled" contributions to support a given candidate's bid for office—but nonprofit coalitions should consider all their options when they create their foundation structures.

527 ORGANIZATIONS

The IRS provides that a Section 527 political organization is exempt from federal taxation (except the tax on investment income). A political organization is defined as a party, a committee, an association, a "fund," or other organization (whether or not incorporated) organized and operated primarily for the purpose of accepting contributions, or making expenditures, or both, for a specified exempt function. And one exempt function is defined as influencing, or attempting to influence, the selection, nomination, election, or appointment of any individual to any local, state, or federal public office. A 527 organization may really be a PAC by another name. The difference is that it isn't subject to the same contribution limits imposed on PACs by the Federal Election Commission (FEC). The prohibition bans any coordination or link with the candidate's election committee.

It can, however, raise funds and, hypothetically, take out an advertisement in support of a specific candidate as long as there is no direct connection with that candidate.

A 527 organization is permitted to accept contributions of any amount from any source. However, it's required to make regular reports to the IRS of its funding and expenditures. It can spend money to elect or defeat candidates, but it can't give money to the candidate or be directly associated with the campaign. Depending on the outcome of the court challenges to the Bipartisan Campaign Reform Act of 2002, 527 organizations may also be prohibited from certain types of "electioneering communications" immediately prior to elections. There is the presumption that any communication that refers to a specific candidate for office is considered express advocacy for the election or defeat of a candidate. As such any communication within thirty days of a primary and sixty days of a general election, targeted at the relevant electorate, is considered an "electioneering communication" and subject to limits under the FEC regulations.

Section 527 organizations may engage in issue advocacy (including education of the public about officeholder voting records, positions on issues, views, and qualifications), and in voter-registration drives. Thus, they are in vogue as a way to raise unlimited funds to engage in these permissible activities, which are often related to candidate campaigns indirectly.

Rules of the FEC effective from January 2005 imposed new regulations and limitations on solicitation, segregation, allocation, and expenditure of funds raised that identify, in the solicitation communications, all or part of the funds that will be used to support or defeat candidates (even by inference), and require new reporting by the 527 organization. Section 501c(3) and 501c(4) nonprofits are not directly impacted by these rulings, but PACs are. There are likely to be continual proposals for reforms in this area, and it will be incumbent on nonprofits to monitor legislative action that might change the current rules and regulations.

THE RIGHTS OF INDIVIDUALS

Finally, there is no ban on individual members, board officers, staff, volunteers, or other supporters of the mission or specific programs of any nonprofit organization directly supporting, working for, endorsing, or contributing funds to the campaign of anyone running for public office. There is also no ban on their opposing any candidate, or making that candidate know that the individual's support or opposition is based on the candidate's support or opposition to the goals and needs of the nonprofit and its mission. As long as individuals do not purport to speak for, or on behalf of, the nonprofit with which they are affiliated, or use the nonprofits' means of communications to make known their stand, it's their constitutional right to lobby and support or oppose candidates. There are ceilings on the amounts they may contribute, as set forth in state and federal election laws.

Unfortunately, most individuals involved with nonprofit organizations are not directly involved in the election of individuals to office, and, of those that are so involved, few make it clear to the candidate that their support is conditional on the candidate's support for the nonprofit or its mission. Wealthy contributors often keep

Table 1   IRS nonprofit categories for advocacy/lobbying

Organization	Contributions are tax deductible	Limits on contributions and/or source of funds	Limits on spending for lobbying	May contribute to candidates and still maintain tax-exempt status	May lobby for or against legislation and still maintain tax-exempt status	Reporting requirements	May spend money on influencing election/appointment of candidates for local, state, federal office
501c(3)[1]	Yes	No/No	Yes	No	Yes (up to 20%)	Yes	No
501c(4)[2]	No	No/Yes	No	No	Yes	Yes	No
PAC[3]	No	Yes	Yes	Yes	No	Yes	Yes
527 orgs[4]	No	Yes[5]	Some	No	No	Yes	Yes (indirectly)

1. Organizations governed by 501c(3) face no limit on their educational efforts, and they may lobby (up to 20% of the $1 million ceiling subject to the limitation of 25% of the total on grassroots lobbying) if IRS election is made. Otherwise the test is "not substantial" activity. Contributions are tax deductible for donors. Organizations are income-tax exempt.

2. Organizations under 501c(4) may engage in unlimited lobbying (but not candidate support). Contributions are not tax deductible for donors, but the 501c(4) may only solicit its own members for contributions. Organizations are income-tax exempt.

3. Political action committees may engage in direct candidate support (up to prescribed limits). Contributions are limited and are not tax deductible for donors. Organizations are income-tax exempt.

4. Organizations under 527 may engage in unlimited issue advocacy, voter registration drives, ballot initiative support and opposition, and indirect candidate support. No link or coordination with candidate's campaign organization is permitted. Contributions are not deductible for donors. Organizations are income-tax exempt.

5. Proposed legislation to change rules governing 527 organizations are currently under consideration.

any favors they might be owed from their support for candidates for the sake of their own business interest. That ought to change.

SUMMARY

To avail itself of the full range of opportunities to advocate, lobby, and participate in candidate elections to the same extent as every other segment of society, public or private, nonprofits need to consult with qualified attorneys and accountants and take the following steps:

- **First,** band together with other nonprofits within their field and form a 501c(3) nonprofit organization to manage and direct the coalition's general advocacy efforts. The income of the 501c(3) is not taxable and contributions to it are tax deductible. If it makes the 501(h) election, and it should, it can spend up to 20 percent of its income on lobbying (up to 25 percent of that amount on grassroots lobbying) and any amount on nonlobbying advocacy (e.g., education). It can't engage in candidate support or opposition, directly or indirectly. While it could form a PAC or a 527 fund, this is best left to a 501c(4). See next bullet point below.
- **Second,** the new 501c(3) advocacy coalition can then form a new 501c(4) non-profit organization. Its income won't be taxable, but neither will donations be tax deductible for the contributor. It can spend all its income on lobbying, but it can't engage in candidate support or opposition, directly or indirectly.
- **Third,** the 501c(4) organization can then create a tax-exempt PAC and solicit donations (not deductible for the donor). It can't use the general funds of either the 501c(3) or the 501c(4)—only funds it can show were donated by individuals. The PAC can spend the money raised from members of the 501c(3) or 501c(4) on supporting or opposing candidates for office—but there are prescribed limitations as set forth in the McCain/Feingold Act (which also prescribes limitations on the contributions by individuals). The reason for creating the PAC is to be able to provide financial support to candidates for office (within the prescribed limits set by the governing laws). The PAC can recruit new members from the general public, and the dues those new members pay to join can be used to support candidates for office within the rules governing PACs.
- **Fourth,** the 501c(4) can also create a tax-exempt 527 organization/*fund* and solicit donations (not tax deductible for the donor) from the public. The money may be spent on supporting "issues," which may include, indirectly, money spent to support or oppose a candidate in a federal election so long as there is no link or coordination whatsoever between the 527 fund and the campaign organization of any specific candidate. There are rules and regulations governing the solicitation, characterization, and expenditure of this money that must be followed. The reason for creating the 527 fund is to allow for solicitation of contributions from a wider pool and for wider support or opposition to issues and to office seekers, provided there is no coordination between these office seekers, their organizations, and the nonprofit that created the 527.

Many nonprofit advocacy-based coalitions may not opt to create a 527 fund right away, but they can still raise funds and support or oppose both specific legislation and candidates with broad latitude as long as they adhere to the rules and regulations governing contribution and expenditure limits, reporting requirements, and segregation of funds for 501c(3)s, 501c(4)s, and PACs.

These structures and the rules and regulations governing them (insofar as supporting or opposing candidates and lobbying in support or opposition to specific legislation) relate primarily to federal candidates and legislation. While nonprofits are sometimes permitted a wider latitude of activity with respect to state candidates and legislation, at least by the omission of federal statutes and regulations specifically governing these areas, there exist state laws and regulations that may differ from the federal guidelines. Thus, as nonprofit advocacy/lobbying/electioneering strategy will doubtless include a major percentage of activity on the state level, coalitions need to check the situation in the state in which they intend to operate. And as the rules and regulations governing lobbying and supporting candidates by nonprofits are likely to be amended or changed over time, every nonprofit coalition should determine, on an annual basis, what issues it wants to lobby for, what legislation it favors and opposes, and which candidates it wants to support and oppose. Then, with the advice of counsel, it should map its strategy in each area, and plan what each of its structures—501c(3) and 501c(4), PAC, or 527 political organization—can do so as to comply with the rules and regulations governing each structure, including separating fundraising, the funds collected, complying with the reporting requirements, and adhering to the rules governing the purposes and allowable amounts for each expenditure.

It's necessary to be scrupulous in maintaining accurate and complete books and records of the source of funds for each of these structures and how the money was spent. Funds will need to be separated and the coalition must not commingle these funds. There are also certain reporting requirements that must be met on an annual basis. None of these requirements are that burdensome. The IRS already requires accurate books and records of nonprofits engaged in any lobbying efforts, and annual reports of all nonprofits.

Individual 501c(3) organizations that make up a coalition should continue to be involved in advocacy and lobbying to the extent permitted, *as individual organizations,* and their membership and supporters should, *as individuals,* be actively involved in the support of candidates who are generally supportive of its mission.

While all this seems a confusing labyrinth, in fact compliance with the seeming complexity of the requirements is a relatively simple job for an attorney and an accountant, and should not discourage the leadership of the coalition from utilizing all of the tools available to it to mount an effective and competitive advocacy and/or lobbying apparatus. Annual legal and accounting advice and counsel shouldn't be a major expenditure, and many nonprofit coalitions will be able to get pro bono legal services. Whatever the minor cost, it's simply another cost of doing business. Nonprofits must stop pretending they cannot lobby to the same extent as the private sector. They can, and their continuing to behave as if they cannot is crippling the effectiveness nonprofits have, and might have, in impacting government decisions. This is the core argument of this book.

CHAPTER 5

BUILDING AN ADVOCACY FOUNDATION

INTRODUCTION

Our greatest glory is not in never falling, but in rising every time we fall.

Confucius

This section and subsequent sections assume that some type of collaborative effort is necessary for most nonprofit organizations to mount even a semblance of the comprehensive advocacy/lobbying/electioneering effort envisioned here. Individual organizations that have the perceived need and the requisite resources to go it alone can apply to the internal operations of the single nonprofit advocacy and/or lobbying model much of what is discussed in the following sections, which deal with the collaborative coalition.

BUILDING A COALITION OF THE FIELD

The best way to have a good idea is to have lots of ideas.

Linus Pauling

In today's political world, successful lobbying interests have substantial resources, including, as part of the overall strategy, funds to contribute to candidates' campaign war chests. In every state capitol and in every big city, including Washington, D.C., there are endless $1,000-a-plate breakfasts, lunches, and dinners attended primarily by lobbyists. Interests that lack the financial resources to attend these functions, engage media relations and public-opinion sampling firms and pay for professional, full-time staff to manage every aspect of their advocacy and/or lobbying effort are simply playing a different game than those who have the resources to do these things. Increasingly, those who cannot afford the admission price of these functions have less chance at the outset that their objectives will be realized. But nonprofits can form coalitions of like-minded individual organizations and compete more effectively with private-sector groups in the lobbying arena.

BUILDING ON A SOLID FOUNDATION

Few nonprofits can muster the funds and other resources required anywhere near the level required to mount an effort as substantial as, say, that of pharmaceutical companies or their counterparts in other industries (at least not yet). For this reason, they must form coalitions both with their counterparts within their areas of interest and with stakeholders outside those areas. Thus, for example, if the arts sector wants to further arts education, then symphonies, theater groups, dance troupes, museums, and every other arts discipline group must form alliances with arts educators, artists, and other segments of the arts community to form advocacy groups that have as their goal a comprehensive K-12 curriculum-based arts education program in every school in the United States. In turn, these coalitions must form an alliance with the tourism industry, the wider education community, and any other potential stakeholder group that will be impacted by the success or failure of arts promotion. These alliances are the only way that individual nonprofits or groups of nonprofits can raise the necessary funds to compete with large, powerful interest groups plying the political scene. But even a coalition of nonprofits may not be able to raise funds sufficient to make itself the equal of the players with deeper pockets. Some individual companies, organizations, and even individuals play the game successfully as well, but increasingly, coalitions, unions, trade associations, and other affiliated groups dominate the scene in both the public and private sectors.

Coalitions are necessary for another reason—they make it easier to muster a grassroots effort of the public that is large enough to make its presence felt among elected officials. The NRA has both the funds (according to opensecrets.org website, the NRA ranked 30th among the "all time" special interests donors since 1989, ten points ahead of the American Dental Association and ten points behind the National Auto Dealers Association) and the citizen army to ensure that its interests are protected in the halls of government. Nonprofits need the same resources and can compete effectively if they choose to do so.

Every nonprofit interest-area field ought to have an advocacy and/or lobbying strategic plan *as a coalition* that includes a representative body composed of all the sectors of the given field. The real strength of nonprofits comes from their ability to collaborate and cooperate with one another and join forces in advocacy and lobbying for common objectives. The easiest and most logical platform on which to build such collectives is the geographical territory—the local town, city, or county, from where the effort can be extended to the state and national levels. It is critical that all sectors of a given field buy into the legitimacy of the representative body at each level, and that each member organization carry its own weight so as to support the larger body. But it is also essential that the larger bodies on the national and state levels don't neglect or forget the needs on the local level Asking people to support a national or statewide objective without allowing for, and being reciprocally supportive of, the objectives on the local level is a myopic policy that will probably send the larger coalition to its doom, as all self-interest begins to take shape at the local level.

Trust among members is the hallmark of effective representative coalitions. Territoriality among nonprofit coalition members—the urges and forces that pressure organizations to go it alone and to refuse to yield control to a larger body—and the collective suspicions, jealousies, and fears between nonprofits that are often competing in the same arena are poison to effective nonprofit lobbying. Separate, multiple advocacy and/or lobbying efforts aimed at essentially the same objectives diminish the power of the effort and minimize its chance of success. This doesn't mean that competition between nonprofits isn't the norm, or that it isn't healthy. Private-sector interests are also in competition, but they still manage to band together as "industries" for mutual benefit.

The danger of unilateral action and backdoor deals by dissatisfied members of a coalition at odds with the will of the majority is real, but it can be minimized by being aware of its potential for harm, by communication by and between all sectors, and by creating an environment where there is a sense of the greater good. Obstacles must be openly dealt with, and collaboration must triumph. The first level (the local level) of representation is the best place to nip the problem of territorial thinking in the bud and prevent its growth and expansion. Nonprofits can never be truly competitive if they engage in advocacy and/or lobbying efforts only at the individual organization level.

Solid, coalition-based representative groups are not always easy to build and are even harder to maintain. A group of like-minded nonprofits with common mission statements and perhaps based on similar disciplines still does not take shape necessarily of its own accord—affiliations and alliances must be built and nurtured. Building the requisite trust to create a true sense of community takes time and effort; it takes a strategy that spreads a sense of ownership and the benefits of success among all the participants. A coalition thus requires full-time functionaries whose job description precisely matches its work. It will likely work better if it is not a wholly volunteer effort.

Trust is based in large part on personal relationships. Once it is established, a "sense of community" can be fostered that works against territoriality and allows individual organizations to make the necessary commitment to the group as a whole. A sense of community implies that everyone gains from the effort, and it is this self-interest that facilitates united efforts and promotes optimism, discipline, and flexibility. People naturally gravitate to united efforts, but only to the extent that there are some successes along the way.

BUILDING A SUCCESSFUL COALITION

Successful collaborations and alliances are based on mutual interest and trust. They use the language of "we" and "us" and are built on mutual respect and common objectives. Here are a few ways nonprofits can establish alliances:

- Start with an assessment of historically successful alliances. Who has the nonprofit organization or field previously worked well with?
- Involve people in the community who are perceived as leaders, because co-opting them to the objective of building a coalition will make it easier to sell the idea to those who are reluctant to endorse the concept.
- Base the coalition on self-interest to ensure that it lasts. There must be a tangible benefit for all the participants, which needs to be clearly understood at the outset: who benefits, and how, from success in the lobbying effort must be spelled out.

- Assign responsibility for who will do what and when, as coalitions must have clearly defined roles and responsibilities. There should be no confusion. A written strategic plan helps to codify the roles. Coalitions must create a timeline to implement the plan and ensure that commitment to it is serious. They should make specificity the watchword.
- Ensure flexibility and adaptability, with built-in mechanisms that facilitate compromise—these are features of successful coalitions. That said, the coalition does not need the help of supporters who exact too high a price for their joining the effort. It should keep its eye on the ball—that is, it should weigh the supporters' benefits.
- Facilitate frequent and open communication, as no coalition can succeed without it. Everybody needs to know what everybody else is doing. Communicating roles and responsibilities helps to sustain motivation and commitment and to trigger ideas that are creative and expansive. Every group or field, and every organization within those groups and fields, has its own internal culture, its own way of doing things, its own customs, and even language, and a nonprofit needs to learn to talk to potential coalition partners in their own language, conveying respect for their values. Self-centered approaches language in which "me" dominates doom the coalition from the beginning.
- Invest in people and *personal* relationships. Coalitions that are led by people who have strong personal relationships fare better than others.
- Make the objectives and goals of the coalition specific, concrete, and reasonably attainable. They cannot be unrealistically ambitious. The message behind the lobbying effort should embrace the limited goal and succinctly repeat this goal over and over again.

Coalition members should have a shared vision about the areas of commonality—not every detail or nuance has to be shared, but there should be a general agreement about what is of the highest priority to areas of mutual interest.

The two most important elements of a successful coalition are

- a firm commitment by all members to spending the requisite time, energy, money, and other resources, agreed upon *at the outset,* in furtherance of the lobbying objective; and
- a real passion for, and belief in, the mission among both the leadership and the base members of each participant in the coalition.

A successful coalition, then, is characterized by the following:

- **Cooperation replacing competition:** working together with mutual respect to accommodate differing ideological positions, setting the goal(s) together, merging expectations about the results, and making a commitment to work for the objectives of a coalition and to contribute time and money.

- **Inclusion rather than isolation:** many working together instead of everyone working alone. This makes it easier to resolve power struggles and the conflicts that usually occur when different cultures come together for a single purpose.

The "big picture"—how everyone involved benefits over time—should be the guiding focus. Successful coalitions find ways to get beyond differences.

- **Orientation to short-term results:** keeping an eye on the goal, and not getting distracted.

There are two types of coalitions—ones that are ongoing and permanent, and ones formed for a limited duration, usually with specific objectives in mind. While limited-duration coalitions can be a valuable tool for nonprofits, some form of the permanent type is necessary, if only because a coalition that exists at least in the shell form can be revived more easily when nonprofits are under the gun and the response time is limited. It is difficult to reassemble a coalition every time there is a specific objective to pursue or an attack to ward off. Other important reasons for maintaining permanent coalitions include the following: (1) raising funds to professionalize and support lobbying efforts and to contribute to candidate campaigns is an ongoing process that is made easier by a wider potential pool of supporters and contributors with whom contact and communication is constant; (2) it is impossible to retain qualified staff without ongoing employment opportunities, and systemic turnover in staff is harmful to sustained capacity; and (3) a lack of permanence makes institutional memory impossible. (The memory of any organization often resides in the memories of its long-term leadership. It would be wise if every nonprofit wrote down its history—for example, what battles it fought to get specific legislation passed or defeated, including all the details as to how it won or lost those battles. But, in fact, few nonprofits do this. Even those with permanent staffs don't record their histories as much as they should. Thus, much of the wisdom gained from experience, the "institutional memory", as it were, is lost when leadership is transitory or when it moves on after short periods of time. Institutional memory is *only* possible when there are ongoing, stable personnel, and even then, more often than not, it is lost.)

An old story suggests that *"too often people in the nonprofits world, when asked to form a firing squad, make a circle."* Nonprofits can be their own worst enemies. A solid coalition based on consensus is the antidote to solo flying by nonprofits.

All coalitions should have

- **A network-wide communications plan:** This plan should include specific, ongoing mechanisms to keep every member informed and to mobilize action when needed. The same kinds of mechanisms and the same needs for effective communication for individual organizations are even more important at the representative-body level.

- **A media/public awareness education effort:** Media efforts at the field level should be more than just the sum of the efforts of the individual organizations. There needs to be an effort to make the case of the value and benefit of the wider field of the coalition in which numerous individual nonprofit organizations operate and present themselves to the public via the media. In most instances the benefit of the greater field is easier to demonstrate.

- **Ways to fund the effort at a meaningful level:** Funding is the key to effective, competitive lobbying efforts at every level. It is impossible to employ an adequate level of qualified staff and operate at even the minimal level of competency without first securing continual funding to cover the base costs. Efforts that rely on volunteers from coalition members to staff the operation are doomed to failure. Lobbying cannot be a volunteer effort.

Clearly, there will be individual organizations that choose not to participate in the coalition's strategy for designing and creating the representative model, because they have higher priorities, because they lack, or perceive that they lack, the necessary resources, or because they believe that the strategy rules, and operational levers are controlled by those they disagree with. This situation may be unavoidable, but successful lobbying is exponentially increased to the extent a higher percentage of the component members of a given field are brought into the fold. Not every organization must be on board, but deep divisions and vivisectionist trends will sound the death knell of effective nonprofit lobbying.

The importance of the foundation of lobbying at the individual nonprofit organization and local field level being solid, comprehensive, well-oiled, functional, adequately funded and, most importantly, ongoing cannot be stressed enough. The success of lobbying efforts of coalitions is built on this foundation and it is easier to achieve if the base machinery is in place.

The function of the coalition is to serve as the managing clearinghouse and central focal point for the entire lobbying effort. The tasks at hand are a priori too burdensome for most individual nonprofit organizations, and hence the need for the representative group in the first place. Once the coalition is formed, the biggest obstacle to success is maintaining the express understanding among members that each of them is expected to contribute to the effort on an ongoing basis. No group will survive if individual constituent organizations believe that it will handle things well even without their involvement, and that they need not do anything further after the formation of the group. No coalitions can sustain full support and participation over time, but those that can exact commitments that are honored by a high percentage of their memberships have far better success ratios than those who can't.

ORGANIZING FIRST STEPS-SUMMIT MEETING

Whatever the status of the advocacy and/or lobbying efforts in the general area in which a nonprofit operates, a good first step to launching a new advocacy and/or lobbying apparatus or improving the one existing is to hold a summit meeting of all related nonprofits or their representatives.). This applies to all nonprofits, irrespective of whether they are organized on the basis of geography or area of interest or on other lines.

It is important for groups that are yet to form an advocacy coalition to schedule an initial summit meeting to which all possible potential members are invited. The agenda for this meeting should include the various elements that are central to the formation of a permanent representative group, but it should not be presented as a fait accompli or be too rigid. The first meeting should be called not by one single group but by the several groups that have previously met to begin the process of building consensus and buying into the advantages of the formation. A clear understanding is needed among all the parties to the initial formation of a coalition so as to avoid problems later. Things should be discussed specifically, particularly leadership and responsibilities, for every coalition needs a clear definition of who is in charge of what, and how decisions are made. A coalition needs to be mindful of the tendency of people to see and interpret things from their own perspective, which may not always give the full picture accurately. Future dissension and disagreement can easily undermine the foundation. The best way to avoid resentment is to include all members in planning how the organization will be created and how it will be run. Successful representative groups are those in which everyone contributes and decision making is not in the hands of one faction or another. Thus, a shrewd leadership recognizes that its job is primarily to keep the coalition together and ensure everyone's participation. In the final analysis, groups come together and *stay* together because they perceive it is in their interest to do so. It is wise to maintain this emphasis.

Because trust and participation of all members are essential, it is important to revisit this issue when reinventing or restructuring an ongoing effort. Unless a nonprofit field has a representative body at the local level that is functioning at full capacity and is flawlessly deploying all its various parts as previously discussed, an annual interaction of the leadership of the various component groups is essential to allow for fresh ideas, to renew commitment to goals and objectives, and to improve communication and understanding of the issues involved. All structures need to be revamped and improved from time to time, and an annual gathering can be an excuse to address the issues of universal trust and support, commitment, motivation, preparedness to tackle crises, and the general state of readiness of the machinery.

An annual lobbying summit meeting—where the leadership of all groups involved in a given nonprofit field comes together to reinvigorate the lobbying effort and commitment—is a good device not only to sustain performance but also to avoid the natural tendency for advocacy coalitions to devolve into structures run by a very few people. Unless there are mechanisms to involve all segments of a field on a regular basis, it seems nonprofit advocacy coalitions have a historical bent toward shrinking every few years. It is hard work to continually seek out the widespread inputs of the members of a diverse constituency in an effort to retain their trust, support, and commitment, but that is the only way to ensure that the coalition stays alive and healthy. Establishing a culture, over time, that values commitment to a shared workload; to lobbying as a basic, core function, high on the priority scale; and to compromise in pursuit of defined, mutually beneficial objectives is the key to successful coalition lobbying efforts. This does not happen of its own accord; people must work at it.

For long-dormant lobbying efforts or those that have begun to atrophy for one reason or another, the summit meeting is a chance to begin a dialogue with other nonprofits to identify how, together, a new, improved, and united effort can be crafted either from whole cloth, as it were, or by reinventing what exists. For minority interest areas that have viable, fairly sophisticated advocacy and/or lobbying efforts, the summit meeting is an excellent vehicle for fine- tuning, further refinement, and team motivation.

The summit—a good term to use as it elevates the gathering's degree of perceived importance—should be a formalized affair so as to accord it some cachet. It should involve all the leadership of the particular field. The agenda should include

- a brief discussion on the current status of the field's advocacy effort, including what is and what isn't working, and the coalition's recent successes or failures in the advocacy and/or lobbying arena;
- consideration of a needs analysis as a means to further the assessment of the situation;
- identification of the major issues the field faces;
- identification and assessment of current advocacy leadership;
- a discussion on what funds are available, what funds are needed to raise the capacity of the advocacy effort, and what can be done to raise additional funds;
- identification of the field's major assets and whether or not each is being fully utilized;
- a discussion on what advocacy areas might be beneficial to consider prioritizing;
- a discussion on incorporating a 501c(3) nonprofit umbrella advocacy group (if one doesn't exist already to support the coalition effort) and a 501c(4) subsidiary lobbying organization, accompanied by the creation of a PAC and perhaps a 527 organization to serve as the structure for the coalition's efforts;
- a discussion on who would be willing to participate in further meetings, in strategic planning, and in the development of a steering committee or take other additional steps to increase the field's advocacy competency;
- a discussion on the next steps, including a meeting, and on assigning individual responsibilities and assignments.

Here's some advice. The end of a meeting is arguably the most important part—where conclusions are drawn, consensus can be reached, and decisions can be made in preparation for the next steps. Nonprofits try to include too many items on the average agenda, which leaves too little time to adequately address important issues or results in meetings that last too long. Such meetings don't have enough breaks, exhaust the participants, and compromise their level of thinking and the quality of their contributions. When the participants are exhausted it is not possible to maximize the potential of the meeting. Therefore, participants must be given time to thoroughly vet an issue from all sides and reach reasoned conclusions, even if this means limiting the agenda of each day of the meeting and stretching the agenda over many days or different meetings. Nonprofits should enable the participants to stay productive by helping them to stay sharp.

NEEDS ASSESSMENT

It is a good idea for existent structures that are renewing their advocacy and/or lobbying campaign to take a detailed look at the history of the lobbying efforts, level of participation, and the general status of advocacy at the coalition level. This exercise is beneficial at any stage of a coalition's history. (Individual organizations that make up the coalition can conduct their own internal needs assessment as part of the process and should be encouraged to do so.) A preliminary discussion and review of the current advocacy situation can serve as the basis for evolving a comprehensive strategy to assess the performance of the coalition. A needs assessment first inventories the assets of the coalition or, in the case of a new advocacy effort, the assets that can be easily tapped. Based on the inventory the coalition can easily identify the additional resources it will need for the future. The second step is an evaluation of performance and how the assets have been, and are being, deployed. An assets inventory and needs assessment are basically two sides of the same coin. This process can help pinpoint barriers and obstacles to success, aspects of the effort that needs bolstering, and assets that are not being deployed to full advantage.

ASSETS INVENTORY

The assets inventory should include a detailed listing of structural, managerial, lobbying, funding, communications, volunteer base, and media relations pluses that are immediately available to the coalition effort. Thus, if a 501c(3) or 501c(4) organization for advocacy, which is a structural asset, already exists, a new one may not be needed.

Any needs assessment must have widespread participation of the sectors involved to ensure that it is comprehensive and thorough. This can be difficult if there is no immediate crisis to spur the individual organizations to make the time to participate in the assessment. If periodic review can be instituted as part of the culture of the field or coalition, the assessment will be easier to carry out.

An advocacy and/or lobbying needs assessment is a snapshot of the status of the coalition's effort at one point in time. It need not be difficult or time-consuming to conduct. By calling a summit meeting where all the parties are represented and involving them in a survey, a large portion of the needs assessment can be completed in a single day. It is also easy to distribute the survey to large numbers of people and invite them to share their thoughts and observations by e-mail, the coalition's website or more traditional ways. The survey can be a small part (thirty minutes to one hour) of every coalition member organization's Board of Directors meetings, or it can be assigned to these boards' advocacy subcommittees or chairs. The staff of individual organizations can probably complete the lion's share of the survey in a very short period of time. The problem usually lies in getting an adequate number of individual organizations to complete the survey in a given time period. Without a crisis, the survey is likely to be put off. Follow-up telephone calls to remind people to complete the survey are essential.

In addition to identifying a coalition's assets, a comprehensive needs assessment should include an analysis of how involved the coalition's members have been. The process should also involve a review of the coalition's past stakeholder involvement, the current status of fund-raising, and what capacity exists for research and communications.

The needs assessment process can include the following:

- **A survey of the constituent base:** This survey can include a sampling of the coalition's member organizations (which have already sampled their membership bases), the individual members of the whole of the coalition base, or a combination of the two. The survey should be easy to complete, or the returns will be small. It can be e-mailed, posted, or put on the nonprofit's website. The survey can even be conducted via telephone, but the callers have to be trained so that they are knowledgeable and efficient.

- **Focus groups:** Nonprofits can gather representatives of the different sectors of their constituent base and survey them in person. A focus group allows for discussion and expansion of information obtained via a simple survey mechanism so that details of responses can be fleshed out and a more complete picture developed.

- **Summit or other meeting:** needs assessment and review can be an agenda item of a specially called summit meeting or of any other gathering or series of gatherings, the aggregate of which would constitute a fair, representative sampling of the constituent base as well as stakeholders.

The results of the needs assessment/assets inventory should be shared widely and should serve as the basis for any reinvigoration of the program that is warranted. Seriously flawed and resource-depleted advocacy and/or lobbying efforts require holding of a summit meeting of all involved sectors and the launch of a strategy to correct the deficiencies. Where the effort is in relatively good shape, self-congratulations are in order, but minor adjustments should still be made. Again, the time to make the assessment and take corrective action is before the apparatus is put to use to address a crisis. The health and strength of an advocacy and/or lobbying arm are arguably as critical to the organization/field as are sound fiscal policies and the maintenance of accurate books and records. They are as important as fund-raising and as basic as strategic planning. If the coalition treats advocacy as a core function, its successes will grow; if it treats advocacy as an afterthought, its efforts will reflect its weaknesses.

Once established, the coalition machinery needs to be continually assessed and fine-tuned so that it is responsive and adaptive to ever-changing external circumstances. The annual review is like reconstructing war-making machinery immediately after a war so that the machinery will be ready when it is needed again. The lobbying foundation cannot be established and then operated on the assumption that it will continue to function as designed and conceived, on its own, for ever. The exact opposite is the reality—like a high-powered luxury automobile, it must be constantly maintained and fine-tuned. The follow-up essential to effective lobbying cannot be initiated unless the base function of lobbying has already been integrated with the core objectives of the individual organization. The needs assessment should be the platform on which the organization begins to build or retool its strategic plan.

STRATEGIC PLANNING

When the coalition begins to take shape, when enough members of the field are willing to join together, when the parties have met and have come to a consensus on the general vision of a united advocacy effort (or when those forces coalesce around the need to reinvent a dormant or insufficient advocacy effort), the next step is to begin the strategic planning process. The strategic plan should set forth the organization of the structure—what form it will take, how it will be organized, what functions will need to be overseen and by whom, what capacity it is likely to need, what overriding level of professionalism is desired given the current political situation that the coalition faces (and its financial realities—what it can afford), what are its short- and long-term objectives, and what are its other goals. The mission statement should be a one- or two-line sentence encapsulating the purpose of the organization. The vision statement should be a brief elaboration of the mission and the objectives of the organization.

The plan itself should be broken down into logical sections that detail what is expected to be accomplished, by whom, and by when. It shouldn't be too vague, but it needn't be too specific. It should cover a one-year or two-year period. Given that the world is changing rapidly, planning for longer than two years is really an exercise in speculation. Too much detail locks the organization into specifics that may not turn out to be even relevant down the line. The goal is to cover the objectives in all areas, with as much specificity as possible, and to find out what must be done to realize them. But there must be enough leeway in the implementation of the plan to allow for changing circumstances. A strategic plan is a guideline and roadmap for the organization. It allows for an overview of what should happen, can happen, will happen—and, at the time it is created, how it will happen; it both gives form to the enterprise and informs the membership, providing for a sense of community, optimism, and establishment of the general principles that will govern action.

The plan should have inputs from across the spectrum of the coalition's field of interest and should be the product of many minds debating the reasonableness of desired outcomes and the steps necessary to convert those desires into deliverables. It is a chance to look at the whole picture from a detached vantage point. But it isn't the Holy Grail—avoid the mistake of spending inordinate amounts of time on the plan, and remember, it doesn't have to be perfect.

THE BASICS

Effective lobbying requires more effort than just sending out action alerts and urging supporters to write letters to their representatives. It involves creating an apparatus, broken down into all of the various functions, of a comprehensive advocacy strategy—fund-raising, volunteer/stakeholder management, communications, lobbying, research and materials preparation, candidate election campaigns, and media relations. An effective advocacy strategy must be built on a solid foundation of committed resources—money, personnel, time, and participation. It requires organization, training, at least some full-time staffing, willing foot soldiers, readiness to put aside territoriality and suspicion among coalition members, and the commitment to the long haul. The strategy cannot be an ad hoc thing, created and resurrected only when a crisis looms; it needs to be constant over time so that it can meet the demands placed on it. It needs to be flexible, adaptable, and ready to move in new directions. Building the foundation and initiating the expansion of the effort, so that over time capacity grows continually, takes time and the right strategic planning at the outset. But it is attainable by every sector of the nonprofit world if people recognize and embrace its necessity and value, and begin the process with smart planning.

One central tool of nonprofit advocacy is the *mobilization* of grassroots pressure, but the mobilization tool should not be confused with the principle of *organizing* people, which is not as much a tool as it is a precept of management. Mobilization may be essential to realize one or more specific objectives, but it can be difficult to accomplish, and its benefits can be transitory and short-lived. But organization of the advocacy machinery, which is a prerequisite for mobilization of grassroots pressure, must be methodical and continuous.

Every nonprofit organization ought to have a public-policy strategic plan that provides for basic organizational elements including the following:

- **Defined roles:** It is essential to define the roles, responsibilities, and duties of all segments of the organization. Advocacy and/or lobbying, if it is to be effective, cannot be assigned to one group of people exclusively—it must be shared by all persons involved in the coalition, each contributing to an effective campaign. This is not to say that no one is in charge of the effort. It is important to create some sort of hierarchy to ensure leadership and accountability, but too often nonprofits delegate the advocacy function to one staff member or board committee and ignore the daily requirements of launching and sustaining an effective lobbying capacity. The roles of each segment should be written down where possible, and new entrants to the organization should ideally be both briefed about and trained in the strategies, techniques, priorities, and approaches that the organization (the coalition and its member organizations) has formally adopted as its lobbying protocol. Moreover, as the membership of nonprofit organizations changes more frequently than that of some private organizations, it is important that briefings and training are ongoing and updated on a regular basis. The first step in integrating the lobbying function with the core objectives of the organization is to ensure that all members know and accept that it is critical to the organization's health and well-being and to the success of its mission. While organizational members that are part of a wider coalition can share successful models of incorporating the advocacy function as a core priority, each individual organization must ultimately develop its own model. This essential task is the foundation on which successful coalitions are built. It is a precondition for success. If member organizations don't believe that advocacy is one of their primary functions and act on that belief, it will not be possible for the coalition to do the same thing on the larger level. If all coalition members do is "join" the coalition, expecting it to effectively assume all advocacy and/or lobbying functions, run itself, and succeed on its own, both the individual organization and the coalition efforts will fail.

- **A board of directors:** There must be some sort of permanent structure to oversee the lobbying effort over time. Note that the *oversight* function (performed by the board) and the *management* function are completely different and separate. The buck must stop somewhere; governing policy must be created somewhere; direction and planning must originate somewhere, and these responsibilities constitute the oversight function—that is, to make broad-based policy. Legally, the board of directors is ultimately responsible for the organization. The 501c(3) needs a board of directors (as does the subsidiary 501c(4), although there may be overlapping of memberships), which needs to meet regularly, devise some means of monitoring government action that might affect the organization, and reach out and network with other nonprofits at the local, state, and national levels that share similar goals and mission statements. But the board must resist the temptation to micromanage the staff leadership in the interpretation and implementation of broad policy outlines. Meddlesome boards do not attract superior talent. Insecurity manifested by interference is the antithesis of effective decision making. If board members want to govern in the trenches, let them resign from the board and apply for positions on the staff. Boards that do not understand and honor the differences between their role and that of management are a characteristic of amateurish and weak organizations. No lobbying coalition can function effectively under an interfering board. Board members are volunteers—they have their own lives, their own organizations to run, and other demands on their time and energies, and they cannot "run" the advocacy and/or lobbying coalition. Professional, paid, full-time staff must be hired—as full a complement as is affordable, and at least the bare minimum required.

Note: For most nonprofit incorporated organizations, the minimum number of board directors required by law is three. Nonprofits have any number of board seats, with some including as many as fifty or even seventy-five. The purpose of large boards is doubtless to ensure full, inclusive representation of all sectors of the organization and to provide expanded board resources based on what the members bring to the table. But large boards can easily become paralyzed and the decision-making process choked by factions and the failure to achieve consensus. The ideal alternative is to have very small 501c(3) and 501c(4) boards—umbrellas for the advocacy coalition—comprising highly respected and trusted representatives of the parts of a coalition, and a larger, inclusive advisory committee to counsel the organization (but not with voting authority that can render the entity hostage to infighting and cause too wide a divergence of opinion). Achieving this compromise of limiting the board size may be difficult, as suspicious coalition members may not want to yield authority and power. Another approach is to construct the board on the basis of the by-laws and delegate much of the decision-making authority to either the chief executive officer or subcommittees of the board, each charged with the oversight of a specific aspect of the lobbying effort, and with near-absolute authority so as to avoid disputes at the larger board level. However, this alternative is much less workable than the advisory committee approach. The 501c(4) board should be small and its seats occupied by those in control of the 501c(3) to ensure that the two organizations are really part of a larger, whole effort. Again, an advisory panel can guide the efforts of the 501c(4) in alignment with a strategic plan and thus ensure that all voices are heard.

- **The advisory board:** An advisory board can be an effective means to ensure inclusion of all segments of the coalition (and the outside community) without paralyzing the board's decisions by including too many voices. Advisory boards need to be composed of more than trophy members—those whose marquee name value is the primary reason for inviting their participation (a typical nonprofit advisory board is often packed with trophy members). The lobbying coalition is too important to leave to people who have no intention of contributing anything more than the use of their name. An advisory board should have a regular meeting schedule and defined roles and areas of operations. Members should be advised about what will be expected of them so that the final board will be fully committed to defined roles. The board can consist of any number of people, but it should not be so large as to make it ungovernable. The right number of members should reflect a balance between the imperatives of including the various segments of the coalition community, augmented by stakeholder members, prominent people who will raise its visibility and cachet, and others with whom the coalition might be closely aligned, and ensuring that the board is not too large to continue to function as a working entity. Including people with marquee names within the community—because of their positions and titles, their activities or their wealth or other status—is a good idea, but if the coalition wants them to be included in the "working" membership, it will need to identify ways to entice them to make a commitment to the organization. (It is perfectly acceptable to include "celebrities" of one stripe or another, even if they are not full working members, because there is value in having their names associated with the effort. It is, of course, of greater tactical advantage if they also join in the actual work of the advisory board.) Naming a prominent, well-respected person as the chair or two people as cochairs may make the recruitment of other people easier by giving the panel a little cachet. People tend to agree to provide this kind of service if (1) they genuinely care about the cause; (2) they are invited by someone whom they respect or wish to please; (3) politics of one kind or another is at play; or (4) it is a prestigious thing for them to do. In large geographical areas, meetings can be problematic because of the members' hectic schedules, which make it difficult for them to travel. Therefore, venues should be selected by rotation within the territory, or teleconferences should be held. Advisory committees can be valuable in providing perspective and new ideas, vetting proposals, raising visibility, and facilitating fundraising strategies.

- **Management staff:** The day-to-day operations of the coalition advocacy effort must be managed by a dedicated, paid, professional staff and not by the staff of a member organization assigned to the task part-time. Staff that consists of a single, part-time employee is preferable to one comprising only volunteers. Nonprofit advocacy will not work without its own staff, and failure to provide for dedicated staff is an admission that the advocacy and/or lobbying function is *not* a core responsibility. Any strategic plan must therefore determine what staff is essential and from where the funds to cover the costs will come. The more ambitious or important the objectives, the greater the need for a larger staff. The staff reports to the executive director, who reports to the board of directors of the 501c(3) formed to house the advocacy effort. A separate 501c(4) organization can function with staffing by the parent 501c(3), as can the adjunct PAC. A good advocacy staff consists of at least five full-time employees:

- the executive director
- the development director (fund-raising)
- the volunteer/grassroots coordinating manager
- the legislative liaison officer and
- the communications manager.

Complementing these positions, the next additions would include a media relations manager, an operations administrator (books, accounting, etc.), and clerical staff.

- **A communications networking plan:** Nothing is more important than the establishment of a permanent communications system that keeps every sector of the coalition organization up-to-date on advocacy and/or lobbying issues. Communication must be comprehensive, constant, quick, and immediate and should allow for feedback and interaction. In today's increasingly high-tech world, the communications system ought to include both a dedicated website and an e-mail listserv protocol (independent of and distinct from any member website or listserv) to allow for instant communication. Faxes, newsletters, telephone calls, and letters may augment the high-tech system. And in addition to all this, there needs to be at least occasional personal interaction among all the organization's segments at, say, meetings, conclaves, conferences, and summits. As the coalition is probably composed of sectors that do not interface with one another on a regular basis, nothing can replace face-to-face communication and the personal exchange of ideas and thoughts, and recognition of this fact requires periodic (the more frequent the better) gatherings that focus specifically on the lobbying arena. Trust, commitment, motivation, and faith in the effort are all improved by effective communication.

- **A media/public awareness strategy:** Part of the function of lobbying is to build and mobilize grassroots public support and, therefore, strategies to garner media coverage and public awareness must be part of the lobbying arsenal. Like the relationship with elected officials itself, media competence and capacity require *relationships* with people in the media and attention to the details of managing the enterprise.

- **A volunteer mobilization effort:** Few nonprofits or their fields can demonstrate widespread constituent support to an elected official without help from the wider community. Employment of professional lobbyists is effective only if the client can support them by mobilizing support in the home area. Effective lobbying is built on solid, broad-based people support, and volunteers are the key to establishing, nurturing, and maintaining this grassroots support.

- **A fund-raising support plan:** This plan must be part of the strategic plan. Because nonprofits are basically small organizations, it is virtually impossible for them to manage all of the work and functions that lobbying requires of them; thus, they need to form coalitions. The coalitions will need to fund paid help (if possible, both professional lobbyists and staff or quasi-staff). Lobbying that is entirely volunteer dependent is, more often than not, doomed to failure. There is simply too much at stake, the turnover in volunteer ranks is too systemic, the workload of paid staff from the membership already too great, and the demands, schedules, and deadlines too onerous for lobbying to be an afterthought of volunteer management. Volunteers have their own lives and other responsibilities, and lobbying needs people who are committed to only one master. There are also real and fixed costs associated with lobbying—from basic overhead (postage, printing, mailing, website maintenance, research, travel) to personnel. And finally, if nonprofits are to gain the advantages of involvement in candidate campaigns through 501c(4) organizations and PACs, there need to be ways to raise the funds required. Advocacy fund-raising is a full-time job.

The component of a strategic plan should include the following:

- **A mission statement:** a one- or two-line summary of the reason the advocacy organization exists

- **A vision statement:** an expansion of the mission statement that includes what the organization hopes to accomplish over time; a broad summary of the desired objectives, goals, and outcomes of the organization's efforts; and a set of deliverables if the goals are met

- **Breakdown of job functions:** management/administration; lobbying; making the case (subsection research); communications; grassroots/volunteer management; stakeholder relations; and media relations(with the specific tasks of each)

- **Breakdown of areas of involvement:** local, state, federal—monitor legislation, draft legislation, and lobby for funding support/increases (with the overarching activities in each)

Therefore, it is through individual organizations' solid commitment to advocacy that truly effective coalitions of nonprofits, together with stakeholder support, can become powerful advocacy machines. The efforts of the few must coalesce into a single effort of the many.

STAKEHOLDER TRUST

Stakeholders are organizations, areas of interest, and coalitions that are not directly involved with, or tied to, a nonprofit organization, field, or coalition. They benefit to one degree or another from the nonprofit's success, but it is not one of their primary focuses or priorities. Virtually every nonprofit mission will have other nonprofit organizations in different fields and other sectors of the community hoping that it succeeds. Thus, for example, an arts organization that promotes the value and benefit of arts education might count on teacher groups, the parent-teacher associations (PTAs), the business community, the police and sheriff's department, the juvenile justice system, and other civic groups that can be called on to support its goals. These groups have an interest in the success of the arts community, because arts education benefits students, teachers, employers, and communities. Arguably, participation in arts programs is effective as a gang-activity abatement tool and helps youth at risk with an alternative to drugs. It is incumbent on nonprofit lobbying efforts to identify the groups outside their immediate area of dominant interest that have a "stake" in their success and reach out to them for support. Everyone needs some help, and no one should be afraid to ask for it. But nonprofits must remember that if someone, particularly a politician, helps them, they must be prepared to return the favor when it is needed. Politics has long been the stuff of "you scratch my back, I'll scratch yours."

Two principles govern effective alliances between nonprofits and potential stakeholders:

- **First**, these kinds of collaborative alliances don't take shape by themselves. A nonprofit group must reach out to potential stakeholders, initiate contact, and bring convincing arguments as to why it is in the stakeholder group's interest to support an agenda or a specific goal;

- **Second**, effective collaboration involves reciprocity—if a nonprofit seeks active support from a potential stakeholder, it must be prepared to return the favor in kind. Stakeholder support can range from simple advice or endorsement to active lobbying support. More often than not, the specific agenda and goals and objectives of the nonprofit organization or field that is seeking collaborative support do not dovetail exactly with the potential stakeholder's agenda and interests. Therefore, the nonprofit coalition seeking collaborative support has to justify to the stakeholder the expenditure of precious time and other resources it expects for the furtherance of its mission.

One advantage of securing stakeholder support is that often this group has resources beyond those of the nonprofit that is in need. Thus, the PTA has a substantially larger membership base and apparatus for support than the arts education group. The teacher's union has extensive paid lobbyists and perhaps even an advertising budget (probably owing to mandatory dues exacted from its membership), which the arts education organization does not. The PTA and the teacher's union have an interest in arts education, which is, however, pitted against a whole slate of other priorities. It is the job of the arts education group to convince them that arts education must be a high priority for each group. It can do this by imparting education and information, by providing the findings of studies on the value to students and teachers of inclusion of arts education in the curriculum, and by showing that students who take arts education perform better in other academic areas, that they have higher attendance rates, and that they are less likely to be disruptive in the classroom. In a sense, convincing stakeholders to be actively supportive and to enlist their member bases' support for the nonprofit's lobbying efforts is a form of lobbying in itself, subject to all the rules that govern lobbying.

Many nonprofits make the mistake of assuming that once they have a potential stakeholder's support on record, their job is done. They don't realize that motivating the stakeholder's core base or a wider constituency is even more difficult than motivating their own base. This is so because these people have less commitment to the nonprofit's cause, they are not as passionate as the nonprofit's core supporters, and they have already allotted much of their available time to lobbying for the stakeholder group or some other entity to which they belong. To get them to take on a greater workload, even if they understand and appreciate the advocacy coalition's benefits to them, the nonprofit has to "sell" them the idea and convince them to undertake the work. This takes constant attention and time and involves ongoing communication and lobbying. The end result of a wider coalition of support can be worth the extra effort, but in some stakeholder situations, the most the nonprofit can hope for is help from a stakeholder group's leadership, but not from the group's member base.

Effective stakeholder affiliation is a high-maintenance task. For this reason, stakeholder involvement in a coalition of like-minded nonprofits should never be relied on as the linchpin of a given effort or specific campaign. Such support is too fragile. It can make the difference between success and failure, but it is unlikely to carry the day if the primary body cannot muster support within its own constituent base. While stakeholder groups may benefit from the nonprofit/coalition success and may therefore care about the issue at hand, it is likely that the benefit will not be of primary importance to them. Realistically, they have their own issues and do not care as much about the nonprofit's issue.

Rule 4: Coalitions must be built and maintained. Coalition members must commit themselves to the enterprise.

Rules 5: Coalitions must attract strong stakeholder support.

CHAPTER 6

MANAGING THE LOBBYING EFFORT/ORGANIZATION

> You do not lead by hitting people over the head—that's assault, not leadership.
>
> Dwight David Eisenhower

Once an advocacy coalition has been established and has garnered the requisite commitments from its member base, created its legal framework, and drafted its strategic approach, it needs to set up its operation and network. The same sequence of steps applies to reinventing or rejuvenating advocacy efforts. On the national and state levels, the coalition network must have a geographical, district-type structure so that all areas are represented and the barriers of vast geographical spaces and diverse populations are addressed. The larger the geographical or numerical base, the greater the need for some decentralization of authority so as to ensure trust, support, and the capacity to be effective and relevant (remember, all politics is local). On these national and state levels, it is critical that all geographical areas are involved. It is also important to involve the elected officials from the rural areas because the legislative chambers, particularly the Senate chamber, are frequently based on the need to ensure representation of these areas and to strike a balance between the Senate chamber and the House or the Assembly, both of which have a more population-proportionate representation. Another reason for involving rural legislators is that legislatures that still honor the seniority system will often have key leadership positions (on committees and other bodies) dominated by such legislators, who are more likely to be reelected over time than the officials in the more politically competitive urban areas. (However, this trend is declining in jurisdictions where there are term limits or where gerrymandering has resulted in safe districts.) Generally, rural areas throughout the country tend to be more conservative and thus Republican strongholds, and urban centers tend to be Democrat controlled. Voter registration and voting history favors Democrats in the larger states and Republicans in the smaller states. As it is important for a nonprofit to avoid having its issue cast in partisan terms on the national and state levels, it needs to include all areas in its strategic thinking. On the local level, geography isn't often as major an issue as it is on the national and state levels because the jurisdictional territory isn't necessarily as vast (though it can be), and thus, at-large representation suffices over a district-based system. The point is that a network needs people in charge of and responsible for all the territories and the elected officials who represent each territory. The purpose of the coalition and the network is to cover targeted elected officials and to manage the lobbying efforts so that they have the widest reach and impact to leverage the maximum influence on decision making. A nonprofit cannot afford to exclusively target any one segment of elected officials, even if such a strategy might yield enough votes for victory on the specific objective at hand. If it does so, the nonprofit may be making future victories more difficult to achieve by casting its lot with a too narrow pool of support. Effective advocacy dictates both short- and long-term strategic thinking.

Coalitions, then, must divide the myriad tasks that exist into an organized scheme. Advocacy involves fund-raising, research and preparation of evidentiary materials, communication, media and public-opinion management, grassroots and stakeholder organization and coordination, and the actual lobbying of elected and appointed officials. Each specified job ideally needs someone who will oversee and guide it. Networks do not necessarily have to be elaborate, but leaving areas uncovered, delegating oversight responsibility to a committee, or taking other ad hoc approaches can lead to problems in execution and torpedo an entire campaign at just the wrong time. As previously discussed, it is best to have full-time, paid staff. But even volunteer oversight is preferable to having no one in charge of key areas, and volunteer management of some functions is probably unavoidable at the individual organizational level, where it is unrealistic to hire several full-time employees. All the above areas are essential; they can't be easily prioritized. General Motors can't sell cars without a design team, a sales staff, an advertising department, a manufacturing wing, and so forth—remove any one critical function and the whole thing falls apart. So it is with the advocacy function.

Remember, the prime objective of any lobbying effort is to leverage influence with decision makers. Building relationships with these officials is essential and allowing for the time it will take is important. In the beginning of any advocacy effort, the most important legislators to target and begin to form relationships with are those with the most power—the leadership, the committee and subcommittee chairs, and the key members of the Administration (Executive). Once these areas are covered, the network can grow to encompass a wider selection of elected officials. None of these approaches is possible if the advocacy effort's leadership comprises part-time functionaries or changes constantly. Building institutional memory and developing meaningful relationships take time and need a consistent approach.

The linchpin of this book is that nonprofits need to raise the funds to hire people whose sole function would be to guide the lobbying efforts and coordinate the work of the volunteers and the coalition members. Indeed, volunteers have something extra to offer in expanding the network's reach of contacts, experience, knowledge, and resource base, but an all-volunteer effort in place of full-time staff is hard to sustain on a permanent or semipermanent basis, and part-time advocacy suffers from too great a handicap to compete in the current arena.

It is unlikely that all but a few nonprofits or coalitions of nonprofits will have anywhere near the resources required to put together a full complement of paid, full-time professional staff to implement an advocacy and/or lobbying strategy, but the need is apparent to anyone who has ever been involved in such an effort. Drafting an organizational chart on the basis of a realistic plan will allow each effort to prioritize personnel needs. Hopefully, each effort can then try to arrive at a solution to its needs, given the available resources. Volunteers can then fill the posts for which full-time staff cannot be hired for lack of sufficient funds. But the pressures and stresses of the workload will obviously play heavier on a volunteer who has other job obligations. Each campaign will have different priorities based on individual strategies, but each must consider the functional areas set forth here and make hard choices. To some degree, the likelihood of success may make it easier to raise funds to improve the effort, and individual coalition members can justify the expenditure of time, resources, and money on the basis of what success means to their missions and objectives. Hopefully too, a full and exhaustive analysis of what is needed will motivate increased fund-raising efforts.

BREAKDOWN OF THE JOB FUNCTIONS OF THE COALITION

Below whoever is charged with oversight of each function of the coalition, particularly on the state and federal levels, are district or area captains. If a campaign is well-funded, support for certain functions may be outsourced. Depending on the degree of expertise needed, retaining outside support in the following areas may be appropriate: website management, media/public-relations efforts, campaign contributions solicitation, research/public-opinion sampling, and professional lobbying services. Whatever functions are supported by outside firms or consultants, there should still be someone on the staff who oversees these paid efforts and acts as a link to each firm or consultant. The operative word in connection with outside consultation is *support*; these people *support* the staff, not replace them. A study of what jobs need to be undertaken by paid employees and an estimate of the cost may help to persuade more people that a minimum staffing complement is required and that fund-raising is necessary.

HIERARCHY

Widespread participation of coalition partners, active stakeholder support and involvement, substantial volunteer activism, and resources to engage a lobbying firm and to employ other tools are advantages nonprofits in many areas can only dream of. The larger the advocacy and/or lobbying effort, the greater the need for layers of functionaries to manage the effort, and the greater the need for full-time employees in posts that help coordinate all the various tasks the effort demands. At the apex of this hierarchy is one or more boards of directors (for the PAC and the 501c(3), 501c(4), and 527 organizations), and perhaps some kind of working or advisory steering committee that includes all the sectors of the coalition. The primary function of these boards and committees is to set the overall policy for the effort at hand, to liaison with the full-time staff managing the effort, and to ensure that all sectors of the coalition are on board, participating and involved (see chapter 5).

Immediately below the governing board is the one person who is, at the least, the titular head of the whole effort. As previously argued, even in small coalitions, it is much better if this person is a full-time employee who has experience and the requisite set of skills to guide an enterprise that is not always easy to manage. If this person is a volunteer with other duties that his or her "real" job entail, the effort has little chance of achieving the level of competence and professionalism that is possible when at least one person has no other masters. Several full-time posts will need to be filled with qualified leaders—including oversight of the 501c(4) and PAC/527 organizations' operational efforts (assuming there are such efforts) and the five major functional areas of the ongoing apparatus: volunteer coordination, communications, fund-raising, legislative liaison (lobbying oversight), and media/public relations. What follows is the *ideal*—each coalition needs to determine where to apply its scarce resources. But it should remember that *somebody* has to do these jobs.

MANAGEMENT

> A camel is a horse designed by committee.
>
> Sir Issac Issagonis

The management function includes oversight and coordination of the whole of the advocacy and/or lobbying strategy and machine. Each separate role is important to the overall success of the effort.

Executive Director

Every enterprise needs a captain, a point where "the buck stops." While a governing body makes the policy that guides the advocacy effort, this body should not be involved in the actual day-to-day operations of the machinery or the effort. One person has to be in charge and call the shots—otherwise the staff will have no direction. Committees are not suitable for running an advocacy effort. The ideal candidate for this position will come from within the ranks of the nonprofit coalition area of interest (e.g., an advocacy coalition of arts groups will benefit from having a point person who is familiar with the arts and culture issues, the field as a whole, and the network of people within this arena). The candidate will have experience in advocacy and lobbying, including a thorough knowledge of the decision-making process at the local, state, and federal levels; familiarity with how influence is leveraged within the political process; preferably some experience in candidate campaigns and party politics; and more than passing knowledge of nonprofit administration, fund-raising, and volunteer management. The ideal candidate will be a visionary, an optimist, a cheerleader and effective motivator, a consensus builder, and a champion of team play. He or she will be a good listener with excellent oral and written skills and will also be an effective public speaker. Advanced degrees and familiarity with media relations and research techniques are other advantages. The candidate will have a sense of humor, some charisma, and an eye for detail, and will be an organized person who is able to make decisive, strategic decisions under pressure. Of course, every organization wants an executive director who is, as described, only a step or two away from sainthood. Recruitment of such people isn't easy, and therefore each coalition should prioritize its needs in the context of its strengths and weaknesses and settle on the candidate it believes embodies the qualities it truly needs. Great leaders start somewhere, and nonprofits shouldn't shy away from investing in someone who will grow into the position.

Executive search firms can be helpful in this process, but are not necessary. They are retained in the belief that they can mine the best slate of candidates and recruit potential leadership that otherwise might not be identified. This may or may not be true. Another reason people want to employ a search firm is based on the belief that somehow the firm's experience will allow it to narrow the field of candidates to the one or two who are the most qualified and are the best fit. Again, this may or may not be true. A search firm should be a valuable adjunct to a nonprofit's own efforts, not a replacement for its involvement. There is no way a search firm can possibly understand a nonprofit's needs and what is required of the successful candidate as well as the organization itself.

It is important to identify the qualities most important in the candidate, to advertise the availability of the position as widely as possible, and to vet and interview final candidates as thoroughly as is reasonable. As the executive director is the key, pivotal position, the compensation package should be as generous as possible. Nonprofits get what they pay for, and they want the best they can get. They should not nickel-and-dime this position and should invest in people, not just in structures and programs.

Director of Administration

The director of administration, the second most-important administrative position, is someone with experience and training in financial oversight. A coalition wants someone who can keep the books, pay the bills, complete the required reports and forms on time, and otherwise manage the nuts and bolts of the operation efficiently and precisely. Organized and professional advocacy and/or lobbying must be run like a business—it has an income and expenses like any other business. And because of the legal requirements of separation of funds raised and funds expended on the various 501 structures, this post needs somebody who is sharp.

Director of Development (Fund-Raising)

Funding, at a meaningfully adequate level, is not easy for nonprofits. And a first-rate advocacy and/or lobbying capacity is not cheap. Lack of adequate revenue streams to fund the effort has been the primary obstacle to effective nonprofit advocacy. Raising funds to contribute to candidate campaigns, as one of the planks of an overall lobbying strategy, requires additional fund-raising resources and expertise that are generally foreign to the nonprofit experience. Thus, if a nonprofit field is serious about mounting a competitive advocacy machine, the director of development is the second most-important person in the whole organization and ought to be a seasoned, knowledgeable veteran. As competition for development professionals among nonprofits of every description is intense and frenzied, this is another position for which the compensation should be at the highest competitive level possible.

There are now more nonprofits competing against one another and with other sectors than ever in U.S. history. There are more real and legitimately important causes than ever. Organizations need every dollar they can raise for operations and programs, and unrestricted funds that can be used for overhead and operations are harder to realize than securing programming funding, leaving many nonprofits with continually expanding programming unsupported by a simultaneous expansion of operational funds to implement that programming. Nonprofit organizations have, of necessity, had to increase the time and resources committed to basic fund-raising over the past decade—in response to expanded activities, increased competition within the nonprofit/charity ranks, and periodic cyclical decreases in available private- (foundation and corporate philanthropy) and public-sector funds.

Nonprofits have had measurable success in their fund-raising efforts over the past decade. Americans are, by and large, a generous people. The success of groups whose agendas call for an increased percentage of government funding in the public-safety area (defense, police, terrorism, crime) and other arenas have resulted in a reduction in the funds available for the other public-benefit areas that are the concern of a large majority of nonprofits (education, healthcare, arts, the environment, etc.). For nonprofits that rely on government support for a major portion of their budgets, a catch-22 situation has arisen—they must spend more time and resources on fund-raising to compensate for decreased government support, which, in turn, makes it more difficult to raise the funds necessary to mount and sustain advocacy efforts that might increase or reestablish adequate government support. Success in raising funds to make good the lack of government support may offer "proof" to government decision makers that the nonprofit/field didn't really need the support in the first place. There is a second catch-22 in this situation: the additional negative consequence of pitting nonprofits against one another for shrinking available funds makes the formation and operation of potentially successful advocacy coalitions more difficult. But if advocacy is a core management function, and if there are substantial benefits to be derived from engaging in the activity, then it makes no sense to do a half-hearted job. Coalitions allow the additional burdens, pressures, and stresses associated with mounting a professional advocacy effort to be spread among many tiers, thus lessening the otherwise impossible demands on individual organizations. *If* there is commitment and acceptance of responsibility on the part of all the coalition partners, raising the funds necessary to hire full-time staff will be much easier than if the same small cadre of people within a given field is the only group to actively work toward the lobbying apparatus goal.

If advocacy is a core management function, a part of advancing the mission statement, and impacts the nonprofit's funding directly or indirectly, then it must be included in the organization's strategic financial approach. The better the foundation that the nonprofit builds for pursuing its objectives, the better its ability to realize its mission. The only exception to this maxim is in the isolated situation where the nonprofit's basic mission is to render some service or accomplish some goal within a limited time period, and once this goal is achieved the reason for the nonprofit's existence will cease and it will wind up its operations. Most nonprofits have long-term agendas. They have very real and pressing current needs that they want to address. But building the solid foundation should take precedence over seeking short-term success in addressing specific objectives of the mission. Even if one disagrees with this premise, it is true that government action or inaction will impact the nonprofit organization in some way, and the nonprofit needs to have some capacity to deal with this situation. Ignoring this impact is like building one's house on a known geological fault line and hoping an earthquake never occurs. That isn't strategic.

Director of Communications

Nothing is more important in the advocacy game than communications by and between those comprising the coalition, between the coalition and its stakeholders and supporters, and between the coalition and the targeted decision makers whom the coalition is trying to influence. Communications need to be continuous, clear and concise, accurate, and interestingly presented.

Ongoing communication is the operative factor. It is impossible to build a sense of community, of common plight and action, to build motivation and commitment, without ongoing communication as to what the issues are, the necessary actions in response to them, the importance of victory, and what is at stake. But there is a thin line between too-frequent communication and too little contact. Life is ever more complicated, and people are, understandably, increasingly resentful of annoying intrusions. The best rule of thumb is to communicate on a regular basis (weekly, biweekly, monthly) and more frequently when there is specific, important news to convey or when a call to action has to be made. Each set of circumstances will be different, and the person charged with coordination of communications needs to know the "community." Given the advances in listservs, e-mail has become the device of choice—it's fast, reliable, nearly universal, and can handle attachments. It can be made personal and presented in a way that grabs the reader. It is also relatively cost effective. But respect for the intended recipient of communications from the coalition should be a factor in how, when, and how often to communicate. The person overseeing communication must be sensitive to the nuances of what makes it effective.

A coalition that has narrowed its objectives and focus won't be caught asking people to do too much. While people want to help, and will, if approached in the right way, they will resent being asked to do more than they were expected to do or more than they perceive as reasonable. The coalition cannot afford to alienate those willing to help and support it. Therefore, it is important for the coalition to inform people via its communications that their help will be sought, but that they will not be asked to do too much. This strategy prepares people to expect a request for help and also reassures them that their privacy and busy schedules will be respected. The communications director needs experience in people management.

Communications also involve regularly scheduled meetings of the leadership and, as realistically feasible, the rank and file for review, sharing of information, situational analysis, and adaptations to strategic plans, and, if for no other reason than for getting together with one another. Such meetings help to build a sense of community, put faces with names and voices, allow for the type of casual contact impossible over the Internet or the telephone, facilitate new ideas, and motivate people to stay the course by reinforcing the sense of "us." Interactions can, of necessity, be by telephone (but that is no substitute for gathering in person). Either sectors or the whole of the group can convene. The steering/advisory committee(s) should meet regularly during an active campaign to influence a specific piece of legislation. Other committees or subcommittees can meet as needed. Thus, management of communications is both a technical and strategic function.

The linchpin of effective grassroots coalition lobbying is continuous communication with the volunteer field. Communications keep the coalition informed and educated about the issues and strategies, alert the field about actions needed, and serve as a tool for mobilizing sustained mass effort. It is also the key to managing motivation and commitment and the mechanism best suited to building a sense of community and keeping splinter groups from fracturing the coalition.

Communications need to be easy to manage and capable of disseminating information at short notice to the whole of the field or targeted at specific segments. Effective communicators operate in a theater of communications that recognizes that informational overload reached critical mass sometime ago. We all are inundated with information and requests of one kind or another every day. We simply don't have enough time to absorb all the information relevant to what we do or to respond to all of the very valid requests for action we receive each day. Huge amounts of carefully prepared material go forever unread by a large segment of the audience to which the material is addressed. That is the unfortunate reality. Thus, effective communications must be concise, clear, brief, and always to the point—not only because you don't want to alienate those you are communicating with, but because you don't want the communication lost in the mass of other messages sent daily and hourly. Communications must be transmitted in ways that entice the recipient to single them out from all the others they receive. In part, the original construction of the coalition and effort, with shared objectives that benefit everyone and a focus on issues of universal appeal, should help to create a situation where communications about these objectives and issues are priorities to the field you are communicating with. Creative approaches to the style, design, and means of communications may help to keep this appeal and commitment at a high level. For all these reasons, an advocacy organization must have a very intelligent, creative, knowledgeable, and qualified communications person on board.

Webmaster

The increasing dependence on the Internet, e-mail, and websites for organizational communication in today's world has elevated the webmaster position considerably. Websites are ravenous mechanisms that demand an endless supply of new information to attract and retain visitors, and visitors are the only benchmark measurement that counts. Content input is time-consuming. Data input, website design, and content management are now skills easily taught, yet highly in demand. Creative people are not as easy to recruit as before, but they are a critical factor in maximizing the potential of the website and ancillary tools to the coalition's goals. Numerous firms offer sophisticated Web and online software tools and management to nonprofits, many at almost no cost at all. But the bottom line is that if the organization can afford to do so, it should recruit a capable and preferably creative webmaster full time to help it engage in serious grassroots advocacy.

Director of Volunteer/Grassroots Coordination

Critical to the success of a nonprofit's advocacy and/or lobbying effort is the design and management of volunteers' roles in support of the group's efforts. Even the wealthiest nonprofits, with the most experience and buoyed by talented and skilled leadership, will still be wholly dependent on volunteers' efforts both within the organization and field coalition and outside it. There is simply far too much to do in any given effort or campaign for paid, professional staff to cover exclusively. The only things that neutralize the advantage of private-sector interests and their large financial contributions to officeholders' or office seekers' campaigns are volunteer-contributed time and the groundswell of massive voter sentiment that the volunteer base can help to organize and make a reality. What nonprofits lack in dollar-for-dollar fund-raising, they can frequently compensate for by having large numbers of volunteer foot soldiers.

Any strategic plan should pay careful attention to how the volunteer effort will be organized and deployed, how motivation can be maintained at a high pitch, and how the effort will adapt to unforeseen, but certainly likely, circumstances that will arise. Foot soldiers and the mobilization of voter opinion are the nonprofit's "ace in the hole." Communications, research, fund-raising, media relations, and even the engaging of professional lobbying firms are all basically support mechanisms and tools designed to equip and empower a vast army of volunteers in the demonstration of public support for a given objective and the communication of this support to elected officials. The strongest case for a coalition's position and the most persuasive arguments in favor of that position are weakened if an elected official doesn't believe there is any groundswell of public sentiment in his or her district for that position. Volunteers are absolutely indispensable in helping to move the voters, and thus oversight of the volunteer function is as important as fund-raising and deserves the best candidate that can be identified.

There are numerous critical areas in the volunteer management function:

Recruitment: The most important goal of volunteer management is recruiting as many volunteers as possible. The larger the pool of volunteers, the more expansive can be the agenda, and the more likely calls to action will be heard by a meaningful percentage of the total.

Training: After an effective recruitment drive that yields a pool of volunteers, the next important job is to provide them with some basic overall training in advocacy and lobbying protocols. Training is likely to be an ongoing function as recruitment of volunteers is likely to continue over time. Training must therefore be simple and easily accessible to the volunteer. It can take the form of workshops, seminars, printed manuals, or online tutorials. It should be consistent over the range of volunteers and designed for the subsets of the main group (e.g., younger people, older people, etc.), if possible. Effective training empowers your volunteers, and empowerment helps to sustain their involvement over time.

Coordination: Perhaps the most time-consuming and unwieldy of the volunteer management functions is the day-to-day coordination that is necessary to keep volunteers involved, informed, motivated, responsive to calls to action, and on message. The larger the pool the more expansive the coordination effort. The volunteer coordinator should be a respected leader—someone very organized, with attention to detail and people skills. It is also important to ensure that the post does not suffer from high turnover. Coordination becomes easier if there is delegation of authority and the structure allows for local decision making.

Information: In any volunteer pool there is likely to be a wide spectrum of people, ranging from highly motivated and committed individuals to those who question themselves as to why they are a part of the effort at all. It is a critical mistake to assume that volunteers are universally as interested in the advocacy effort as is the leadership, or that there is uniform understanding of process and implementation. Neither should the nonprofit assume that once it has explained things, directly answered questions, or otherwise painstakingly and thoroughly addressed each issue, everyone in the pool will be brought up to speed and then will be on the same page. It simply doesn't work that way. No matter how many times any given message is repeated, there will be a bloc that will not hear it, understand it, remember it, or internalize it. For this reason the nonprofit must repeat important information over and over again in a continuous 24/7 stream.

As people hear selectively and remember very little, each message, regardless of to whom it is addressed, should be *simple, direct*, and *concise*—at all times—and repeated as often as is necessary. On matters of urgency or the highest priority, care should be given to prod people into the desired action with step-by-step guidance. And beware of "crying wolf" too often; if everything is labeled "urgent," the term soon becomes meaningless, and your credibility is weakened.

While word of mouth is often an excellent way to expand the base knowledge or awareness of an issue, in terms of volunteer communication management it is a dangerous practice. Like the children's game of "telephone," in which a message is whispered in one person's ear at the front of the line and passed down to the end of the line one by one, and where the final message is usually garbled and bears little, if any, resemblance to the original message, so too will be the result if word of mouth is the primary means of disseminating information. While a nonprofit cannot (nor would it want to) avoid all word of mouth communication, paying attention to the importance of a single message can help to ensure that word of mouth does not undermine the overall effort.

The larger the volunteer base is, the more it will need to be coordinated on multiple levels to make it effective. Communicating with the hierarchy of volunteer coordinators is a task separate from that of communicating with the whole of the field. The two objectives in communicating with this group are to transmit to them *accurate* information on a *timely* basis and to facilitate those activities aimed at keeping a field organized and motivated. The mechanisms available, the necessity of outstanding presentation, and the need for brevity are the same as those for communicating with any other sector, but more attention should be paid to how the messages will or will not impact volunteers' motivation. The tasks of motivating the volunteer base and keeping it informed are so critical that continuous adaptation of these ground rules may be necessary.

To the extent time and resources permit, in larger efforts, the organization of volunteers benefits from tiers and levels. Dividing large numbers of people into smaller units with a hierarchy of responsibility is a principle of organizational dynamics. But it is important to bear in mind that dynamics change and that some degree of independence is necessary to facilitate rapid response and creative ideas, which ensure ownership and motivation. Any system must allow for creativity, initiative, and on-the-spot decision making, while there is still order, accountability, and follow-up. This is another area where balance is needed, and prior thought about the circumstances and situations that might arise can help in striking a workable and successful balance. Some kind of delegation of authority to allow smaller cells to govern themselves is necessary to build trust, to tap into people's skill sets, and to get things done. Often, a "bottom up" approach works better than a "top down" strategy. Total control freaks don't usually run effective grassroots campaigns.

Volunteers can fill many spots, including support staff for the various paid positions, researchers, fund-raisers, event planners, and more, but the transitory nature of volunteers may compromise the advocacy effort in any number of areas by leaving critical functions without oversight at exactly the wrong time. Volunteer management then involves a complex set of priorities and pressures; it needs a full-time, experienced, capable manager.

Baby boomer note: With seventy-seven million baby boomers set to retire in the next two decades, this group should be considered a prime source of volunteer support. Many of these retirees will be actively seeking new, meaningful work to fill their time, and many will be highly qualified, experienced, and disciplined workers with extensive networks of contacts. Many of these highly qualified workers will be more interested in how their assistance might facilitate positive changes in their communities rather than in payment for their service.

Interns
Unpaid internships, filled by college or high school students, that afford the student the opportunity to learn on the job and be exposed to the political system, are an excellent way to provide the struggling advocacy organization with some of the help it requires. There are numerous internship programs that provide brokerage between students and organizations looking for interns. Some college courses or degree programs require students to perform some sort of internship work; others may give course credits for these internships if the program meets academic requirements. While summer programs are more frequent, there are other seasonal possibilities to recruit interns. All nonprofit advocacy efforts should explore the possibility of recruiting one or more interns to work for them. Students who fill these posts tend to be bright, eager, enthusiastic, intelligent, and hard working, even if they are inexperienced and sometimes a little rough around the edges. Involving interns has the added advantage of acquainting younger people with the nonprofit field and may address the issue of future leadership. This is a subject of interest to some foundations as part of their concern with the capacity and sustainability of nonprofits, and for this reason, they might consider awarding a grant for an internship program. Colleges and universities are also a good source of interns as many programs have internships as part of the curriculum or as a requirement for the degree.

Manager of Stakeholder/Partnership Relations
Active stakeholder support, as opposed to mere stakeholder endorsement, can be a deciding factor in the success or failure of many nonprofit advocacy campaigns, but such active support is hard to secure and sustain and difficult to manage. It is valuable to have someone who is specifically charged with the oversight of this area.

Success in securing stakeholder support depends in large part on two factors: how closely aligned the nonprofit is with the stakeholder's priorities, and simple goodwill. Keeping stakeholders actively involved in the nonprofit's advocacy efforts is time-consuming.

Where a nonprofit's objective intersects perfectly with the stated goals of another nonprofit (or field) or with those of the private sector, it will be easier to convince the stakeholder to deploy its advocacy and/or lobbying resources for the advancement of the nonprofit's objective. Moreover, there will be less ongoing monitoring, management, and effort in getting the stakeholder to use its maximum efforts for the nonprofit's benefit. Such dovetailing of objectives may, however, be far more the exception than the rule, and thus the nonprofit needs to make a very convincing case as to how the stakeholder benefits from supporting the nonprofit's objective and why it is in the best interests of the stakeholder to utilize its advocacy and/or lobbying resources and grassroots member bases on the nonprofit coalition's behalf. If a stakeholder group does use its strength (whatever it might be) in favor of the nonprofit, then by definition it is losing the resources that could be used in support and furtherance of one of its own objectives.

Even if the initial commitment is secured, the nonprofit must continually monitor and optimize the stakeholder's involvement to ensure maximum benefit. Such monitoring is tricky, and it takes time and some expertise. If communication is confined to the stakeholder's leadership, there is no guarantee that its rank and file will necessarily follow suit; if the nonprofit tries to cajole, encourage, motivate, and involve the stakeholder's rank and file, the stakeholder's leadership might take umbrage and see this as interference. It is a delicate and thin line to walk, and thus the steps involved need to be strategically considered in the nonprofit's initial plan of action and reviewed on an ongoing basis. Stakeholders can be of great benefit to the nonprofit advocacy coalition, and thus it is worth the effort to put top-notch people into the positions that help manage the relationship. Because of the precarious nature of the relationship, it is a common mistake for nonprofits to overemphasize the projected benefit of stakeholder support and to rely on it more than they should.

Director of Media Relations

The media is both a means of communication and tool for mobilization. Because it changes the dynamics of support, and because it can directly influence an elected official's stances on nonprofit campaigns, it is potentially extremely valuable to the effort. It impacts image, financial contributions, and election outcomes. It is far more sophisticated an art and science than the mere issuing of press releases. Dependent on relationships and networks as well as legwork and research, its practitioners have experience and skills honed over time. They have long-standing relationships with the key media persons who determine what is covered and what is not. Skills that make a good PR person can be learned, but it takes time and on-the-job experience, for which there is no substitute.

Manager of Research/Case Making

In a perfect meritocracy, groups that present the best and most convincing arguments, backed by rigorous evidentiary support data and studies, have an inside track on a decision maker's support. But the sad fact is that while a strong case is necessary for every nonprofit campaign, it isn't enough to win the day, and it probably plays a secondary role to money and politics. Still, the stronger the case the easier it is to garner public support and media endorsement and sympathy. The job calls for someone with extraordinary written skills, research ties and experience, and an innate ability to capture the big picture of things. Even if the ideal candidate cannot be hired, somebody still has to manage the task of assembling hard evidence in support of the coalition's position. This function is part research, part data management, and part presentation.

Director of Lobbying/Legislative Liaison
Ideally, the person charged with oversight of the actual direct lobbying of a legislature, city council, board of supervisors, department, or agency comes from the political world and has knowledge and experience of the process and familiarity with the players. It isn't likely that one person will have substantive experience on both the national and state levels, so the position should be filled by someone with the requisite experience with the legislature that is the focus of the nonprofit's advocacy efforts (e.g., on the national level the likely focus will be on Congress). If the paid staffer in this post is not a veteran of the advocacy world, it is highly recommended that the coalition hire a professional lobbying firm or lobbyist to work in tandem with the coalition. Having both an experienced paid staffer and a firm on retainer is the best of both worlds and is within the grasp of a high percentage of serious nonprofit coalitions. The sheer size of the member composition of most state and national legislatures makes it impossible for one person to adequately service anything other than a fraction of the total members. Ideally, the lobbying director's job is to manage the efforts of others.

Outsourcing
Lobbying firm: Retaining the services of a lobbying firm to work *with* coalition staff (not replace them) is an advantage. The firm can provide a host of services otherwise difficult for the coalition to duplicate and advise and counsel the nonprofit coalition through the labyrinth of government politics (see chapter 7 for more on employing a lobbying firm).

Public relations firm: As media coverage can be a critical factor in leveraging influence and in mobilizing all-important public opinion, employing a public relations firm that works hard for the coalition can be of great value in increasing the potential impact of the issue on the public. Care should be taken to interview prospective firms and find out where they have the best contacts, what they think they can specifically, get for the nonprofit, and exactly what will be the cost, including incidentals (printing, copying, travel etc.) related to the services to be rendered. Though it is not likely, established media firms may sometimes provide their services pro bono (at least in part and for a limited time), and so it doesn't hurt to look around and see if this is possible. Such willingness is probably enhanced if the issue at hand is near and dear on a personal level to someone at the firm who has decision-making authority, or if there is a relationship between people at the firm and the organization.

It is a mistake to assume that outsourcing of the media function relieves the coalition of the burden of recruiting its own internal staff to coordinate the effort. Outside firms are adjuncts to in-house operations, not substitutes. A paid, experienced staffer is ideal, although the function can be carried out by a volunteer who has some experience in the area. If all media relations will be handled in-house, the person charged with oversight of the function should have at least rudimentary experience in the nonprofit's discipline and some personal contacts with people in the media. The position requires a full-time employee, and even with a paid professional staffer and an outside consulting firm, media coverage of nonprofits' issues is often difficult to achieve. Successful media management is a sophisticated enterprise (see chapter 7 for a further discussion).

Legal advice: As there are legal considerations for a coalition beyond the structural formation stage, professional advice is essential. With the vast number of attorneys, every coalition should have access to qualified, practicing lawyers within their support ranks, and while a paid relationship is best, pro bono support here is also possible.

Tax preparation: Every coalition should have outside tax preparation/accounting support where appropriate. Because the IRS rules for nonprofit advocacy are likely to be in flux in the near term, and as predictable attacks on the nonprofit sector's move into politics are likely, as discussed in this book, maintaining scrupulously clean records and books is important. Therefore, on the question of taxes, nonprofits should adopt the motto, "Pay as you go."

Advertising agency: If a coalition is fortunate enough to have raised enough money to support a meaningful advertising plan as a component of its overall strategy, the assistance of an advertising agency to help create the campaign material and place the media buys is essential. Again, some part of their services might be discounted, if not provided pro bono.

There may be a number of other areas that can be outsourced, if not wholly, then in part, and these include graphic design, database management, clerical functions, and fund-raising. It is always advisable to have paid staff to liaison with the retained outside support.

Support Staff
Every enterprise needs support staff—clerical and secretarial staff, assistants, researchers, gofers, and bookkeepers. Some of these positions can be filled by volunteers, interns, or temporary help. Computers have helped even small organizations organize and manage files and records, and other office machinery now makes it possible for fewer people to accomplish more. But support personnel are the backbone of an organization's effective productivity; they are part of long-term institutional memory and experience, and they are professionals too. Nonprofits must always look to cut costs wherever and whenever possible, but they should not forget that "the devil is in the details" and "you get what you pay for." Determine which support-staff positions are the most important, and to the extent the budget permits, fill these posts first. It may be that one or more critical support-staff positions are more important to the nonprofit's situation than one of the managerial positions, and it may be entirely reasonable to fill these support-staff positions before filling management posts.

Search Firms

As stated earlier, retaining a search firm to help identify and recruit the best possible candidates for the executive director's post and perhaps other key posts can be very helpful, but, if finances won't allow the expense, it is not absolutely necessary. Careful thought should be given as to what a search firm can really do for the coalition that the coalition cannot otherwise do for itself.

If retention of a search firm is an option, the choice of which firm to engage should be given serious consideration. Too often, someone in the organization knows of a firm, and on the basis of that relationship there is no "search" for the search firm. This is a mistake. There are a number of search firms that specialize in searches for nonprofits, and the process of selecting one of them should start with the preparation of a master list of five or more possible choices. This list can be compiled based on recommendations, canvassing on the Internet, and inquiries with other nonprofit groups.

Once the list is compiled, the nonprofit should interview each of the short-listed firms and ask them how they would organize the search and what other related services they would provide. Ask them for a sample draft of a job description and announcement. The nonprofit should consider the size of the firm (whether it is too big or too small), the firm's experience and track record, the person who would be in charge of the search, and any other element that might have a bearing on the success of the search.

Once a firm has been selected, the nonprofit should negotiate the fee. Remember that the firm is being hired to help in the search, not necessarily to assume all responsibility for every aspect of it. The nonprofit doesn't want to interfere with the firm's work, but it doesn't want to be absent at every step that leads to a final two or three candidates. It should find a way to work with the search firm to maximize the chances of a successful result.

As qualified candidates often have a choice of more than one job, a skilled search-firm person may be able to help the nonprofit to both find the right candidate and convince the candidate to take its offer above others.

Board of Directors Advocacy Roles

Individual Coalition Member Organizations

Each nonprofit organization that is a member of the coalition should either create a board of directors advocacy and/or lobbying subcommittee or name a board member as its advocacy coordinator. Some official involvement by the board will help to signal the importance the organization attaches to the function. Board involvement shouldn't be in name only—it should actively use its skill sets, networks/contacts, and authority to involve the whole organization in

1. Raising funds to support the organization's advocacy effort and collecting the members' proportionate share of the advocacy coalition expenses
2. Making sure all members of the organization participate in the lobbying process as requested
3. Educating and informing the larger community about the relevant issues of the nonprofit

4. Expanding the audience for the lobbying coalition's "message"
5. Recruiting volunteers
6. Reaching out to potential stakeholder groups and other supporters
7. Building relationships with elected officials and with the media

If the board creates a lobbying subcommittee, this committee should comprise representatives of the various areas of the nonprofit, including staff, volunteers, supporters, clients, and constituents, in addition to the board representative. If there is no board subcommittee, the board member in charge should create an ad hoc committee. This ad hoc committee should meet regularly to review the current advocacy agenda; review action alerts from the coalition and respond to them; and identify people who can facilitate training, act as spokespersons for the organization, engage in fund-raising, and monitor ongoing strategies to build relationships with local elected officials and with media persons.

Even where boards are not directly involved in the mechanisms of the lobbying effort, there should still be institutional avenues for them to contribute their thoughts and ideas on how to advance the organization's public-policy agenda and its priorities and how to increase the capacity of both structures. Advocacy and/or lobbying should be a regular item on each individual organization's board-meeting agenda. Board members should participate in the advocacy and/or lobbying training, as should all staff, volunteers, and supporters. The coalition effort will ultimately be no better than the sum of the efforts of the individual organizational members.

STAFF SUPPORT

Nonprofit executive directors should make sure all board members are continuously informed about advocacy and/or lobbying issues. If the organization is large enough to have a staff member appointed as the board liaison, this person (or someone assigned to the task, if there is no official liaison officer) should communicate with the board about pending legislation, any other government action that impacts the nonprofit, and officeholder positions on matters important to the organization. A well-informed board is more likely to be active and contribute meaningfully to the overall advocacy effort. The mere act of continually updating the board signals that this is a priority area.

COALITION BOARD

The coalition board should have representation from a wide cross-section of the coalition's membership, but the number of members should not be so large as to make governance difficult. Boards with twelve to twenty members are workable. An advisory board can be created to augment the representation of all sectors. The board should establish standing committees for (a) communications; (b) fund-raising; (c) media relations; (d) volunteer coordination/grassroots mobilization; (e) finances; (f) public policy; and (g) lobbying. Officers of the board should include an elected chair, vice-chair (one or more), secretary, treasurer, an appointed PR spokesperson, volunteer coordinator, and public policy committee chair.

Most nonprofits struggle to recruit board members who will function as ordinary workers and make sacrifices on behalf of the organization; business, civic, and other prominent local leaders for these positions. Boards that have high-profile members, including leaders with notable, recognizable names, many of them with "deep pockets," can trade on this cachet in many ways to advance their purposes. On the other side of the coin, board members who are willing to work regularly on behalf of the organization can often accomplish more for the organization than those who are essentially only "trophy" members.

The board should meet regularly and rotate the meeting venue among membership locations. The board's deliberations and its identification of issues should be circulated among the membership as widely as possible so as to create a sense of community, ownership, responsiveness, and involvement.

ONLINE TECHNOLOGY

One of the most significant developments in efforts to equalize the playing field for advocacy has been the advent of increasingly sophisticated, affordable software programs that allow organizations to develop and manage large field databases and employ a variety of devices to facilitate interactive communications of all kinds. Online technology is being used to recruit supporters and, with their help, to recruit still more supporters, then to motivate their online contacts to get in touch with legislators personally. Some organizations use online capacity to encourage massive e-mail contact with legislators, but suspicion of spam and questionable communications render this approach only marginally effective. Arguably the most beneficial use of online technology is in building relationships between the organization/coalition and supporters and donors over time, and in integrating advocacy with other functions of the nonprofit, the online capability being but one arrow in the quiver. Online technology also helps in getting people to respond to specific action alerts and in raising funds to pay for targeted advertisement campaigns and other tools.

Online management of certain advocacy functions (getting the word out quickly, encouraging people to act in response to an alert, targeting specific segments of the total supporter base, researching arguments, and analyzing backup data as part of *making the case*) can be made much easier by software applications designed for advocacy member management. A nonprofit can seek demographic and other information from supporters who are registered with it online, and use this information to specifically identify how these supporters can be of service to it. Several companies (e.g., Convio.com) provide software to do this, and as competition is driving down the price, usage is growing. Of course, a nonprofit still has to solicit supporters to join its campaign and to register with it online, but once they do so, the software allows management of far larger numbers of people by fewer people, and more efficiently and effectively than before.

Software can also be used to improve fund-raising—from prospecting for new donor support to tailoring messages to suit target audiences; from sending multiple, sequential e-mail messages aimed at these targets over a predetermined period of time as part of an overall strategy set in motion at one single point in time, to continuously posting appeals on a website. Highly creative messages that focus on specific individual interests and concerns and that will capture a higher percentage of donations in response can be crafted.

The 2004 presidential campaign established conclusively that solicitation of both financial support and individual action was not only possible via the Internet, but that this type of solicitation is likely to become an indispensable tool in the future (at least at the national level). Tens of thousands of individuals were recruited by both the Republicans and the Democrats to host small fund-raisers, operate telephone banks, rally supporters, and work for their candidate in other ways previously unimagined. Online fund-raising yielded significant amounts in campaign contributions (according to an article by Jim Barney on the "click and pledge.com" website, over 100 million dollars was raised in small online contributions in the 2004 presidential race.). Constant communication made millions of supporters feel more connected to these campaigns, and as a consequence more of them became involved, including large numbers of people previously uninvolved in campaigns on any level. While it is still doubtful whether the Internet and e-mail protocols will resonate with the public in campaigns other than those at the national level, political campaigning will likely never be quite the same, and neither will advocacy and lobbying of any kind that have a grassroots public component to them.

Doubtless, there will be continual refinement and growth of these online applications and increased multitask capacity, enabling, as never before, nonprofit lobbying to tap into its greatest asset—its potential base of volunteers and supporters. Databases are now easier to create, keep up-to-date, and utilize for various purposes based on specific criteria. Nonprofits cannot afford to climb on the technology bandwagon late; they should become competitive and remain so, and for this they need the full array of available tools.

Motivating people, monitoring the political situation, and courting and developing relationships over time will all be made easier by advances in Internet software. These and a score of other functions will always require planning and execution. Use of the Internet should never be thought of as an alternative to the development of a comprehensive overall lobbying strategy, but rather as a valuable tool and adjunct.

Today it is relatively easy to create, launch, and maintain simple websites that can serve as clearinghouses for information. These sites can be continuously updated and can handle massive amounts of traffic. Websites should be easy to navigate, and visitors should be able to quickly find what they are looking for. If a website has too many bells and whistles or extends the connection or downloading time in other ways, people will leave. Once they leave unsatisfied, they are not likely to return. Creativity in website design is important, but not as important as the website being user-friendly.

Listservs allow for direct communication to part, or all, of a given field instantaneously for the rapid dissemination of large volumes of data, research, and other materials. As broadband usage expands, soon the old limitations of download times will be a distant memory.

Newer software allows nonprofits to send messages to their base memberships and solicit messages from these constituents to targeted officials, enabling supporters to respond with ease. With a few quick clicks on the computer, people can now compose, address, and send messages to a virtually unlimited number of elected officials and tailor the messages to individual recipients. Cut-and-paste techniques can allow for at least semipersonalized messages to be created quickly and without too much effort. Moreover, the messages to the supporters of the coalition can be designed in ways that grab their attention, stay in their memory, and thereby increase the reach and effectiveness of these communications. Creative messages that persuade the reader/viewer to read them *and* respond to a call to action are invaluable. A nonprofit's simple goal of getting its core supporters to read its message and respond to a call for action will likely get harder to achieve owing to universal suspicion of spam and unsolicited junk e-mails.

Software can track responses and create sub-databanks of those who have responded to calls to action in the past, thereby providing the lobbying arm with information about who sent e-mail letters to decision makers when requested to do so, where those letters came from, and to whom they were sent. Information is the key to effective mobilization efforts. The greater the store of information, the more effectively the lobbying arm can target and control its efforts.

ONLINE RELATIONSHIP BUILDING

Databases: Online relationship building starts with the nonprofit compiling profiles of as many of its core base of supporters as possible to make the information an asset in the advocacy and/or lobbying function. Refinement of data can help to determine what strategies will motivate people to act and what strategies won't. Declarations of support can be widespread, but there will likely be far fewer people who will actually act when asked to. In building a database, solicitation for information should be initiated by any means possible—both online and offline. But it should be a continuous exercise. Newsletters, listservs, event recruitment, traditional mailings, and advertisements should all be employed as tools to build the initial database.

Ideally, the database will include demographic information as well as likes, dislikes, preferences, priorities, and other information about the individual that will allow the nonprofit to tailor messages to specific audience sectors. One problem for coalitions is the reluctance of organizations to share existing databases. Such reluctance can be based on the feeling that the information is proprietary and confidential and that it will end up in the hands of people who will use it for unauthorized purposes, thus alienating those who gave the information and compromising the holder's use of the information for purposes it considers a priority. There may be fear of competition, and in the case of databases related to fund-raising that contain donor profiles, the fear of having key supporters "stolen" might be real. Nonprofit advocacy coalitions need to address this issue and find out ways to prevent unauthorized usage of databases.

Relevant information can be gathered through surveys sent to individuals when they register themselves or when they enter information into the database via the nonprofit's website or other online interfaces. Not everyone will reply to a survey or participate in it, but with a concerted, ongoing effort based on the presentation of clear reasons for seeking to acquire the information, coupled with assurances of strict confidentiality, a comprehensive database can be created. This task harkens back to the issue of "trust" in coalition formation, as the nonprofit is asking people that it will respect their privacy. Posting a privacy policy with assurances ...d will not be sold or transferred to any third parties is a good approach.

A comprehensive database with demographic and other profile information can be cross-integrated over several functions of the organization (i.e., a database can be used to mobilize grassroots lobbying activities and to organize fund-raising efforts).

Use of the database: The most common use of an advocacy database is to send out e-mail alerts that the coalition needs support. These e-mails need to convey urgency, be concise, be specific in terms of what action is being requested and why, and be worded and presented so as to optimize the odds that it will persuade people to respond. Providing several options as to how the recipient can help will increase the scope of participation. Thus, someone may not be willing to make a telephone call, but will send an e-mail. Whatever is being asked for, the request should make *immediate* compliance as simple as possible for the recipient. Supporters appreciate that their privacy and their time are being respected and that those making the solicitation understand that this is an imposition of sorts. Such requests should also be accompanied by *talking points* or other support material that will make it easier for the recipient of the message to respond.

There will always be a debate as to which is preferable—a larger quantity of responses or a few responses that are of a high quality (e.g., one hundred written, personalized letters as opposed to one thousand form e-mail communications). It is also important to remember not to abuse access to potential supporters—not to go to the well too often. Don't ask people to communicate with decision makers constantly, don't characterize everything as dire and urgent; in other words, don't cry wolf too often.

Software that allows e-mail messages or portal gateways to be personalized with the respondent's name can be obtained, and such a personal touch helps to nurture the relationship. Sending messages that provide information but do not ask for anything in return ensure that the recipient is respected. Today, sending out online questionnaires or surveys seeking people's opinions and advice on issues helps to forge a relationship on deeper levels, and many people are flattered when their opinion is sought. But asking for too much of a person's time (completing surveys takes time) may adversely affect this relationship.

Requests for action can be very specific—the coalition can ask its supporters to communicate with targeted legislators or with the media, or to spread the word about individual bills or other matters. They can also ask for contributions to be used for either general and/or specific purposes. Action requests should be crafted differently for legislators (and within the legislature, committee chairs, members, etc.), staff, media, agency heads, and so on. Messages requesting action need to stand out from other messages. Depending on the level of software resources available, nonprofits can make very creative presentations on the issue and explain why the target's support and help is important. Mini visual/audio presentations can be sent online that grab the recipients' attention and interest and motivate them to action. As broadband usage expands and download time decreases, more visually creative messages with higher production values will become the norm. The day will come when each inbox receives a number of mini movies a day.

People identified as sympathetic and supportive of the nonprofit are important because they care. This doesn't always mean they can comply with a request, but they are, at least, already somewhat motivated. The trick is to turn the motivation into action at the earliest possible moment before it is lost. People need to be inspired; their passion needs to be triggered. A stunning visual/audio message can be autolinked to a web page that will identify the e-mail and site addresses of the targeted decision makers (so the supporter doesn't have to); help the supporter craft a personal letter or response; enable a hardcopy of a finished letter to be sent via e-mail, fax or post; send a copy to the database administrator; and facilitate a host of other tasks that can be accomplished on a one-stop basis, all with just a few clicks of the mouse by the original e-mail recipient.

As a rule, support response will be higher if the targeted person can be enticed to complete the requested action immediately, and there is a greater chance of this happening if what is requested is made simple to do or multiple ways to comply are provided. The drop-off rate is significant if the target, for whatever reason, decides to postpone the action. People get busy, they forget about the request or it seems less urgent, and for these reasons it is necessary to repeat the request after a specified time period if the database information indicates that no response has been received. Because a reminder is a form of pressure, it should be done tactfully. It should not be used for every single request that fails to draw an immediate response, but saved for very important occasions.

After a period of time during any campaign or ongoing advocacy effort, software that tracks responses to requests for action will help identify which presentations were the most effective, and this can help the nonprofit or coalition to refine its approaches and increase the level of response. Tracking can identify people who are likely to respond and those not so likely to do so. Surveys can be effective devices to engage supporters and make them more interested in the nonprofit's issue and more responsive to its requests for help. Surveys can also be used to determine if there is any way nonresponders can be converted into active supporters. As online advocacy management is permission based—meaning that the people whose information is stored in the database have opted in, are interested in the issue, and have volunteered to be kept in the loop—time that would otherwise have been spent on communicating with people who have no real interest in actively joining a campaign can be put to better use. Periodic summary reports, including measurements against specific criteria, can provide information and insights into several aspects of an advocacy effort and help make the nonprofit or coalition more effective. And online tools for communication and database management are faster and much more affordable than traditional tools.

Acknowledging the support of people who do respond helps cement relationships. Individuals can be thanked via an automatic e-mail reply that is sent when tracking alerts the database administrator that the individual has taken action as requested. Their names can be added to a list of persons to whom thank-you communications are sent from time to time, they can even be sent a downloadable, printable certificate of commendation, or some other ways to acknowledge and honor their support can be found. People like to be acknowledged and thanked, and a simple gesture takes relatively little effort and is invaluable in building goodwill.

All of this new application technology is still in the embryonic stage. The future is likely to see both unimagined new possibilities and problems.

WEBSITES

As a central clearinghouse, websites are now irreplaceable tools for nonprofit advocacy. They can be accessed at any time by any of the nonprofit's fields; they facilitate easy downloading of massive amounts of information presented in a professional manner; link people to scores of other sites with related information; and register people for a variety of things—from e-mail newsletter subscription to events, rallies, and meetings of all types. Websites provide tutorials, seminars, and other technical assistance, education, and training. They also allow for interactive communication, opinion sampling, polling, news, live feeds of hearings and other events, relevant media coverage, and more—all easily accessed, centrally and conveniently organized, and always available.

Of course, the essence of better websites is that they are, above all else, designed well—easy to navigate and comprehensive enough to provide the users with what they want. Attractive graphics and all kinds of whistles and bells may be of value, but the most important thing to users is that they can find what they are looking for quickly. Thus, websites need to be comprehensive and user-friendly, and above all, quick to identify and provide the information or area requested. As a rule of thumb, if visitors have to click the mouse more than three times to get to where they want to go on a site, a substantial portion of the initial audience will be lost. Making certain a site is easy to navigate and comprehensive, with one-stop shopping for all the information or services desired, takes many hours of programming. The cost of personnel time will thus determine the level of sophistication of any website. But with increasing options to outsource these tasks on an increasingly affordable basis, the time and level of competence required is falling as well. A number of nonprofit service organizations are providing website software and experts pro bono or at a low cost to help nonprofits develop sites.

While it is easy to develop and launch a new website, constant updating of content is more difficult as it requires more personnel time. To maintain its relevance, a website must have a never-ending stream of new content; dated sites that do not change content regularly lose visitors quickly, and it is difficult to lure them back. All of us, as Internet users, have voracious appetites for new content.

Care should be taken to ensure that credit is given prominently on the site to all participants and supporters of the coalition. Care should also be taken in naming the site—the ideal URL for a website conveys clearly what the site is about, is easy to remember, and is as short as possible—for example, www.savetheriver.com is easier to remember than a longer, more complicated name, though a name that is unique may stick in the memory longer. Be particularly careful about words that are difficult to spell. A nonprofit should remember that it also wants people who probably know nothing about it or the issue at hand to visit the website, and that there is no reason for them to do so except for recent interest. If they can't find the website easily, they will give up the effort, and the nonprofit will lose a potential supporter, donor, or volunteer.

THE INTANGIBLES

IMAGE

Each lobbying interest group or coalition has an image—not always accurate, and often based on perception, not fact. The decision makers the group or coalition seeks to influence will ask: Is the group a player or not? Is it powerful or weak? Does it have powerful friends or not? Is the group rich in resources or poor? Does it play hardball or softball? Is it reasonable or unreasonable? Are the people behind the group knowledgeable or uninformed? Does the group play by the rules or is it a maverick? Can it be trusted or not? Does it return favors or not? Can it be manipulated or is it strong? Will the group compromise if necessary or not? Does the press love it or ignore it?

An image once created can survive a change in circumstance and either work to the advantage of the nonprofit or hamper its chance of success. Cultivating and managing the exact desired image is an important strategic issue and should not be ignored. Image and perception are based on the press's observations of the coalition's behavior and those passed on by word-of-mouth; they are established over time and are part attitude, part reality, part mystery. Many activities will have an impact on a coalition's image. For example, letter writing, telephone calls and other campaigns strategies need to enjoy widespread participation to be effective. Too few letters, for instance, send the wrong signal—that the coalition can't muster the support of its own people. This will impact its image. A coalition must never appear weak and ineffective.

The coalition should seek to be thought of as serious, honest, realistic, resolute but not unwilling to compromise, loyal, and skilled—regardless of the degree of power that it may wield. If it has power—funds, machinery, foot soldiers, the press, and powerful friends—it will get even farther if it is held in high regard as a reasonable and professional group. Reputation can only be established over time, through multiple battles and skirmishes. For most nonprofits, the lobbying game will be long and ongoing. They will win some and lose some, but they should grow with each campaign, each year—learning from their mistakes, honing their skills, building their assets, and cultivating their supporters so that the advocacy organization increases, over time, its power and the likelihood that it will prevail on critically important issues. The only way to get there is to start now. All of what the organization does will create its image. The greater the power or the perception of its power, the better will be its image.

A weak effort telegraphs the wrong signal, and some consideration should be given to making no effort at all as opposed to a weak one. If the coalition generates ten telephone calls asking for support and another group generates one thousand calls for this group's cause, who do you think will be taken more seriously? The coalition doesn't have to win the numbers game, only generate numbers that indicate widespread support in the district for its position. That's the whole point of the grassroots component of the overall lobbying campaign.

The nonprofit coalition's image is created by its own people—how they dress, their demeanor, their knowledge, and their attitude. Each of them is an ambassador of the coalition, and it is wise to make at least the board, staff, key volunteers, and other prominent actors on its stage aware of this fact.

To the extent the nonprofit can reward supportive elected officials by working for their reelection—and by inference punishing those who opposed it, by either withholding any reelection support or moving support to an opposition candidate—it will establish in the political culture that the organization/coalition is a serious political player. Of course, 501c(3) organizations cannot fulfill this function; it must be done either by individuals operating as private citizens or by a PAC or 527 subsidiary of a related 501c(3) or 501c(4) nonprofit. But it is easy to make clear what action or inaction brought forth the support or withholding of support. There is no need for such reward or punishment to be acrimonious or even impolite—as in *The Godfather* movies, this is "strictly business." The nonprofit, like any other entity, has the right, nay the duty, to protect its own self-interest and work for decisions it believes is in its overall best interests and those of society. This is true even if not every member of the organization or coalition agrees. The organization/coalition exists apart from the sum of its members and constituents. American law recognizes it as a citizen.

IDENTITY

Maintaining a positive self "identity" within the coalition is extremely important in keeping the coalition solidly together and motivated to take action. The identity or sense of community is paramount in forging alliances that can withstand stress and attacks. The sense of community—"we are in this together"—is what motivates people to work hard and continue to do so even in the face of overwhelming odds and defeats. Often, the coalition is composed of people whose work is interconnected, but who do not, because of distance or for other reasons, have many opportunities to interact with one another. Thus, a sense of isolation and aloneness can often permeate the coalition. Believing that one is part of a greater whole is comforting, but without occasional tangible evidence of the connections, it is easy to feel one is working in a void. Effective and continual communication helps in solidifying an identity. For a large-scale effort, some type of district system that allows for frequent interchange among members of local chapters reminds participants of the bigger picture. It is important that there be actual evidence that the larger army of soldiers exists, that it is real, for this allows people to believe it can succeed. Similarly, it is important that the members of any organized lobbying effort enjoy, from time to time, a victory in their efforts so that there is a sense that what the group is trying to accomplish is possible. People won't stay long if they think a cause is hopeless. Every group needs to think of itself as a "winner."

QUALITY/EXCELLENCE

One part of a nonprofit's image/brand is the attention it pays to its work, its own sense of quality performance. Are its graphics first rate or mediocre? Is its correspondence always spell-checked first, or is it sloppy? Are the nonprofit's people on time, or habitually late? Is the organization professionally run, or is it an amateurish operation? These things all create an image of the organization and its people and how it is perceived. Everybody holds quality-conscious organizations in higher esteem than those that are not professional.

A second part of the nonprofit's image comes from observations of how it conducts itself— really, how its people conduct themselves. Are they patient or do they make idle threats? Are they mature or petulant? Are they calm under pressure or do they come apart? Organizations and people that conduct their affairs with some degree of dignity and maturity will get much further, everything else being equal, than those that are thought of as poor players.

Establishing excellence as the standard and insisting on professionalism will also help establish the internal and external image that each segment of the coalition has of the whole coalition, and this will encourage all those involved to take pride in the way they conduct the coalition's business.

The external identity is much like a "brand" name—it is the image people have, in a general sense, of the organization. It is collective recognition of what the organization does, and a perceived sense of "how" it does it.

Identity can be established and image enhanced in a number of ways:

Logo: If there is easy access to someone with artistic ability (and virtually every organization has someone who knows someone with such ability), ask this person to try to come up with a logo for the advocacy coalition or the lobbying purpose. The logo can then be used on the organization's website, its printed materials, its merchandising, and so forth. Branding the effort in this way helps to build identity, which then helps to build the sense of community necessary to motivate the members of a coalition and to improve awareness of the issues and the campaign among the wider public. Repetitive use of the logo over time is the key to recognition.

Slogan and symbols: A one- to four-word slogan or a symbol that encapsulates the issue/lobbying purpose can complement a visually appealing logo to build identity, expand awareness, and serve as a rallying point. The slogan can be the essence of the message. The most obvious examples of effective slogans from the recent past include the "Got Milk" slogan and the Clinton election cry, "It's the economy, stupid." Both grabbed the public's attention, are eminently memorable, and perfectly summarize their message – all of which helped to plant them in our collective psyche in a relatively short period of time. The United Negro College Fund's "A mind is a terrible thing to waste" is an almost perfect slogan for an enormously effective fund-raising campaign. "The Arts Mean Business" effectively sends the message that supporting the arts is equivalent to supporting business, and is designed to both inform the public and solicit the support of the business community. Seemingly less-than-perfect slogans become more highly regarded after repetitive use over time. Familiarity is the factor that enhances the genius of a good slogan in retrospect.

Symbols may take longer to establish in the mindset of the public, unless they are particularly memorable and unique. One of the most successful symbols ever created (which was developed virtually without any cost) is the AIDS Red Ribbon. The impact of this simple symbol on creating awareness, recruiting support, garnering media attention, and forging commitment to the cause is incalculable. This symbol is so successful that it has been appropriated by numerous other efforts (green ribbons for environmental causes, pink ribbons for breast cancer research, and so forth). The Chinese Panda Bear symbol of the World Wildlife Fund works because it elicits a sympathetic emotional response. Recognizable symbols can connote empathy, sympathy, anger, incredulity, or any of a host of other responses useful to the coalition in advancing its message and expanding its power base. They aren't essential, but they make things easier. Identity is important to distinguish an organization from the already crowded sea of organizations; a positive image can help in the motivation of the core base and play a role in creating momentum for the campaign. These factors shouldn't be underestimated as one of the areas planners should consider when arriving at strategies for success.

MERCHANDISING/IDENTITY

Symbols, including logos, and the merchandising of those symbols and logos on T-shirts, mugs, buttons, bumper stickers, posters, banners, jackets, caps, and the like can help create the sense of community as visual reminders, can transmit the message to the public, and can also help raise funds in the process.

MOTIVATION-RALLYING THE TROOPS

Keep your fears to yourself, but share your inspiration with others.

Robert Louis Stevenson

There are whole fields of study in psychology, marketing, advocacy, and other areas devoted to effective motivation of groups of people for an endless number of purposes. Given hectic schedules, pressures of job and family, myriad competing causes—besides limited financial resources, general ennui, and apathy—how does the nonprofit go about motivating both its volunteer base and the general public to support its lobbying efforts?

The nonprofit's core constituency needs three resources to become politically effective: *money* to support the coalition's efforts and to contribute to candidates for office (in varying amounts, but some); *time* to become involved in the coalition's work and in the campaigns of candidates for office (again, in varying amounts, but some); and the *skill set* to work the political process (and if the volunteers don't have the skills, training can easily equip them with the tools needed to make them effective for the nonprofit's purposes). The key element is the *motivation* to part with hard-earned cash, to make the time to participate, and to accept training—in short, a compelling *reason* to extend themselves.

Theoretically, belief in and support for the nonprofit's goals and missions, respect for the success of its programs and services, involvement in the nonprofit in some capacity, and the desire to make a difference and advance something positive in the community are all motivating precepts that can be mined to move individuals to action—first the core constituency and grassroots coalition volunteer base and then the general public. Idealism and passion are alive still. But this is often not enough.

The first question to ask is: What's in it for them? How do they benefit directly? If the nonprofit is environmentally based and its goal is to reduce car emissions to improve the air quality—the direct benefit is cleaner air to breathe—for the individual, and, perhaps more importantly, for his or her children. If the nonprofit is arts based and the goal is more money for theater groups, the indirect result will help the area to attract more tourists (and, as tourism is increasingly important to the economic health of most areas, everyone benefits). The more direct the benefit, the better.

Bear in mind that daily schedules are increasingly hectic; none of us has time to get done all we have on our "to do" list. The nonprofit should take into consideration what it is asking people to do, and try to find ways to make the task easy for them.

It helps if the leadership, or at least one person, is obsessed with achieving the desired result—someone for whom the objective is a preoccupation and who is willing to follow that obsession. Successful advocacy and lobbying is replete with examples of one or two people whose single-minded dedication to passing a piece of legislation was the driving force behind ultimate success (Mothers Against Drunk Driving grew from the effort of just two people, and the passage of Megan's Law was spearheaded by one lone person). Such a belief in, and commitment to, a *cause* can be contagious; it can set the "tone" for an entire effort, steel the resolve of thousands of people who join the effort, and motivate them to stay the course until victory is at hand. This kind of determination is a form of the American entrepreneurial spirit that we so value; it can inspire and motivate huge numbers of people and intimidate legislators. Not all advocacy objectives, no matter how laudable their purposes, lend themselves to such single-minded devotion, but those that do touch such a chord, even if in but one person, have a distinct advantage. One person *can* change the world. Sometimes the one person who will not be deterred becomes an immovable force.

COMMUNICATION

Out of sight, out of mind. When trying to motivate people to support the advocacy and/or lobbying effort, the nonprofit must maintain constant communication with them. It must inform them as to what is happening at each stage of the process, let them know the bad news and the good news, and involve them by keeping them informed. This will instill in them a sense of "ownership" in the nonprofit's effort. They will have a greater sense of this "ownership" if they feel they are part of the "insider" strategic planning. Sometimes developing an "us" and "them" environment can help the nonprofit to secure the trust of its support groups; the more these groups buy into what the nonprofit is trying to accomplish, the less the nonprofit has to worry about motivating them to stay the course.

STRATEGIES

What else can be done? Successful nonprofit lobbying efforts need to be

1. **Easy, simple, and clearly defined:** It is essential that what a nonprofit asks people to do is clear and understandable, that its goal is attainable and realistic (thus not a waste of their time), that it will provide them with the background and the tools to do the job, that what it is asking is only minimally intrusive into

their time and/or pocketbooks, and that they will be part of changes that dovetail with their priorities and interests. It is important for a nonprofit to address
concerns of scarce time, lack of skills, or any other fear, trepidation, or barrier
that keeps its targets from giving it an initial "yes" to a solicitation for help.

2. **Based on a sense of community:** People are more likely to participate in the
effort if they perceive that they will be acting in concert with others and not
alone. Even though much of what the nonprofit needs them to do (writing
letters, contacting legislators, etc.) may be solitary activity, there are ways to
network people in the process and establish the perception that even if they
are acting alone they are part of a larger whole—a *community* of people—and
that they, as members, are contributing to a bigger picture. It is necessary to
reassure people of this fact repeatedly.

3. **Organized on the principle that everybody counts:** One of the most preva-
lent excuses people make for not responding to action alerts is that in the context of large numbers of people necessary to a purpose, their role is not crucial
and that their participation will neither be missed nor make a difference. This
belief must be addressed and eliminated. Convince your base supporters that
their involvement is absolutely essential. Identify them by name at all times,
personalize the cause to their priorities, recount defeats and threats past and
present, and educate them that every additional letter, fax, phone call, or
e-mail makes a difference.

4. **Fun and pleasurable:** The advocacy enterprise should not be so serious that
there is no room for fun. Fun and laughter are always possible in any situation,
and if the monotony of daily minutiae can be broken up by people enjoying
the camaraderie and fellowship of the process, it will help build morale and
optimism, which in turn increases productivity and facilitates solicitation of
new people. While all activities are not inherently fun, an atmosphere of enjoy-
ment and an openness to laughter are valuable assets. Somber situations and a
crisis mode of operation should never be allowed to become systemic and permanent. A casual atmosphere is conducive to having fun; a casual attitude permits fun; and a casual approach encourages having fun. Serious business and
purpose does not have to exist at the expense of having fun.

   More people will participate in the nonprofit's effort if it can make the
process and the activity enjoyable. It should hold letter-writing house parties
instead of just asking people to write a letter. The group should make training
events social affairs—it should unite friends, neighbors, and coworkers, and
involve families and children. Rallies don't have to be a political confrontation;
their main purpose is in amassing large numbers of people. Food, music, and
social activities are the elements that bind people together and make drudgery
enjoyable. Getting people together, when and wherever possible, advances the
sense of community, of the "we"; it promotes commitment and dedication
and enhances motivation and the satisfaction of being involved.

5. **Contagion:** Involvement in a "community" of like-minded people can be contagious, and can help to expand the nonprofit's base and maximize the individual efforts. Nothing is more contagious than success, which is another
reason why goals and objectives should be realistic and attainable—kept

simple and doable. Any victory along the way helps to energize the troops. On the opposite side, too many defeats can decimate participation in a campaign. Leading a nonprofit advocacy coalition is a little like being a football coach—much of the work is cheerleading.

6. **Able to tap into the sense of outrage:** People need to relate to what they do personally; they need to have a stake in the success of the mission. Emphasize how they—or their family, friends, workers or community—benefit by supporting the nonprofit's effort. Point out the downside—what they stand to lose by the mission's defeat. One effective motivational tool is the cultivation of a sense of outrage. Countless governmental actions can be portrayed as forms of senseless and thoughtless injustice and, when made public, can outrage people. We are, by and large, a nation that values fair play and lofty aspirations very highly. We don't like it when the underdog, trying to do the right thing, gets the short end of the stick. We identify with *David* in his struggle against Goliath. We want the "good" guys to win, and the "bad" guys to get their comeuppance. The nonprofit should tap into this sentiment to personalize the issue.

    Outrage moves people to action and can swell the ranks of a movement overnight. Not every government action, even though it negatively impacts the good work of a nonprofit, is, of course, outrageous. Many are simply difficult choices between competing goods. But many of those choices *are* outrageous and ought to be seen as such. Nonprofits are often too meek and mild for their own good. Ideally, the choice that threatens the organization threatens the individual constituents. The nonprofit should involve all supporters in the process—seek their ideas and opinions, integrate them throughout the hierarchy, and delegate authority and responsibility.

7. **Training-Oriented:** If people feel that they lack the skills and competency to participate in a lobbying activity or that they will fail in that activity, they may be reluctant to make the attempt. Training supporters to be competent advocates and lobbyists and providing them with tools and information so they are confident in their knowledge and capacity will help to move them to action. Training also helps to demystify the lobbying process and gets people to understand that influencing legislation and government action is basically achieved through common-sense mechanisms. Many people are easily intimidated. Providing them with knowledge and skills can allow them to overcome these feelings of inadequacy. The nonprofit should make sure there is a mechanism in place to answer questions as they arise. If people can't get an answer to their question, they may simply abandon the group's effort.

R.E.S.P.E.C.T. . . .

A nonprofit's support base, including volunteers, is its most valuable asset. It should take very good care of these people. The organization's attitude toward them, the way they perceive how it views them, and the respect it accords them will all determine in part how they respond to it. Their privacy should always be respected, and thus the nonprofit should prevent its databases from falling into another's hands. It should temper what it asks of them, so that the supporters sense that it respects their schedules and the demands on their time. The organization wants its people to know it appreciates what they do on its behalf, and that their efforts make a difference, and it should acknowledge and thank them whenever possible. The organization wants them to feel competent, and therefore it needs to provide them with tools and training to boost their confidence.

RITES, RITUALS, AND CEREMONIES

One of the timeless tools for building group solidarity is the adoption of rituals and ceremonies and the inclusion of rites in the folklore of the group. Events or devices welcoming new initiates, ceremonies honoring people's contributions, gatherings of the whole membership, and other ways to mark and celebrate the existence of the group and the people belonging to it are essential to keeping up morale, creating a group identity and dynamic, and forming bonds that will motivate people to take action. Victories, even small ones, can be good reasons for celebrations.

CONSISTENCY

The nonprofit must repeatedly tell its core base of supporters how they benefit, how they are joining like-minded people, how the organization/field positively impacts them and the community, why their support is critical, and whatever else they need to know to be motivated to help the nonprofit when requested to do so. Nonprofits need to understand some of the ways to achieve this motivation and acquire some of the skills requisite in this art/science. Nothing is more important than keeping the motivation of the effort high and stable and those involved optimistic.

Volunteers need to be continually motivated so as to keep them involved. Nothing destroys a sense of community quicker than the epidemic of loss of hope. For this reason all advocacy campaigns need built-in victories that the base can celebrate and that can reenergize the field. One simple means to keep spirits high is to continuously thank the workers, and the more creative these thank-yous can be made, the better.

CREDIT

My friend and noted advocacy guru Paul Minicucci says that one of the basic rules of successful advocacy is to *"give credit where credit is due, and to give it even where it isn't due."* In other words, successful advocacy leaders know that they don't need the credit for success—those to whom it is important to know where credit should lie, will, in the final analysis, know who did what. If spreading credit around—even where it is a little gratuitous—increases people's motivation to work, expands the circle of support, and enhances the chances of success, then it's a good move. People like to be credited and acknowledged for their participation and the value of their work.

One of the most important roles for senior leadership in advocacy and/or lobbying efforts is that of *cheerleader*, urging the field to act, to stay resolved, to go the extra mile. Cheerleading in this sense is a balance of nurturing, thanking, supporting, cajoling, "guilting," and otherwise moving people to action. Ennui is the enemy. Delay is the virus from within. Bystanders are of little help.

PASSION

It is difficult to even quantify passion as an element in the advocacy process, let alone "manage" it, but there is no dispute that passion will move staffers, volunteers, and core base constituents and supporters to work harder and longer. Passion can be encouraged; it is certainly contagious. Some causes will excite the passions of members and the public alike because of their nature (Save the Panda is one such organization that has successfully fanned the passion of those for whom such a cute and cuddly animal simply demands action); other causes are not by nature as likely to spark such a passionate response. Passion can be borne out of anger or frustration, hope or belief, a sense of equity and fairness, or the feeling of rightness or wrongness. Whatever its genesis, whether or not it can be manufactured, a conscious attempt to fan its fires is smart management.

In any case, the opposite of passion—"indifference"—can be particularly dangerous for any nonprofit advocacy coalition; it leads to apathy and must be fought at every level and at all costs. Virtually everything an advocacy coalition attempts— from fund-raising to volunteer recruitment, from lobbying to media management—is dependent on making the issue(s) at hand meaningful, relevant, important and, to some extent, urgent, so as to be able to move people to action. If a nonprofit can't convince people to care about what it cares about, it will have to fight its fight all alone—and more often than not, this ensures defeat in the advocacy arena.

On the negative side, unbridled passion may cloud decision making and perspective; it may get in the way of methodical planning. Advocacy and lobbying need passionate advocates and lobbyists, but their passion must also be tempered to promote deliberate and calculated planning, and therefore the nonprofit's leaders must be realistic and practical in their approach.

ENTHUSIASM

Enthusiasm is different from passion. Exuberance and ardor are assets that bind people to the mission and motivate them to work harder. Enthusiasm is infectious in the workplace and beneficial to the working environment. In some senses, enthusiasm is more fragile than passion. Passion exists in the belly of the beast and exists in the best and possibly the worst of times. Passionate people may be optimistic or pessimistic, they may be motivated to work hard or depressed to the point of sitting on the sidelines, but they usually stay involved. Enthusiasm comes from the heart, and can also ebb and flow at different times. Enthusiastic people may not have the depth of belief in the "cause," but enthusiasm almost always increases productivity. Again, the periodic victory is essential to maintain enthusiasm.

THE VOLUNTEER LEADERSHIP

The senior leadership will face more pressure and endure more stress than the rank-and-file volunteers and membership, and this is particularly the case for volunteer-filled positions whose labor is gratis. Thus, the organization's governing board and the executive director need to nurture these key people in any way possible.

Acknowledging their contribution, honoring their commitment, and thanking them for their service can all go a long way in balancing the negatives associated with the intensity of this kind of endeavor.

STAKEHOLDERS

Stakeholder bases are more difficult to motivate because they are not a part of the core constituent group of the nonprofit, and therefore motivating them takes extra effort and vigilance. One factor that influences the willingness of stakeholder group rank and file to make the effort to become active is the example of their leadership. If their leadership is committed, active, and motivated, the perception of their endorsement of the cause helps them to legitimize their involvement and justify their commitment. Accordingly, it should be played up at every opportunity. As stakeholder bases are one step removed from the core base, the individuals in stakeholder groups need to be thanked, acknowledged, and honored more often, and communications to them need to be more frequent and comprehensive. Stakeholder members should be physically integrated with the coalition's members whenever possible to promote the contagion of the core base enthusiasm. Outside stakeholder members should be made to feel they are a part of the "us" of the effort. Having at least some of a stakeholder group's membership involved in the hierarchy of the nonprofit's advocacy apparatus is a smart move.

THE GENERAL PUBLIC

Securing general public support is difficult; motivating them to action on an ongoing basis is a Herculean endeavor. The nonprofit has to make the public aware of the issue(s), give them a reason to act in its support, and then provide them with the means and tools to act—all on a timeline.

If the nonprofit has succeeded in getting a member of the general public to sign on in support, via its website or in other ways, and the individual has expressed interest and voluntarily provided the contact information, then it can move this person to its volunteer base. Such a person is then not only a member of the public, but also one of the nonprofit's volunteers. The rest of the public has less of a tie to the nonprofit's cause than does its core constituency and volunteer base.

The first essential strategy for the nonprofit in trying to get the public to act in its support or to become part of its core base is to determine exactly what it would like them to do (Write a letter? Make a phone call? Come to a rally?). Whatever the nonprofit's specific goal for the public is, it must repeat this message to them over and over so as to maximize the chances that someone will learn of it and react. Repetition of the message can be accomplished by having it sent from multiple sources—thus a request for people to show up at a rally should be sent out by the coalition and by the stakeholder groups, announced in newspapers, passed on via e-mail, and spread by posted flyers, word of mouth, telephone calls, and any other means available—not just once, but several times.

The second essential strategy for moving the public is to convince them that the nonprofit's cause is reasonable and of value to the "public good." They must perceive its needs as something that warrants their involvement, that *their* interests are really the same as *the nonprofit's* interests. Different sectors of the public will respond to different messages. Thus, parents may be moved to support the nonprofit if they feel that what it wants positively impacts their children and has value for them; senior citizens may join the cause if they feel that what it wants relates to their needs. While the nonprofit can't be everything to everyone, it increases the chance of having its plea heard in a positive light if it can tailor messages to specific audiences.

CREATIVITY

Nonprofits are, more often than not, at a competitive disadvantage on a number of fronts, including funding and available resources. On the other hand, nonprofits have certain assets and advantages, including an attractive "product" and the skills and talents of a potentially wide field of supporters. All nonprofits need to think out of the box in terms of the design, style, type, and method of delivery for their lobbying strategies, their communications, their fund-raising pitches, and so forth so as to maximize the success of their message and to engage the volunteer base. If a nonprofit does the same thing it has always done, it is likely to get the same result. It should take some risks in terms of strategies—it should be creative, be different, and find new ways to address the various issues and challenges facing the effort.

Here are a few ways in which nonprofits can increase their creativity:

- **Design:** Websites and listserv e-mail messages should always take advantage of the myriad ways they can be enhanced creatively with interesting layout, color, fonts, photos, and presentation. Messages that stand out visually, that are easy to read and, in the case of websites, easy to navigate may increase the percentage of people who read them and motivate more people to take action. Remember that ease of navigation—the ability to find what one is looking for—always trumps design. If people get a message or go to a website, they want to find what they want as quickly as possible, and if the design interferes with their accomplishing this, there is a greater chance that they will not try. But if navigation is easy, *and* the message or site is visually pleasing, stimulating, and memorable, then it will resonate better and be more successful. Don't make the messages *too* slick, as it is necessary to retain some sense of David versus Goliath.
- **Brevity:** Communications should always be brief, concise, and to the point. They may still be creatively presented, but they are more effective if they cut to the chase at the outset. People don't like intrusions into their private lives. Avoid "information overload" and creating chaos by providing too much information for people to consume.
- **Simplicity:** Keeping messages simple doesn't mean that they can't be creative or comprehensive. If a communication is designed to inform and educate the recipient about an issue, keep it to this one issue. If a communication asks the recipient to do something, make sure there is a specific request and only one "ask" per communication.

Create an environment in which new ideas are welcome, where people feel comfortable putting forth suggestions, even though some of these suggestions will not be workable. Value the membership's opinions and thoughts and institute ways to demonstrate that the more the input into the process the greater the likelihood of increasing effectiveness and participation. Encourage people to help, create mechanisms that nurture their brainstorming about how to improve the nonprofit's systems, and establish the means for them to do so. People are often hesitant to make suggestions and share observations because they think they will appear stupid—a nonprofit can avoid this if it chooses to do so. I have seen countless lobbying and advocacy efforts as well as political campaigns and business enterprises suffering, and even failing, because they deny themselves the opportunity to see and hear the one great idea that would help to ensure their success. They miss this one great idea because they don't take the time and effort to listen to everyone, to hold the process "open" to every possible idea. They fail to provide for people who want to help by failing to provide them an entry point into the process. They often take their own core base for granted. Nothing could be more myopic.

Organizations don't usually set out to be elitist, but unless they consciously address the issue of how to promote new approaches, the net result may be the same. No one knows where the next hit record will come from, where the next dot-com revolution will start, where the next leader will emerge. Smart entities, be they political, business or philanthropic, provide to the greatest extent opportunities to capture ideas. Nonprofits may not be able to create a milieu that guarantees the genesis of great ideas, but they can certainly create environments that will stifle and crush these ideas from coming forward. Instead, they should devise a few ways to enable volunteers and supporters to improve their systems. While some centralization is essential in a lobbying effort, most efforts can afford to delegate powers and decisions across the spectrum, and by so doing, they will be strengthening involvement and action. A well-run lobbying effort is the province of the many, not the few. Control is not the issue, but influencing decision makers is. Staying on message is the issue. Expanded support is the issue. The more ideas that are generated, the greater the likelihood that some of them will be good.

LEADERSHIP

> The key to being a good manager is keeping the people who hate me away from those who are still undecided.
>
> Casey Stengel

Volumes have been written about effective leadership, the attributes charismatic leaders possess, the manner of their actions, the way they motivate people, and the like. Effective advocacy leaders know how to get the most from their troops. They know how to set guidelines, as opposed to giving orders; they know how to encourage, rather than demand. Hold out the carrots, lots of carrots, but throw away the stick—it doesn't work in these circumstances. Be a real leader by leading—people will follow you if you are optimistic, resolute, organized, and value their contributions. Conversely, they will abandon you if you are unsure, disorganized, wavering, indifferent or patronizing. Your job is to grow the coalition, keep motivation high, secure the best tools you can, and be as thorough in your efforts as is possible. Advocacy and lobbying are two enterprises that cannot be done by a single individual or a handful of individuals—they are team efforts. As previously discussed, they can be *launched* and *led* by one lone person, and this person can make the difference; but ultimately this person needs an army to win—from visionaries and practical strategists, to spokespeople and researchers; from those who can goad and energize the base to those who understand the realities of the game as played in the political corridors. Most importantly, the advocacy and lobbying enterprises need people who generate infectious optimism and enthusiasm.

ADVOCACY FINANCES

BUDGETARY CONSIDERATIONS

Ongoing advocacy and/or lobbying and the advantage of having paid, professional staff for this activity (which may or may not include a separate lobbying firm or contributions to candidates) require an annual budget apart from the budget for the pursuit of any specific advocacy objective. Budgets need to include all costs of personnel, benefits, overhead, office rent, telephone, postage, supplies, travel, and so on, and the sources of income. Pursuit of a specific advocacy objective or campaign (passage or defeat of a particular bill in the legislature) may require a separate budget setting forth the specific costs that will need to be covered. Revenue streams should not be cavalierly determined. It is important to be realistic, even cautious, in making projections as to where the money will come from and how much can be raised. Overly optimistic or Pollyanna projections will impede strategies that were carefully arrived at. There will need to be as many as three potential funding streams: (1) to pay for the basic costs of ongoing advocacy, both overhead and personnel (including the optional retaining of outside professional firms); (2) to cover the additional costs attendant on one or more specific campaigns geared toward a specific advocacy objective during any given fiscal year; and (3) to fund a war chest from which to make campaign contributions to candidates. Most nonprofits never get past the first item, and even there, revenue to adequately cover the costs associated with merely maintaining an advocacy structure is frequently not achieved. The hallmark of the voluntary nonprofit advocacy effort, and one of the reasons why nonprofits continue to be at a competitive disadvantage, is the failure to pony up an adequate amount of money to cover the costs of the effort. The nonprofit can't mount an effective lobbying effort on the cheap, and the nonprofit universe *must* accept that, in large part, they have to pay for the effort themselves.

This money can come from the core base supporters—the coalition members themselves—augmented by other sources. For most nonprofit field areas, raising funds to a level that is sufficient to pay for a meaningful advocacy effort is realistically possible for a coalition of organizations, *if they are willing to make the commitment and invest the time and resources to do so.* It will be time-consuming and taxing, and will require a mindset shift from traditional conceptions of how to pay for advocacy, but, unquestionably, it can be done. If the nonprofit universe will collectively resolve to make it happen (as people resolved post-9/11 or post-tsunami to raise funds for the victims' relief), it will happen. Many other sectors of society with fewer resources than nonprofits possess have done it with great success.

Until a sector accepts the advocacy role as fundamental to its existence and forms a united coalition committed to raising the minimal funds to hire competent, full-time staff, successful lobbying, over time, will not be a viable option; its vulnerability will increase with a lack of weapons to fight attacks.

THE BUDGET

An ideal budget for a large lobbying apparatus, exclusive of contributions to campaigns, can run into the single- or even multimillion-dollar range per annum. This kind of money is generally beyond the reach of the average nonprofit coalition, and thus it is essential to prioritize the strategy to be used so as to determine what the coalition needs, and does not need, can and cannot afford. Employment of at least a full-time executive director is nonnegotiable—filling this post is essential to any advocacy effort. Of the five critical advocacy functions, each coalition must weigh the relative needs of its situation and prioritize which posts to fill first. Theoretically, advocacy can be advanced by filling all the posts with volunteers, but realistically, such an effort will be handicapped from the outset and unquestionably at a competitive disadvantage compared with others lobbying in the same political arena. I argue here for a minimum of three full-time, paid employees—the executive director and any two from the other five areas (development, communications, liaison/lobbying, volunteer coordination, and media relations).

Expenses such as online website/listserv/e-mail capacity can be budgeted for depending on what is attempted or desired. Similarly, printing expenses can be minimal, if very few printed materials are ever used, or very expensive, if these materials are provided to the member base, the target lawmakers, the media, and the public. Some costs vary depending on external circumstances. Thus, travel expenses will depend on the size of the geographical territory and the current cost of oil. The cost of lobbying and other outside services will probably rise with inflation, as will perhaps some fixed costs such as rent, travel, and telephone usage.

SUMMARY

The nonprofit advocacy coalition must draft a realistic budget and then devise strategies to raise the requisite funds. Such strategies will require a major commitment of time and energy on the part of all the members of the coalition in order to succeed, particularly at the launch. Failure to provide an adequate budget and implement the fund-raising strategies to pay for the expenses will cripple the effort to develop a viable, competitive advocacy and/or lobbying apparatus and torpedo the capacity to win specific campaigns at the outset.

The key to competitive advocacy and lobbying is the *willingness* of the coalition to commit to *whatever it takes* to raise the funds to become an effective player in the game; this includes full-time, paid staff and a fund to support specific candidate campaigns.

FUNDING STREAMS

Where then will the money necessary for advocacy and lobbying come from? Government and foundation support normally available for nonprofit programs and, to a lesser extent, operations, is usually not available to support advocacy efforts. Traditional nonprofit advocacy and/or lobbying has relied on member support as its primary funding source. There are two member-support approaches:

- **Organizations** within a given field are solicited to join and pay dues, usually on the basis of a sliding scale according to the member organization's budget size; and
- **Individuals** are asked to join and pay dues, and often there are escalating levels of individual membership, with each upward level conferring additional benefits.

Other sources of income include

- donations in addition to membership dues
- grants—public and private (if not for direct advocacy or lobbying, then for organization, education, and training expenses)
- bequests, trusts, appreciation of assets (a minor funding stream at best)
- earned income strategies ranging from bake sales to auctions, and from merchandising to fees for services
- fund-raising events

Raising money to support various advocacy and/or lobbying functions must be considered as merely another cost of doing business. Therefore, a percentage of all the money raised by the nonprofit should be allocated to the advocacy function expense. However, there are problems with this approach: (1) often, funding is restricted (i.e., it can only be used for certain purposes—most often programming-related expenses and not general operating overhead); (2) the public responds sympathetically to programming value and needs, but not necessarily to raising funds for fixed overhead costs (without which programming would, of course, be impossible); and (3) raising funds for one purpose is in direct competition with raising funds for another purpose, and the individual organizations that comprise the coalition will be reluctant to solicit support from their core base precisely because this base is fragile and they don't want to cause *their* donors to reduce their current level of support to their organization. But if advocacy is to succeed, coalitions of nonprofits must find a way around this reluctance to allow solicitation of their base support.

Another potential problem is a public backlash against nonprofits lobbying in the political realm; attacks are likely to be spearheaded by groups eager to stem any rise in the power of possible opponents. The whole of the nonprofit sector needs to address this issue foursquare and devise strategies to educate and inform the American public in a deliberate campaign to win acceptance and approval for the value its advocacy efforts will bring to the public. Winning this "hearts and minds" battle is likely to be a precondition for successful public fund-raising efforts, which might be remarkably easier if the campaign for influence were successful. As discussed earlier, wholly apart from the need for nonprofits to make a major shift in advocacy efforts so that they can advance their causes and oppose legislation not in their best interests, in the long term, it may be necessary for nonprofits to win this struggle if they are to survive. Their ideological opponents are likely to attack their activities on political grounds.

A coalition of nonprofits needs to have some formula that establishes equity between the members of the coalition as to contributions to the advocacy effort. The wider the coalition, the less contribution each individual nonprofit member organization will need to make, and the greater the pool of potential individual members will be.

DUES-BASED SUPPORT

Organization vs. Individual Members. Mandatory vs. Voluntary

The traditional nonprofit approach of soliciting organizational membership through dues based on a sliding scale of budget size has often produced a situation in which very few organizations, notably those with larger budgets, are the primary source of funding. The total of all funding remains inadequate to the advocacy demands and tasks at hand, and understandably, organizations providing the funds sometimes seek disproportionate influence and advantage in and from lobbying efforts as they are the only ones paying for it. This results in a fractionated field, often with members at odds with one another. Moreover, during lean economic times, the boards of directors of smaller organizations, hungry for funds, do not see the long-term advantage of participating in the wider advocacy effort and so opt out altogether. Too frequently, nonprofit budgets make no provision for coalition advocacy efforts.

Organizations such as teacher or correctional officer unions, which deduct mandatory dues from members' paychecks, are the only nonprofit representative bodies that have adequate lobbying budgets. Yet few nonprofits have member bases that are contractual collective bargaining efforts that allow for such mandatory deductions. The typical nonprofit membership or constituent base is voluntary. Soliciting dues from individual members is time-consuming, and where memberships are small, an inadequate approach. If, however, there is a large enough pool for the solicitation of individual memberships, it is possible that enough small-dues payments will be sufficient to justify the solicitation. Individual-member dues are easier to collect in some ways because the organizational budgets of smaller nonprofits are so small that there is no leeway for such expenditure. Individuals, at a small, affordable rate, can pay—it's just a question of whether they will.

Organizations that combine solicitation of both the organizational- and individual-member dues with success are groups where a passionate commitment to the mission statement has been established and where there has been an ongoing legacy of making a financial commitment to advocacy efforts. The willingness of a coalition's organizational membership, the individuals within those organizations, and the supporters outside to shoulder the burden and pay dues to support advocacy is the test of whether or not any field of interest is serious about advocacy as a core function. If the percentage of organizations and individuals who are willing to share the burden is not very high, then the commitment of that field is doubtful and the whole of the advocacy enterprise questionable. Advocacy and lobbying are about self-protection, and if a given sector hasn't yet reached the point where there is near-universal understanding and acceptance of these as core functions, then its members are unlikely to be willing to dig into their own pockets to cover the function. And if they aren't willing to invest in themselves, raising the requisite funds from other sources will be very difficult, if not impossible. Dues from the base are unlikely to be sufficient by themselves to meet all the costs, but they must cover a meaningful proportionate percentage of the total expenses. If a nonprofit doesn't believe in its own efforts, how does it get other people to believe in what it is trying to do?

DONATIONS

Soliciting and receiving donations are even more difficult enterprises for the organization that does not have an adequate budget and a history of supporting this kind of activity. Yet for many nonprofits, donations are a (if not "the") primary source of income. Donations and contributions have been the lifeblood of political fund-raising on all levels and will likely remain the mainstay of nonprofit financing of lobbying efforts. Donor campaigns run all year long and become an integral, ingrained part of the organization's overall development strategy. In an increasingly competitive marketplace where the number of just and valuable "causes" seems to increase daily, donor-based fund-raising becomes more difficult and less reliable during lean economic cycles, with increasingly escalating costs. Donor fatigue means that more energy will be required to maintain donor loyalty. Despite the fact that blind solicitation of the public is even less predictable, out of necessity, this will be the centerpiece of the funding strategy in the future. Nonprofits must succeed at expanding their donor bases and convincing new donors that advocacy and lobbying are legitimate, worthwhile enterprises, the benefits of which justify the investment.

Because the coalition will have two primary lobbying arenas in which to operate—lobbying for or against legislation, and lobbying for or against the election of specific candidates—and because the coalition will likely use multiple structures to support the various efforts made in each of these arenas, who (meaning, which targeted group) is asked to contribute to which structure (the 501c(3), the 501c(4), the PAC, or the 527 political organization or fund), and when (at what point in the legislative and/or electoral cycle) will require considerable strategic planning, coordination, and thought, and will be a major task in the overall scheme of things. Any targeted donor/contributor group will need to be assessed very carefully to determine what will maximize their motivation to contribute (for example, will it be their interest in a tax deduction or other tax consideration? Will it be their passion about the politics of the situation? Will it be their desire for anonymity?). It requires a somewhat sophisticated database and special ability to make this kind of analysis. But meeting this part of the fund-raising challenge is one of the most critical steps for success.

ONLINE SOLICITATION

The Howard Dean 2004 presidential run and the phenomenon of the Move On.org and similar (527 fund) website-based organizations have made it clear that online solicitation of donors outside the base constituency of a group can be highly effective in funding precisely the kind of coalition-based nonprofit advocacy agenda that includes candidate support. The problem of soliciting small donations was always that it was not cost-effective. It was also unreliable and was not the optimum use of limited resources and personnel time. The shrinkage of the world through the Internet has now created the global village, and linking to sympathetic and potentially supportive individual donors is now easier, quicker, and often much more lucrative. Online techniques to reach out and expand the base of a coalition are just beginning to evolve as a tool. They portend new options as they revolutionize fund-raising. They should be explored by all nonprofit coalitions, not only as a potential fund-raising device, but as another media mechanism to inform, educate, and change public attitudes and perceptions.

Given that software to manage website-based donations are now affordable and available off the shelf, and given the current ease of website creation, online public-donor solicitation can become a meaningful part of any advocacy fund-raising strategy—both from within a field's base and outside. There are large pools of people who want to get involved in promoting certain causes. Both the Dean experience and the Move On experiment confirm that this potential market of passionate people can be tapped. The secret is to persuasively state your case, touch a nerve, issue a clarion call, and spread the word far, deep, and wide. Small donations can add up to sizable totals, and first-time donors can be tracked, cultivated, and managed online. New donors are potential new volunteers and supporters as well.

PATRONS

Soliciting patrons has become such a basic fund-raising tool for nonprofits that much of the approach was codified long ago. Money from individuals or companies is the mainstay of philanthropic work in the United States, and outside of earned income, it constitutes the historically largest percentage of nonprofit operational income. Anyone who has ever donated to a nonprofit has been solicited by countless other organizations in the same field. Lists of major contributors are dearly held, and the biggest individual donor patrons are wined and dined extensively. Like big bettors in Las Vegas, referred to by casinos as the "whales," these people are sought after, courted, and treated as high maintenance. It may be possible, at least for those nonprofits that already have patrons, to appeal to these large donors to help with the advocacy expenses, which may be one way to protect and maximize their main contributions and the intents and purposes they had when they made donations.

ANGELS

One final form of funding is to locate and convince one independently wealthy "patron" of the cause to become the financial "angel" of the nonprofit organization or one of its specific services, projects, or goals. There are a surprisingly large number of very wealthy people out there, and increasingly, they are using some of their wealth for philanthropy while they are alive, rather than waiting until they die to bequeath it. Many of these people prefer to put their money where it will have practical application, as they like results. These people are comfortable in their appreciation of the need to be involved politically, and thus donations in support of advocacy often appeal to them. In any event, it can't hurt to ask.

BEQUESTS/TRUSTS

With the baby boomer generation beginning to reach retirement age, and with a percentage of this generation having inherited substantial sums of money from their parents and accumulated wealth themselves, the beginning of a historic transfer of wealth is about to take place in the United States and elsewhere around the world. Add to this that among a new generation that has accumulated substantial wealth in a relatively short time, we are beginning to see increasing funding of donor identified philanthropic causes during the donor's lifetime. This largess is being allocated on the whims and particular desires of the individual donors, who are now being courted in consideration of where their wealth will go and whom it will benefit. Many nonprofits have benefited from creating mechanisms that allow donors to make gifts to the nonprofit (e.g., the charitable gift annuity), and this long-term potential funding stream might work for some advocacy coalitions. Creation of these types of mechanisms isn't nearly as complex as people might think. But a knowledgeable attorney should be consulted.

GRANTS

There has been a shift in grantor (foundations, corporations, government, and all other bodies) expectations toward an emphasis on measurement of success. Venture capital philanthropy, characterized by an insistence on specified results being achieved as a result of their support, coupled with foundations and government wanting more accountability in terms of whether or not specified programs designed to address a specific need have, in fact, met that need, has forced nonprofits to increase their emphasis on evaluation and measurement of the efficacy of programs. Thus, in applying for a grant, nonprofits would be wise to include an evaluative element in their proposals.

Foundation Support

While foundations have historically shied away from providing funding to programs and projects of nonprofits that had even an element of advocacy or lobbying, there have been some recent shifts in thinking. Foundations seem to be governed by the inaccurate belief that they are prohibited by the IRS from awarding grants to organizations for lobbying. The rules that apply to nonprofits apply to foundations as well, and foundations are clearly permitted to make grants to nonprofits, even if they know that the nonprofit will use the money for a program or project that includes advocacy activities. However, this freedom will continue only as long as the nonprofit recipients act within the limitations and prescriptions generally applicable to the expenditure of the funds, and separate the allocation between advocacy and lobbying activities and the other parts of a given project or service. Lobbying in support of or opposition to a specific legislation or candidate is an activity that may *not* qualify for the use of foundation funds. But foundation funds may be used for training, organization, strategic planning, research, education, volunteer coordination, and other areas related to advocacy.

Many foundations have funded organizational capacity and sustainability as priorities, and advocacy is arguably directly related to the objectives of increased nonprofit capacity and the sustainability of organizations. Thus it seems somewhat incongruous for foundations to arbitrarily exempt advocacy from funding, but as they are essentially private enterprises, it is their right to prescribe allocation of their funds any way they wish. For most the issue is political, and foundations are historically somewhat conservative in wanting to avoid the political limelight. It isn't that foundations do not understand or appreciate the importance of the nonprofit sector having the tools and skills to advocate and lobby effectively, but rather that they want to avoid taking sides in political debates. There is a trend however, toward foundations being amenable to providing grants where the funds are used for indirect advocacy activities, such as skills training workshops, and programs designed to educate and inform the community so as to equip the nonprofits to protect their interests and increase their visibility. As long as the funds are not used to directly lobby for the passage or defeat of specific legislation or to influence candidate contests, many foundations are now willing to at least consider requests for grants.

Thus, there may be aspects or parts of a nonprofit advocacy program that will appeal to foundations as aligned with their priorities and objectives, and nonprofits should look to foundations for possible support for these definable programs within the overall advocacy effort and not just for unrestricted operational support. Other possible areas a foundation might be interested in funding include

- **Educational outreach:** Imparting information and education about the value of a nonprofit or field of nonprofits to a community is a supportable objective because it has an impact on nonprofits beyond advocacy into fund-raising, volunteer recruitment, stakeholder partnerships, etc.
- **Technical assistance:** This may be in the form of skill-set training—via seminars, toolkits, the Internet, or workshops.
- **Communications:** Website development and data management are capacity-building activities.
- **Planning:** Strategic planning and needs assessments are part of planning.
- **Research:** Research comprises Public-opinion sampling, studies, and pure research.
- **Coalition building:** Coalition building is always in favor as it recognizes the need for nonprofits to improve their performance by cooperating with other nonprofits and other sectors of the community.
- **Meetings and summits:** These are a traditional area of funding for foundations.
- **Sustainability/capacity building:** These will always be a priority for foundation funding because the principle of helping nonprofits to stand on their own is a cornerstone of programs that help them to move into the future.

Government Grants
Nonprofits in a number of areas rely to varying degrees on financial support from
government (e.g., the arts). The reliability of this revenue stream is directly corre-
lated to the depth that the nonprofit's mission is regarded by the public as sacrosanct, and a mission that is perceived to be of public importance is not open to
cuts by elected officials. Government support is also subject to the roller-coaster
cycles of the economy—there are more funds available in good times than in
bad zztimes as there is less pressure to prioritize allocation. Finally, the amount of
government support is directly related to the effectiveness of the lobbying effort,
and thus organizations dependent in some measure on government support have
good reason to maximize their lobbying strength. Government money is not available for the advocacy effort, and its use for lobbying or electioneering activity is
strictly prohibited. But this money may be used for some basic operational and
otherwise permitted purposes.

CORPORATIONS

Corporate philanthropic support has also undergone profound changes in the past
two decades—there is increased competition for it, and more corporate giving is tied
to marketing objectives and strategies. Corporations want their philanthropic contributions to work toward some corporate objective, such as building community goodwill or increasing brand recognition. Corporations are increasingly interested in the
demographics of the nonprofit's core base (Do they dovetail with the corporation's
target audience?) in both the local and national perception of the nonprofit's cause (Is
the issue neutral or divisive?) and in how support for the cause can help them achieve
one or more of their definable objectives. Corporate funding tends to shy away from
controversy so as not to alienate any market segment, and thus it may be harder to
raise corporate funds. Increasingly, it is the senior executive team that determines the
areas of funding the corporation will even consider, and it is not uncommon for these
decisions to be influenced by the spouses of these team members.

EARNED INCOME

Earned income strategies are one of the three primary means (the others being dues
and donations) for advocacy coalitions to raise the necessary funds to operate. Some
strategies may be too small for the advocacy coalition organization in terms of how
much money it might generate and the amount of time it would require, but not too
small for individual members of this coalition, who can use even small strategies as
a way of covering their proportionate share of expenses.

Here are a few earned-income strategies:

Fund-raising events: The most common earned income strategy is the event
fundraiser. Often the major event involves the presentation of one or more awards
either to individuals who have been generous to the organization in the past or
to persons who work within the field purview of the organization and have made
exemplary contributions to the cause. This strategy is common because it allows
the organization to identify possible award recipients who have a large network of

people who support them (for various reasons) and thus provide the nonprofit with a built-in potential audience from which to solicit attendance at the fund-raising event. The size and scale of this type of event can range from very small to grandiose. A big event is usually managed by a professional firm that arranges and plans both the logistics and the fund-raising strategies for a fee.

Another type of event is the "benefit" performance, a presentation by a performing group (e.g., concert, play, etc.) where the artists contribute their services and the proceeds of the event (less costs) go to the beneficiary organization. Benefits may be difficult to secure, particularly where the "artist" involved enjoys celebrity stature, in which case artistic ego is involved, and performance artists may be reluctant to donate services if their appearance for the beneficiary means that they are curtailing their own marketability in a given territory for a period of time (i.e., most performers have a limited number of tickets they can sell in a given area—if they appear on behalf of some charity, they are less likely to be able to turn around and sell more tickets for another performance in the same area during the same period of time). Expenses can be higher than anticipated, and these events usually require substantial time and effort to plan and execute.

Fees and admissions: Some nonprofit fields are engaged in services for which they charge a fee (e.g., training programs, workshops, fiduciary agency); others are involved in presentations for which they charge an admission (e.g., arts presentations). In areas such as the arts the piece of the income pie provided by such events can be a substantial percentage of the whole.

Naming rights: Although naming rights are often associated exclusively with capital campaigns, there have been some efforts to sell them to specific projects or services of the nonprofit as a fund-raising strategy. Corporations purchase naming rights to generate community goodwill and to increase recognition of their brand across a wider audience. It remains to be seen whether or not they will want their names and brands associated more directly with advocacy.

Sales: A second commonly employed strategy is "sales" based: merchandising, licensing, and the like, the net proceeds of which go to the sponsoring nonprofit. These can range from the merchandising of products associated with the cause of the organizations (from T-shirts and mugs to buttons and bumper stickers) to the licensing of rights the organization may own.

Raffles or drawings: Raffles do not usually generate a significant income but can be sizable enough to be a mainstay of smaller, community-based organizations (thus a way for coalition member organizations to raise the funds to cover the costs of its' dues or contribution to the larger effort.). A major prize donated to the nonprofit organization, with credit to the donor, and the proceeds from ticket sales to the organization make for a simple (although sometimes time-consuming) project. Television auctions, common in PBS fund-raising, or smaller silent auctions can work for individual coalition members and raise their proportionate contribution to the whole.

Scores of other earned-income devices have been used by nonprofits. Choosing between possible options depends on the amount of funding needed and the time and resources available to the nonprofit compared with those needed for other activities. All such choices should be made in consideration of both the short- and long-term funding needed and the cost of engaging in one activity over another.

INVESTMENT INCOME/ENDOWMENTS

Some nonprofits and fields of nonprofits are in the fortunate position of having been able to raise funds to start endowments or other investment portfolios, and the interest thereon, or the increase in the equity thereof, yields an independent revenue stream. Advocacy efforts should set the long-term goal of creating endowments or trusts or other growth mechanisms to sustain the effort over time. If the whole of the nonprofit sector were to embrace advocacy as a function, educate the public about this function's value to them, succeed in at least beginning to fund advocacy as a professional exercise, there could be a sea change in both the perception of nonprofit advocacy's benefits and the extent of its presence. This would allow for the beginning of the development of endowments and the like by the year 2025. By the year 2050, nonprofit advocacy—advocacy for the public good that counterbalances the private-sector, special-interest advocacy—could be fully financed and become the equal of the aggregate of private-sector advocacy.

The larger the coalition the greater the potential to raise funds from within, but the larger groups are more unwieldy and difficult to manage. There is never enough money to do everything that might help in a given effort. Even the NRA would likely say it needs more funds, for the lobbying effort is a hungry animal that is never really satisfied. There is always more that could be done if money was available. But however it is done, an amount minimally adequate to fund the coalition's advocacy efforts, including staffing, must be raised. Failure to adequately fund the advocacy effort as a professional enterprise will doom any lobbying attempt to failure.

CHAPTER 7

INFLUENCING THE DECISION-MAKING PROCESS

Let no man imagine that he has no influence. Whoever he may be, and wherever he may be placed, the man who thinks becomes a light and a power.

Henry George

SETTING THE OBJECTIVE

The first task in a specific lobbying campaign is to set the objective. This is done by the lobbying group's ongoing steering committee/board of directors, with consensus among the various members of the coalition. The objective may be to achieve a desirable goal, to meet a pressing need of the group, or to react to proposed legislation or other governmental action or inaction that will have a specific impact on the group. The objective should be specific and focused and should appeal to the widest audience, but not so ambitious as to be impossible to attain. It shouldn't be too broad; each campaign must have definable, understandable goals. This doesn't mean the goal itself needs to be less than what the organization really wants, but rather that it needs to be as precise as possible. Goals and objectives that are not formulated in reaction to something need to be inspiring and exciting to the base membership, worthy of the commitment of time and energy, and capable of changing things for the better so as to advance the nonprofit's mission.

There are seven basic questions to ask in setting the objective of a lobbying effort, either long- or short-term:

- What does the coalition want, and why? Asking this helps in determining what the coalition really wants. Needs should be specific.
- Who in government can give the coalition what it wants?
- What message will work with those who can give the coalition what it wants?

- Who is the best person to deliver the message?
- How can the coalition best influence those who can give it what it wants so that they will?
- What can the coalition offer those who can give the coalition what it wants? What do these people want? (When the coalition knows what it has to offer and what decision makers want, it can ask what else it needs and whether it can get it.)
- How does the coalition exert influence on those who can give it what it wants?

Advocacy is an ongoing process; relationships are nurtured over time, issues change according to external circumstances, research advances, the needs of an organization or field change as it grows, and there is turnover in the ranks. Yet at any given specific point in time, there must be clear objectives for building the advocacy machine that can be effectively managed and that are realistically attainable (relationships with elected officials and their staff, fund-raising, preparing arguments in favor of the benefits of the nonprofit field, and so on). This may require prioritization of a number of goals, including choosing between certain objectives, all of which might be desirable or even essential, but which are beyond the capacity of the coalition to manage simultaneously. Assessment of strengths, assets, and available resources as compared with what might be required to achieve any given goal or set of goals will likely result in the coalition having to put more resources into one area at the expense of another area.

The objective (and the strategy to achieve that objective) must be clearly set forth so that everyone understands what it is and how the coalition will go about trying to realize it. This will help to avoid confusion and subsequent misunderstandings and thereby facilitate unification of the effort. Limiting strategy to focus on a manageable set of tasks that can be realistically achieved will help to maintain trust and commitment from the field. Every lobbying and/or advocacy effort needs some success from time to time to ensure its motivation by those who are trying to help the coalition reach the stated goals. If the goals are not clear to everyone on the "team," it will be difficult to implement strategy effectively, and almost impossible to stay on message; if the coalition aims at achieving too high a set of objectives, and makes this its measure of success, success will be too infrequent to maintain motivation and cohesion within the field.

ARRIVING AT THE BEST STRATEGY

Strategy is nothing more than the outline of the methodology that will be employed to realize the stated goals or objectives. Because of constantly changing circumstances, the fragility of coalitions, and the very nature of political action, it is impossible to set forth an exact strategy that will be used in every specific lobbying effort. Advocacy must be flexible enough to adapt to whatever reality exists. This is another reason it is so important to build a solid foundation, to develop a machine that can be used whenever needed, to hone skills, and to establish alliances. Some objectives require long-term strategies, which makes planning even more problematic, but that said, it is still essential for a coalition to set forth, in writing, the outline of how it will achieve its goals. The exercise of developing the strategy helps to clarify understanding, identify potential roadblocks and barriers, and uncover hidden assets and strengths. The process helps to forge bonds and strengthen the coalition's commitment. Having to think about the ramifications of various strategic scenarios at the outset may save valuable time and resources later on. A workable strategic plan helps to delineate areas of responsibility and ensure that there is an equitable distribution of responsibility and authority among coalition partners. Such a plan also helps to establish the lines of authority.

The general strategic approach to building the coalition lobbying machine and the approach for launching each specific legislative campaign should cover the basic elements of advocacy, including communications, the lobbying effort, stakeholder management and coordination, media relations, fund-raising, volunteer coordination, developing the *making the case* arguments, and research/evidence gathering and dissemination. A plan needs to set forth who is in charge of each area, what the various tasks are within that area, and what the coalition needs in each area to succeed. Each step is set forth (in broad strokes) in consideration of a master timeline and budget.

Just as it is important not to attempt to achieve an unrealistic set of goals, likewise it is important to set the goals within a timeline. More often than not, a political objective will involve a timeline that is dictated by existent circumstances beyond the control of the coalition. It is important to allow as much time to accomplish a set of goals as is reasonably possible, and thus overall strategic planning for a coalition should strive to begin pursuit of an objective as early as possible. Too many efforts fail because the advocates waited too long to begin to act. In political matters, it is axiomatic that there is *never* enough time.

FORMING THE TEAM

Specific campaigns necessitate assigning specific individuals to oversee the various component arms of the group's advocacy apparatus. These managers will likely be the advocacy apparatus' full-time staffers, if such a luxury exists, augmented by other appointees (either paid in-house, contracted for, or volunteer) to bring the effort to a fully staffed complement. In most nonprofit campaigns, many, if not most, of these people will be volunteers or staff hired for other reasons. These managers, together with key representatives of the member base, will comprise the steering committee. Other levels of the structure will naturally evolve. In coalitions there must be key people who are the links to the steering committee from each of the coalition's sectors. The important point is that all the coalition segments must share the workload of the advocacy function; too few people committed to the effort will result in failure. Advocacy and lobbying have become too sophisticated and important an endeavor for any group to "bluff" its way through with inadequate personnel and resources, or with only the barest outline or idea of who will do what.

KNOWING WHO THE NONPROFIT IS TRYING TO INFLUENCE

First, the nonprofit must identify who it is targeting with its advocacy and/or lobbying efforts: is it a legislature, a committee, individual lawmakers, the Executive, or an agency, or is it the media, the public, or another entity?

Once the nonprofit has identified and narrowed its target, it needs to know as much about the members of this group as possible. In the case of specific legislators (e.g., committee chairs), the nonprofit will want to know the demographics of their district, key issues in the district, the political makeup of the constituency, the voting history of the individual legislator, and everything that will help it to craft a message and devise a strategy to win the support it seeks.

One of the great values of a nonprofit's personal relationships with decision makers is that it gives it insight into who their targets are as people: What values do they hold? What priorities do they have? How do they make up their minds about something? What in their backgrounds predisposes them to one position or another? The more the nonprofit knows about someone, the more it intuitively knows how to approach that person. Thus, it is a good idea to build files on at least the key decision makers the group needs to sway to succeed in its efforts— that is, the facts about them: Where are they from? Where have they worked? What was their education? How old are they? What are their interests? Who is in their family? Where did they work before assuming public office? What committees do they sit on? What is their voting record on similar issues? Who are their major contributors? The point is to gather sufficient information so as to give the decision maker a face, as it were. When is this person's birthday (send a card)? The more information the nonprofit has, the more it is likely to be able to discern the level of support or opposition it might reasonably anticipate, and how it might most effectively go about bringing that person to its position. The nonprofit should talk to people who know the target (build a database of who knows the target and how well); check out the Web (where virtually anything can be researched today just by Googling the name); and research biographies and databases. It should know its subject. All of this makes the nonprofit's job easier and helps in identifying what help it may need, and from whom, to maximize receptivity to its needs. This is the information age—gather information, study it, use it.

Rule 6: Lobbying is built on personal, ongoing relationships with people.

UNDERSTANDING THE PROCESS

While logic suggests that the stronger the coalition's case is for the rightness of its position, the greater its chances of influencing a decision maker to support it, the political realities of the process may make this assumption a strategic blunder. The truth of the matter may be that while an absence of arguments in the coalition's favor might hurt it, having the best case in the world may not necessarily help it; in fact the people the coalition is trying to influence may not even consider its case—their decision may be affected only by political considerations. It is therefore important for the coalition to understand the process so that it focuses on what will work, not on what seems logical. If it understands the process, it can save valuable time and resources and avoid being surprised or disappointed because of erroneous assumptions.

IDENTIFYING THE OPPOSITION

Often, an advocacy campaign or a campaign for or against the passage of a bill succeeds or fails depending not so much on who supports it but on who opposes it. Co-opting opposition into the coalition's side, or in some other way neutralizing it, is a first-level strategy when launching a campaign to support specific legislation. Some advocacy and/or lobbying objectives clearly don't impact an identifiable group, while in other cases the impact is so obvious and direct that it poses a threat to another group. So, if the coalition wants more money in the state budget allocated to its programs, the money would, of course, come at the expense of some other programs, as there is only a finite amount available. But it is unlikely that there would be a direct connection between one line-item and another, and thus the coalition's objective isn't likely to raise opposition based solely on the fear that the money is coming out of someone else's pocket). Many objectives engender directly related opposition. So an Indian tribe seeking to expand its gambling operations might be opposed by people in the community who are morally opposed to gambling—the church and others; it might be opposed by the people who live near the casino, who fear it will have a negative impact on family values; it might be opposed by the city for fear of increased crime or traffic (or it might also be supported by the city because it might generate jobs and new tax income). There may be others who oppose it. If the sum of the opposition is powerful and can mobilize public opinion, then it may be irrelevant that there are those who support the Indian tribe's objective. If both sides are well financed and have equal public and behind-the-scenes support, it creates a very difficult situation for the lawmaker who will disappoint and perhaps alienate one side or the other. Equality of power happens, but this is more the exception than the rule. More often, opposition is either nonexistent or lukewarm, or its power overwhelms those on one side of an issue. Assessing your opposition is tactically essential.

CHOOSING THE RIGHT MECHANISM TO SUPPORT

It is important to understand that there may be more than one approach to realize the objective at hand. If an ecological nonprofit seeks to protect a specific piece of property, it may be possible to accomplish this goal by a specific piece of legislation, or by some declaratory Executive decree. The reality of politics and budget constraints may make either of these approaches extraordinarily difficult to succeed. If a ballot initiative is available in the jurisdiction where the ecological nonprofit is operating, it might be a better alternative than either Executive action or legislation to protect the property, although the initiative may perhaps involve more effort. Judicial action may trump any lobbying effort. In opting for one approach or the other, the nonprofit should choose the mechanism that is politically realistic to operate, that involves the best solution to its situation, that will be easiest to rally support for, and that is doable within the timeline. The point is to think through all the alternatives.

BALLOT INITIATIVES

Unfortunately, in states such as California, where deficits have run large and resources are inadequate to meet the demands, the ballot initiative process has come to be the preferred device to try to secure state funding and to tackle a host of other political hot-potato issues sidestepping the legislature and the governor. Thus the teachers' unions have succeeded in mandating a percentage of all state income to education. The state's local governments, cities, and counties, which have repeatedly seen the state raid the funds allocated to them to balance the state budget, have succeeded in prohibiting the state from continuing this practice, thus freezing these monies. Other groups have become emboldened by these successes. California's budget is now some two-thirds mandated, and only the remaining one-third is available to fund myriad government programs and address interest group needs. The legislature and the governor have increasingly less leeway as to what they can and can't fund because less money is available for them to allocate, and even this reduced resource is under attack by those whose unheard pleas compel them to use the ballot initiative process to accomplish their ends. Even though most voters are inclined to vote "no" on ballot initiatives, more initiatives seem to be introduced each year. Carefully worded ballot initiatives that satisfy the needs of multiple parties can motivate broad coalitions of potential beneficiaries to raise funds to support an initiative, to reduce opposition, and to appeal to large segments of voters unaware of the possible consequences and ramifications of their support. Some special interests have used the ballot initiative to advance their agendas. (A case in point was the California initiative, Proposition 73, that authorized the state to conduct stem-cell research, which was financed, according to an article in the Orange County Register (July 24, 2005), by twenty-six wealthy couples, most of whom were venture capitalists who stood to benefit financially were the stem cell business to spawn new industries. To the extent voters approve more initiatives over time that mandate state funding, no matter how attractive and beneficial they appear on their face, the percentage of the pie over which elected officials have control will shrink further. This may well result in a "haves" and "have-nots" division, and so the rush to "get what you can while you can" is accelerated. If California is but a harbinger of things to come in other states across the country, which it often is, the very principle of legislative control over the budget may be in jeopardy in jurisdictions with a ballot initiative process. All nonprofits that lobby should keep a close eye on this trend and how it may impact their lobbying strategies in the future.

FRAMING THE ISSUE

Once the issue is set, a strategic plan drafted, and the advocacy organization and its leadership in place, then, and only then, can the nonprofit or coalition begin the planning and implementation of the lobbying effort itself. Before any nonprofit can begin to implement a lobbying strategy, it must frame the issue at hand. What exactly is the desired outcome? What will constitute success? The objective must be stated succinctly and concisely and with specificity; it cannot be too broad or too ambitious. Increased funding is a noble goal, but it is hardly precise enough to be a lobbying objective. How much funding? Where will it come from? Are there strings attached? For how long should funding continue? How will the funds be spent? What happens when the funds are gone? "A one-million dollar allocation from the county budget general funds for each of the next five years to support the ___" (insert: arts, environment, health care of children, etc.) is specific, precise, and easy to understand. Finally, the objective must have some chance of success. Attempting a campaign that has no chance to succeed will cripple an advocacy effort long after the fact. One million dollars in Los Angeles county might be a reasonable figure. It might be unreasonable in Peoria. One hundred million dollars in Los Angeles isn't realistic.

The framing of the issue and objective isn't always as easy at it might appear. There are, naturally, divergent opinions in any field as to what are the most important needs and priorities, the right and wrong ways to proceed, and what the objectives ought to be at the top of the list. While unanimity isn't always necessary, some consensus is. An all-inclusive and open discussion of the issues and how to proceed is the best approach to ensure consensus and trust. Compromise is unavoidable and probably a good thing. Objectives need to coincide with mission statements and current policy, and ought to address the most pressing needs or threats. There must be field and rank-and-file trust; objectives need widespread ownership to garner widespread support, and this is particularly dicey in coalitions of nonprofits within a field of interest. Of course, sometimes, pending legislation is of such a threatening nature, or one need so supersedes all others, that arriving at a consensus isn't a problem. The point is that a coalition cannot just assume that a given objective will automatically generate universal trust.

Questions—as to who benefits and how—need to be asked. It will be exponentially more difficult to enlist the support of constituents and stakeholders that have no identifiable benefit from an effort's success. The objective must be such that a strong case can be made for its support—from within, from the public, and finally from elected officials targeted for lobbying efforts. Some factions of a group or coalition may be less satisfied with a final, agreed-upon set of objectives and priorities, and to keep the greatest number of them involved in the process and committed to the agreed-upon goal, it is necessary to "lobby" them, as it were, as to the benefits to them, short- and long-term. A cohesive group is important—one not harboring any resentments or reservations that might later undermine the effectiveness of the effort. Politicians are adept at distinguishing between apparent community sentiment and deep-seated mistrust.

It is possible to frame an issue in several different ways, depending on how it is packaged, marketed, and delivered. Coalitions should experiment with different ways to frame their issues before making a final determination.

Rule 7: The objectives must be clear, focused, realistic, and simple, and supported by the entire coalition.

TIMELINE: MONITORING LEGISLATION

The second basic task is to draft a timeline as to what needs to be done and when. If the campaign seeks to secure the passage of a certain piece of legislation, the legislative process itself will dictate much of the timeline—what is the deadline for introducing legislation in any given session? (Early in the legislative session, there should be a review of all legislation introduced, identification of bills that may or may not impact the nonprofit's field, which ones it wishes to support, and which ones to oppose and target for defeat. As the capacity and resources of the advocacy coalition will likely have some limitations, prioritization will be an imperative as the nonprofit determines how much can be taken on. As previously discussed, too many nonprofit advocacy efforts try to fight too many battles simultaneously—to the detriment of all of their efforts.)

The nonprofit's timeline will include subcommittees' likely schedule for taking up the matter, whether there will be full committee or floor votes, and so forth. The timeline should be as detailed as possible, with the understanding that it will need to be flexible, as scheduled dates often change at the last minute. It should be specific as to the likely tasks that need to be performed in each of the advocacy areas—communications, media relations, volunteer coordination, and so on. The managers of each section will need to continually refine the timeline relative to their areas, and there need to be updates to everyone else as all aspects of a lobbying effort are interdependent. A master calendar should be created, with the legislative session timeline—committee and public hearing times; dates and places; filing and other deadlines; scheduled votes; and due dates for submission of materials, applications, testimony, and the like to the Executive and Legislative branches—and other relevant dates (meetings, rallies, trainings, etc.). Copies should be sent to all sectors of the advocacy effort, and updates should also be sent out periodically, as dates for committee hearings and other legislature procedures will inevitably be changed, often more than once or twice.

STRATEGY

The next step is to draft an overview of a strategic approach to how the objective is to be realized. This kind of strategic planning is different from drawing an overall strategic plan for the entire advocacy and/or lobbying apparatus; a strategy is needed for specific legislative or other lobbying objectives. This overview will include a look at current assets, available resources, needs, a campaign budget, and other elements that will allow the steering committee to begin the lobbying process in accordance with a battle plan. From the battle plan will stem the myriad specific tasks to be addressed, assignments to be made, people to be mobilized, and assets to be deployed. This is like a war. The specificity of the objective allows for, nay demands, concrete plans. It is thus essential to consider not only who may be enlisted as supporters, but also which opponents loom on the horizon. Ask not only who benefits, but who loses. Whose self-interest may motivate them to stand in opposition? Are they powerful? What resources do they have available to them? What are their major objections? Can they be co-opted? Is there any room for compromise that will satisfy all the parties? Can the nonprofit work around them?

The more powerful the stakeholders that the organization can line up in support and involve in the campaign from the outset, the more opposition it can handle. The greater the nonprofit's resources, the more opposition it can handle. The ideal situation is for the organization's advocacy machine to grow in power to the point where others are more afraid of its opposition than it is of theirs. If the teachers' union has ten paid lobbyists and the nonprofit has one; if the union contributes two million dollars a year to various lawmakers' election campaigns and the nonprofit contributes ten thousand dollars; if the union can mobilize its field to send in twenty thousand letters and the nonprofit can only manage one thousand, the union's opposition to the nonprofit's objective may kill it. If the reverse is true, their opposition may not matter. Although power is measured by recent victories or failures, and is in constant flux, it can also be a constant over time for those interests that have built up intimidating machinery. Indeed, for some groups (such as the NRA), their reputation is sometimes enough to ensure their victory.

ASSIGNMENTS AND RESPONSIBILITIES

Any specific lobbying objective or campaign must put the strategic approach into action by assigning specific people to specific tasks and having these people and the entire membership of the coalition accept the responsibility to support the effort. There needs to be a clear understanding of who is agreeing to do what *at the outset.* Doing so helps to create an environment in which it is more difficult to shirk one's responsibilities and shine on one's assignments. Group consensus and expectations act as motivation for people to perform.

TRAINING

Plans to train members of the coalition, volunteers, and potential supporters among the public in the basic skills and protocols of lobbying as well as in conveying the central message of a specific advocacy campaign are necessary before the campaign starts. These plans should continue while the campaign lasts, to accommodate newer recruits.

MAKING THE CASE

- Step 1 in the advocacy effort is the *making of the case*—gathering the evidence and materials that support the argument in favor of the position taken. The case is then made to the coalition's base of supporters to familiarize them with the arguments supporting the coalition's position.
- Step 2 is in the *presenting of the case to the media and public* so as to build grass-roots support and the volunteer network.
- Step 3 is *presenting the case to the decision makers.*

GENERAL CONSIDERATIONS

In making the case to lawmakers, it is absolutely essential for the nonprofit to link what it is asking for to the benefit of the politician's constituency; there must be some readily identifiable benefit to the people who live in the official's district. The more specific this benefit, the better.

But even if this direct link is forcefully made, nonprofit lobbyists must bear in mind that the reality of lawmakers having to make impossible choices between competing "good" proposals and justifiable needs increasingly results in unsuccessful attempts to win lawmaker support. These failures occur for no other reason than the reality of limited resources, which do not allow all programs to be supported. Thus, nonprofits should never rely on hard evidence, worthy causes, and good products alone to close their "sale"—that is, the efforts to seek support. It isn't always accurate to conclude that this or that argument didn't work; the final decision may have nothing (or little) to do with the nonprofit's arguments. It simply isn't enough that "right" is on the nonprofit's side, that it is illogical not to support the group's cause, that the benefit of its programs and services and proposals far outweigh the cost. In a world that demands priorities and where politics is increasingly the determining factor, all the equities and arguments in the world may not be enough to win the day. The nonprofit needs political power and clout, for the system of lawmaking, rule promulgation, and funding decisions is not always merit or logic based. *Making the case* to legislators may be different from making the case to the Executive; and making the case to the Executive may be different from making the case to the media or to the general public—different in approach, content, timing, and all of the other elements involved. The desired outcome may change how the nonprofit *makes the case* to any of these targeted audiences. Thus, there is no *one single* approach to making the case, no one-size-fits-all approach, but rather many versions and permutations of approaches, each designed to accomplish a specific result, each aimed at a specific target, each with a customized approach.

Circumstances change frequently, and nowhere more so than in the political arena. What previously worked, or failed, may not have the same result now. The nonprofit wants to give legislators as many reasons to be on *its* side as it can, as many reasons *not* to oppose it as possible.

If a picture is worth a thousand words, then a direct contact or experience with the nonprofit and the "value" it seeks to use to persuade decision makers is worth a thousand pictures. The greater degree to which the lobbyist can bring a personal experience to the lawmaker, the easier it will be for that lawmaker to relate to what s/he is being pitched. This may not guarantee a positive result, but lawmakers who can be persuaded will more likely move in the direction wanted if they have experienced firsthand what the nonprofit is talking about.

RESEARCH

Whether the nonprofit's objective is to pass or defeat specific legislation, to increase government funding, or to favor or oppose some change in rules or regulations affecting the nonprofit field, before it can make its case, it must analyze the issues facing the coalition (What will be the impact? Who will be affected and how?). It should then gather and assemble existing evidence (studies, surveys, public-opinion samplings, data, facts—anything concrete that might fit into an argument in support of the coalition's position). Evidence may be of economic impact, social import, educational relevance, or other impact. The Internet is equalizing the playing field, making existent relevant data and information more available than before to nonprofit coalitions that are short on time and funds to outsource the function. There is a surprisingly large inventory of data, studies, comparisons, surveys, and the like on virtually every subject imaginable, and compiling what already exists and tailoring the results to bulwark basic arguments in favor of the coalition are not as out of reach as it once was. This type of evidence gives credence to a nonprofit's argument. Particularly relevant are data that indicate that a nonprofit program, service, or approach to an identifiable societal or community issue has been effective in resolving that issue. Therefore, rigorous evidence of evaluation of a given program or plank, demonstrating its success, is persuasive. Each plank in the *making the case* platform needs to consider how it also benefits potential stakeholders and, ultimately, the community.

Over the long term, coalitions should encourage new, independent research conducted to examine the impact of government action or inaction related to the coalition's sphere of interest. This type of research is often time-consuming and expensive. As its relevance and reliability may be attacked and questioned, it is important that the research be conducted by people whose qualifications, expertise, impartiality, authority, and methodologies are above reproach. Ties to academia may prove promising, particularly for coalitions that cannot afford such research themselves. Reliable research can also be used to increase media coverage, as it is often highly appealing to the news media.

Coalitions must be honest with themselves in setting forth the pros and cons of the group's position. One cannot address potential opposition unless one can state what that opposition's views and reactions are based on (what the opposition perceives as in *its* best interests). Facts speak louder than conjecture. Offering speculative arguments based on anecdotes is not likely to be persuasive to elected officials not predisposed to support the group's position. There is a distinction between the facts and data and the *conclusions* based on these facts and data. The numbers may be beyond question—the conclusions based on these numbers are often subjective and open to interpretation, attack, and outright rejection. Care must be taken to relate facts and data to conclusions drawn in support of the group's position, and attention should be paid to the additional need to have one's conclusions validated by other, impartial third-party entities or individuals.

Authoritatively sound and academically rigorous third-party studies are the benchmarks of supporting research, for this research is less vulnerable to attack and dismissal. Evidence needs to be as unassailable as possible. That said, virtually all research can be questioned. It is almost impossible to design a methodology that is unassailable.

Public-opinion sampling is valuable, for elected officials are always interested in knowing which way the wind is blowing. All studies included in support of a group's position are somewhat self-serving in that they would not be included if they didn't bolster the group's contentions. Thus, even unassailable studies are somewhat suspect in the eyes of suspicious, jaded lawmakers. One method around the inherent questioning of a group's evidentiary materials presentation is to have some of this information presented by third-party groups that are ostensibly less prejudiced and biased, such as stakeholder groups. Thus, if the tourism industry presents studies, facts, and figures about the value, role, and contribution of the arts and the cultural sector to the industry's bottom line, this evidence may find a more receptive and accepting audience in a legislature than it would if the arts field presented the information—or at least it would be harder to reject and dismiss. A second method is to solicit media outrage at rejection of sound evidence and to question the motives in lawmaker conduct that seems arbitrary, capricious, and specious.

There is a frightening trend of lawmakers casually rejecting conclusions based on research that is credible by any standard, and even the data from the research. Politicians will accept research as "fact" when it supports positions they favor, and dismiss it as flawed when it supports positions they oppose. It is increasingly common for them to simply ignore certain evidence that runs counter to a position they have already staked out. Elected officials are increasingly comfortable simply choosing not to believe facts and figures presented to them that contradict their positions or that would require them to question their own assumptions and premises. While this is an astounding trend that seemingly turns advocacy on its head by rejecting facts and logic, the reasons may be practical in the sense that the lawmaker can't please everyone, and the decision to placate one sector over another is, in part, made for political reasons. Politics often demands that legislators support certain positions even if this means other positions must be rejected, and rejecting some of those positions is difficult to rationalize on any basis, and so the easiest way to deal with them is not to try to rationalize them all. This is easier if no one is looking. Thus, yet another burden has been added to the workload of the lobbyist—identifying ways around decision makers' entrenched and illogical positions to at least force them to consider the facts as they are, not as the official has decided they must be. That this trend exists is yet another reason why power politics has increasing sway and importance.

Everyone in the loop of the advocacy effort needs to understand and internalize the basic arguments in favor of the group's objective, the bullet points of the evidence supporting the group's position, and the counterarguments of those who will attempt to attack or question these arguments, so that they may be rebutted. It is a given that such attacks, questions, doubts, and reservations will arise, and so spokespeople for the coalition at all levels need to be prepared to counter these attacks. As is discussed elsewhere in this chapter, it is important that everyone in the advocacy coalition be on the same page and deliver the same message over and over again.

An important reality to bear in mind when gathering evidentiary studies and other support materials to include in a *making the case* presentation is that in all likelihood, the elected officials to whom the evidence and other arguments comprising the *making of the case* are presented *will not read them*, nor will their staff. At most, they may peruse an executive summary. Time is far too precious a resource to legislators and other elected or appointed officials to be spent on even a fraction of the materials presented to them on any given day. The best the nonprofit can hope for is that three to five conclusions from its argument can be presented in a clear, concise, and clever enough way to stick in legislators' consciousness, and accomplishing this goal will doubtless require persistent repetition of its message by a variety of speakers, including those with access to the official. This doesn't mean that the nonprofit need not prepare the case in detail with credible support materials; it simply means that the nonprofit's ultimate target audience will not review the materials with anywhere near the conscientious scrutiny the group would hope for. Each of the arguments needs to be well thought through and organized into the most convincing presentation. Again, brevity is essential.

Ironically, the opposition may familiarize itself with the nonprofit's arguments in greater detail than the decision makers the nonprofit is trying to influence. Opposition scrutiny will look for weaknesses in the nonprofit's position and exploit them. If the nonprofit does not prepare its arguments thoughtfully and in detail, with ample evidence, it will make its opponents' job easier, and its arguments will be dismissed and attacked by others.

Rule 8: There must be credible/substantial support evidence.

SOLICITING EXTERNAL SUPPORT

Part of *making the case* for the nonprofit's position is to align its support so as to demonstrate that its position is the same as that of the community's other sectors. All of these stakeholder groups (industry and trade associations, chambers of commerce, unions, education groups such as the PTA and teachers' unions, civic organizations such as the Rotary Club, etc.) that the nonprofit has courted should be an integral part of its case— who is supporting it and why, and what benefit does the group's promotion of its cause bring for other sectors. Elected officials know their own communities and districts very well—their knowing that the nonprofit's position has widespread support from other sectors in the district puts the officeholder on notice that the issue has wider ramifications within his or her constituency. Beyond stakeholder support, the nonprofit should think about how else it can demonstrate to the lawmaker that its position has been considered by others at the local level, and that they support the nonprofit's position.

The nonprofit must consider the following:

- **Editorial support:** Such support can be an endorsement of the nonprofit's position in local newspapers
- **Individual endorsement:** It means support of other elected officials or leaders within the community (academic and civic leaders, business CEOs, association presidents, former elected officials, celebrities, etc.), as expressed in letters or in campaign literature. Some of these possible supporters may also have a more direct relationship with a particular lawmaker.
- **Party platform endorsement:** Political parties have local, statewide, and national organizations and ongoing business apart from supporting office seekers in election years. Both major parties have regular, scheduled meetings between election cycles, and one of the tasks facing them is the continual rethinking of party platforms. The advocacy organization/coalition should be composed of people from both parties, and members of each should be encouraged to work within their party machinery. There are networks out there of very loyal party members who

remain unseen during election years, but who are the backbone of the work of their parties. Getting to know these people helps to pitch the nonprofit's position with victorious candidates. Forming relationships with party people can be an invaluable networking tool and can also help support the nonprofit's specific efforts to pass or defeat legislation that would impact it later on. If the nonprofit can get support for its position in the party platform (e.g., the party recognizes the value of the arts and cultural sector to life in California and supports public funding in an adequate amount to rank California in the top ten in per capita state funding for arts and culture), it can then point out to party officeholders that support for its position is in alignment with their party platform.

- **Blue ribbon commission support:** Any independent commission or other body that has considered the circumstances and issues attendant on the nonprofit's position on the issue, and concluded that the position is preferable to other options, can be cited as a supporter of the nonprofit. If no such commission existed (anywhere), it is possible to create one , and consideration ought to be given to doing so. Creating such a body, and having it affiliated with some other body (academic, governmental, etc.) to give it credibility and position, is a specific task in itself, but not one that is so complicated as to discourage the effort. The nonprofit should identify a chair or cochairs whose authority, image, and reputation will help in the recruitment of others; solicit people with expertise from among those who support the nonprofit; make sure there is cross-representation of all community sectors, and schedule and hold at least one meeting; invite the media and circulate the final report that will likely endorse the organization's position and otherwise favorably support it.

LANGUAGE

It is important that nonprofits use the language that works best with those they are trying to influence, and not always the language of their "field." Lawmakers are interested in what improves the quality of life for the citizens of their districts, and using language that "speaks" to this need will improve the chances of the officials relating to the value the nonprofit is seeking to establish when it *makes its case*. If the nonprofit is trying to recruit young people to support it, use the language they are most comfortable with.

PRESENTING THE CASE TO THE BASE AND THE PUBLIC

Once the nonprofit has outlined the major arguments in favor of its position, compiled research and data, and aligned endorsements in support of these arguments, it can begin to present its case to its volunteer base, stakeholder coalition memberships, and finally to the public. (The outline should include the positive impact of supporting the nonprofit and the dire negative consequences of the group not prevailing.) Presenting its case will help the nonprofit build grassroots public support that can be demonstrated to the targeted public officials. The case should be first presented to its base, then to its supporters and stakeholders, then to the media, and finally to the decision makers. Presenting the case to the decision makers is part of the lobbying effort and dealt with in subsequent sections.

AVOID CASTING YOUR IMAGE AS ONE OF ENTITLEMENT

Too many nonprofits project the image that they believe their "missions" entitle them to special consideration. This presumption of entitlement reeks of arrogance and invariably falls on deaf ears with lawmakers who must balance a vast array of needs and demands against resources. Wherever possible, decision making left to those at the local level resonates well with politicians. Nonprofits need to avoid being thought of as somehow outside the mainstream; they need to work hard to establish that they are "regular" citizens, dealing with problems and situations that impact the average person. Compromise and accommodation are the hallmarks of successful lobbying, and nonprofits must learn to *really listen* to those that oppose their views so as to fully understand and appreciate what it is about their position that ruffles the feathers of others, so as to find out whether this position might be better received if dressed differently. Negotiation is less about what the nonprofit "wants," and more about what both the group and the other side "need." Invariably, both sides won't get all that they want; but it is sometimes easier to reach a point where they both can get what they need. The nonprofit should remember that what it wants must often come at the expense of what someone else wants.

SECURING STAKEHOLDER SUPPORT

Because the nonprofit's stakeholder groups are outside its base coalition, their voice in support of its position gives credibility to the claim that the nonprofit has broad-based community support. Moreover, some potential stakeholder support may be able to speak with a powerful authority the nonprofit may lack. Thus, arts nonprofit organizations are really small businesses, and they may find it valuable to include city, county, and regional chambers of commerce as stakeholders. While the arts may be perceived as of nonessential value to the community, business is thought of as very important. If the chamber of commerce speaks on behalf of the value of the arts, its voice carries weight the voice of the arts lacks. It is incumbent on an advocacy coalition to convince stakeholders to lend their support, and this is best accomplished if the coalition is already part of the stakeholder constituency, already in a relationship with it. If the arts field were smart, it would join its local chambers and work within these bodies as members of the small business community. When the chamber voice is needed it will then be much easier to rally this stakeholder support. Some stakeholder groups will have more in common with the coalition than will others, and the coalition should prioritize the potential supporters accordingly. The coalition should remember that support is a two-way street, and negotiating a reciprocal trade-off is not unusual.

EDUCATING YOUR BASE SUPPORTERS (INCLUDING STAKEHOLDERS)

The nonprofit should make sure its entire team knows its position, the arguments in favor of the position, and the identity of other sectors that support the position. It is imperative that there be no confusion in the nonprofit's group; every person who is involved, no matter how tangentially, is a potential spokesperson or ambassador for the nonprofit's cause—staff, board, volunteers, and supporters. A fact sheet with the issue, the nonprofit's position, a simple, bullet-pointed summary of the basic arguments and the group's message, a list of supporters/endorsers, and perhaps five frequently asked questions (FAQs) and answers should be widely circulated among the nonprofit's rank and file and posted on its website. The nonprofit will want everyone to convey the same message and to stay on that message.

GETTING PUBLIC ATTENTION

First, the nonprofit must find a way to command the attention of the public (see also the following section on media relations). If the nonprofit can't make the public aware of its issue, it can't make its case to them, and the group wants to motivate them to back it up. Getting the public motivated is no small task. There are two primary ways to try to attract public attention:

1. Word of Mouth

The areas that nonprofits might manipulate to increase word-of-mouth coverage of their issues and that what they do is of value include

- **Expanded stakeholder support:** Any strategy that widens the support for the coalition beyond those groups that have something directly at stake, including the immediate stakeholder group, will help.
- **Expanded endorsement:** Expanded endorsement by other sectors, the media, influential leaders, and business groups can all help to widen the awareness of the nonprofit's issues and situation and persuade people that what is at stake is important.
- **Direct contact:** Direct-contact activities are those that increase the one-on-one contact of supporters with the public, such as, for example, door-to-door education campaigns (more often than not energized by the participation of youth brigades in the effort).
- **Grassroots communications:** Newsletters, speakers' bureaus, online information, announcements, flyers, and other means of communicating with the coalition base, including stakeholder constituencies, can spread the nonprofit's message, and a conscious, concerted effort to spread the word can then reverberate beyond this base to encompass other sectors, over time.

But the problem with this approach is that it is limited in its potential reach because it may not reach enough people in the time frame of the campaign, or, even if the reach is wide enough, those targeted may not respond with action. Moreover, the word of mouth approach is difficult to monitor, track, and manage. It may, however, be the only alternative for cash-strapped efforts.

2. Media coverage

Television, newspaper coverage and editorial support, and other media focus are probably the most effective ways of raising public consciousness of a nonprofit coalition, its programs, objectives, and the issues facing it. Media coverage can be either news coverage or advertising based.

- **News coverage:** Unless there is controversy involved, or there is some other element that the news media considers worthy of attention, it is difficult to get sustained and comprehensive coverage, particularly through the normal channels available to nonprofits—press releases and press conferences, rallies, position papers, debates and town hall meetings, and the like. Even relationships with well-placed people—reporters, editors, other journalists, television anchors, and television and/or radio station general managers—won't generally guarantee coverage as the media is, at heart, a business interested primarily in its bottom line—as evidenced by ratings or circulation (which impacts advertising dollars)—and as issue-oriented items historically generate minuscule additional circulation.
- **Advertising:** Paid advertising can be very effective, yet a full-blown campaign is so expensive as to be beyond the scope of most lobbying efforts, public or private.

Thus, for the average nonprofit, devising media coverage strategies is limited to finding ways to increase the appeal of its message to the media to expand potential coverage.
Media coverage strategies might include

Controversy: As mentioned above, the media thrives on controversy and sensationalism. These two elements of media coverage are not, however, necessarily those a nonprofit wants associated with its position, as they may bring more problems than benefits. The only kinds of controversy that might work to the advantage of the nonprofit would be those that are perceived to unfairly and unjustly harm the nonprofit (the nonprofit as a "victim"), and therefore also harm the public. Thus, a scandal involving elected officials who are trying to manipulate a situation against a nonprofit so as to enrich some private, special interest (at the public's expense) may elicit sympathy and outrage among the public. Failure to correct known injurious harms to the public, such as failure to clean up toxic dumps, may be the type of scandal that interest the media. Anything that can be of demonstrable harm to the economy or to children also works. These types of scandal and controversy cannot usually be created, but are rather developments that can be exploited, if they arise. The possibility of devastation that might be caused to the whole community, or to specific segments within the community, if the nonprofit coalition loses its fight, may also interest the media. Nonprofits are stewards of the public good, speaking for the public, not for themselves.

Sometimes, controversy can be implied by certain actions, and even manufactured. Confrontation is a proven television magnet. Thus, local television news continues to cover picket lines, as representing some dispute, even when those picket lines are manned by fewer than a dozen people. There is something television cannot seem to resist about picket lines, or their 1960's counterpart, the sit-in and rally. The point in garnering television coverage is to think in terms of "visual images" as the content. What will make a good ten- to fifteen-second visual behind a sound bite? The Reverend Al Sharpton has exploited the community rally to new heights of political power.

In the last analysis, what nonprofits can do is manipulate the two primary human instincts that pique the public's interest and therefore might increase media coverage: *fear* of losing something valuable and important, of negative consequences, and *greed* for something valuable and important, for a benefit, and for being enriched by something identified as positive. These two primary human emotions capture people's attention because they are threatening and exciting. Nonprofit causes and objectives can usually be put in either of these two categories—the potential loss of something valuable to the community that will have dire and painful consequences to the community, and the potential gain of something valuable to the community that will significantly better its lot and improve lives. The key is to first establish that what might be lost or gained is extremely valuable, so valuable in fact that the community cannot ignore it, and then that the sought-after government action is reasonable, measured, and worth the cost as a tangible benefit.

The sacrosanct nature of the nonprofit's cause: The long-term goal is to make the work of the nonprofit so essential in the public's mind—clean air, excellence in education, public safety—that it becomes sacrosanct (as apple pie and mom), and therefore elected officials cannot afford to oppose it publicly (and can do so privately only at their own peril). Establishing a nonprofit's public benefit as a core value on which there can be no disagreement isn't easy, and it takes time, but it ought to be a goal of every nonprofit lobbying enterprise, for it makes the lobbying job ultimately easier. It should be part of the ongoing establishment of a solid advocacy foundation, and work toward this objective should be a constant element in the strategic approach the nonprofit adopts.

MAKING-THE-CASE STRATEGIES

The areas that the public already takes very seriously and which, therefore, nonprofits might fit their mission statements and specific goals into, so as to achieve the elevated status of work too important not to support, include

Jingoism: Appealing to the public's or decision makers' pride and sense of place or people is an effective way to state the needs of a nonprofit, particularly when comparing what is being done at home to what is being done elsewhere. Thus, suggesting that New York spends two dollars in per capita support on the arts and California spends only three cents makes Californians think not enough is spent on culture—there is an unspoken competition between states such as New York and California. Suggesting Arkansas or Alabama spends more per capita than California makes Californians think not enough is being spent because they think of themselves as ahead of these states, superior in some ways. Capitalizing on this kind of thinking isn't approving it, it is simply recognizing realities. This tactic may also work in lobbying for more support—thus Arkansas and Alabama can point with pride that they are ahead of California in funding of arts and culture, and appeal to decision makers to keep them at the forefront.

Economics: Creating a link between an objective and some kind of economic improvement is another useful tactic. If the nonprofit goal will spur the economy, create jobs, bring needed money to local or state government, or in some way help business (e.g., the relationship of the arts to increased tourism), then this is an issue to which people in the community can relate. We have all learned that a positive economy determines our standard of living and is one of our highest priorities.

Youth/kids: If there is a potential benefit to kids inherent in what the nonprofit does or is proposing to do, or has done, and this potential benefit is threatened or cannot be gained if the objective of the lobbying campaign isn't realized, this fact can help to persuade people to be supportive and even to motivate them to action they might otherwise not take. People will do much more if they think their kids are impacted than they will if the issue is only about adults. Programs that deal with drugs and addiction, and without which our kids would be more likely to be exposed to or use drugs; programs that prevent kids from joining gangs; programs that deal with the health of kids are all valued by parents. Parents want their children to have *every* advantage and opportunity.

Effect on senior citizens: Because the senior-citizen lobby is so effective (senior citizens are better organized, more likely to vote, and more likely to contribute financially to protect their own interests), issues that deal with them command attention, including primarily health issues (prescription drugs, insurance coverage, heath care) and personal freedom issues (the right to drive and to vote). No one wants to see senior citizens suffering, in part because, like children, they are not able to defend themselves as well as other segments, and because we can all see "ourselves" as senior citizens in the future. The aging of the baby-boomer segment will make the senior citizens' group even more powerful in the next two decades.

Education: For the same reasons people react differently when something positively or negatively affects their kids, or kids in general; people are more supportive of what impacts education than almost any other government function, with the possible exceptions of defense and health care. Education is seen as essential to our future well-being—it impacts job preparedness and qualifications, and is seen as critical to maintaining a leadership position in the world. Programs and services that impact education, and without which the education of our children would suffer, resonate well with the community. There is also a very real internalized sense of obligation to future generations in virtually every population.

Safety: If something can be related to issues of safety—be that by way of health care, public works or regulation (roads, automobiles, airplanes, asbestos, etc.), the environment (air and water quality), terrorism or crime, or natural disasters (floods, earthquakes, etc.)—the public interest can be stimulated and media coverage can be expected. We are all interested in our safety—in our environments and our persons.

Equal protection: Americans value their democracy and democratic rights, freedoms and heritage, and see fundamental fairness, equal protection, privacy and freedom, free speech, the Americans way of life as core issues, and anything that threatens these cherished benefits of democracy can move the public. This area also includes appeals of equity—help for communities that are underserved and at a disadvantage. Appeals to fairness and diversity find sympathetic audiences.

Fear: There is no question that invoking fear is an effective tactic. If people think something bad will happen, or that something valuable will be lost if the lobbying objective isn't successful, this is a powerful motivation to provide support and join action. For example, crime will increase if the after-school program doesn't stay in business, or the forests will be lost forever if we don't protect them now. There are counterbalances at play as well, and use of a fear tactic should be considered from all sides before it is resorted to. Thus, in the first example above, people also don't generally like codling of criminals or gratuitous handouts to people who ought to provide for themselves. It can be a thin line politically, and can sometimes cast the wrong image for the whole of the campaign, but it can also work where other approaches fail.

Values and morality: Family, patriotism, faith, and hard work are all examples of values that we hold dear. Value-based arguments have been used with increased frequency in elections over the past two decades. Unfortunately, playing to the qualities that underpin these values—responsibility, doing the right thing, and compassion—is not necessarily as effective. Americans also have a strong sense of "fair play" and of the need to support "the right thing," although, of course, there is wide disagreement on what the right thing is or isn't in any given situation. Still, attaching an objective to one of the underlying tenets to which we subscribe can be effective in drumming up support. Legislation that redresses in some way an inequity that unfairly harms one group in our society has powerful appeal to our fundamental belief in equality and all segments of society having a level playing field. Similarly, while we have little sympathy for criminals, we can't accept innocent people being wrongly incarcerated. Discerning the dominant value is not always easy, as some values are in conflict with one another. Thus, we sympathize with those who are down on their luck, but we expect people to work for a living.

Vulnerability: Americans are by and large sympathetic to underdogs and those who cannot protect themselves. A protest against abuse of animals (warm-blooded, anyway), particularly domestic animals that are perceived as cute and cuddly, is one example of an action that appeals to the public's outrage when a vulnerable class is being harmed.

SUCCESS BENCHMARKS

One of the most persuasive arguments a nonprofit can make in favor of support for its position lies in the declared success of its past or current programs and services, related in some way to the issue at hand. How success is measured is a function of casting outcomes and results in their best light, without unrealistic exaggeration, as related to specified needs of the communities served. There may be multiple equations to compute a formula to make such a determination, and the nonprofit has the leeway to opt for the methodology that is the most advantageous. People respond to the argument that what the nonprofit has done has worked—and that what it is simply seeking the ability to continue to be successful.

MEDIA RELATIONS AND GETTING THE MESSAGE HEARD

Media coverage of advocacy concerns can be the factor that makes or breaks a non-profit's effort to reach its objective. Gaining media coverage and support is both part of *making the case* and *presenting the case*. Media coverage is also essential to attracting strong grassroots public support. But to be effective, media coverage needs to be substantial and sustained. A single mention is like trying to sell a product with but one television advertisement—too few people will see it, still fewer will remember it. Lobbying the media to win it over is a prerequisite to effectively lobbying decision makers, and most of the same principles apply: cultivation and nurturing of long-term personal relationships; effectively making the case with supporting evidence and demonstrable show of community support and backing; and exploiting the goodwill of friends. The nonprofit should always make a "talking points" or FAQ sheet available to anyone in the coalition who might be in contact with the press, and everyone in this category should be schooled to never miss the chance to have the coalition's "message" picked up by the media. The coalition should always be prepared and ready.

Here are a few methods of media management:

Television: Nothing is more effective than television *advertising*, but only if the advertising is repetitive. Television *coverage* is likewise invaluable, but it must be substantial enough to distinguish the issue from other issues and repeated often enough to sustain interest. Because of the nature of television ratings theories, repetitive television coverage of "issues" is difficult to obtain. Television prefers a visual event to a word-oriented issue—as a "medium" it is about people, not ideas. Good visuals are preferable to "talking heads." Thus television coverage of nonprofit issues is unlikely unless these issues can be presented in a dramatic "people" way that provides good visuals and a "story."

There are a few ways by which nonprofits get television coverage: as mentioned earlier, protest is almost always good television fodder and has a chance to generate coverage. Likewise, any gathering or assembly of large numbers of people—for example, for Earth Day or some other big rally—appeals to television's needs. Release of information or studies about some impact on people's lives—clear air and water, health or safety concerns, economic impact, and addition or loss of jobs—is attractive to television if accompanied by a good visual (a celebrity-packed press conference, for example). To garner television interest, the nonprofit should first think in terms of the "story" it has to tell—is the story dramatic? Does it have a "local" angle to it? And then the nonprofit should think in terms of the "visuals" that will accompany its story—do they work on the six o'clock news? Cultivation of relationships with television news people might help the nonprofit in improving the reception to its pleas for coverage; at the very least, the group will have someone whom it can ask directly as to what it should do to get coverage.

Print: Print coverage lends itself more to issues than does television. *News* items are about the "who, what, where, when, why" and "how", and *features* are about the "story" behind the facts—both are historically "word" oriented, and pictures are not as essential as in television. However, the adage that the picture is worth a thousand words still applies. Both types of coverage can be effective, but again, in a competitive news world, it takes some creativity to build sustained coverage over time. The same factors that promote television coverage are in play with print: anything that demonstrates that the issue is important to a large contingency of the print medium's audience will promote coverage; the more dramatic the story, the better; and, like virtually anything else, if the nonprofit has some kind of personal relationship or involvement with writers in key positions in newspapers, the greater the likelihood of at least making the case for coverage.

Clever, creative, well-put-together press packets and news releases are mandatory in this competitive arena. Press conferences can help to frame and launch issues, but unless there is some reason for the press to attend them, something with potentially high reader-interest—the presence of star power, the possibility of an announcement of a dramatic breakthrough in medical science or of something very basic to the local community being at stake, with possible dire consequences looming on the horizon—it is very difficult to get substantial coverage by way of a press conference.

While it is difficult to control/manage media coverage of the issue important to the nonprofit, there are other avenues for expansion of the grassroots base awareness of the issue that are open to greater control by the nonprofit. They include speakers' bureaus; use of stakeholder communications mechanisms; bully pulpits; and alignment of notable public personalities, celebrities, highly placed business leaders or politicians with the nonprofit. Because nonprofit issues are often deemed too complex, too boring for media coverage, nonprofits must be supercreative in their presentation of their issues, and, if possible, assign to this work only those involved in the media management oversight function who are well placed, experienced, and highly skilled.

Listservs/newsletters: E-mail lends itself very well to alerting, educating, and advising large blocs of people and communicating with them. Listservs are databases of people that one can communicate with via a single e-mail, which can be a one-time message or a periodic online newsletter. The advantage of the listserv is that the message gets to people in the nonprofit's targeted list automatically—they are not required to go to a website or do anything to get the message. Of course, people can be resentful of uninvited intrusions into their e-mail boxes, and therefore, carefully crafted and creative messages that are only minimally intrusive work best.

E-mail is now a given in most people's lives. Because of the rise of spam and junk mail, the increased demands on people's time, and the sheer volume of messages, e-mail messages are likely to be read only if they are brief, concise, to the point, and identified as from a sender the recipient recognizes or at the least feels safe about. Finally, messages sent via e-mail listservs must be in a style and layout that is attractive and easy to read. Self-contained e-mail messages are more likely to be read than those that require the recipient to open an attachment or link to some other page.

Listservs can be created in-house by entering the e-mail addresses into a program, or by soliciting people to subscribe to the listserv by entering their information and then sending an e-mail to the listserv manager. Solicitation can be through a website or by any other means of alerting people of the listserv's existence and the objective of getting people to subscribe. For listservs created in-house, subscription solicitation may augment and expand the list over time. People can easily opt out of a listserv by unsubscribing, and it is a good idea to include, in every message sent, a simple icon on which to click to unsubscribe. Many people will appreciate that they can opt out if they so choose. Every newsletter or message sent to a listserv should also have an icon the reader can click to pass the message on to someone else. One of the best ways for a nonprofit to grow its listserv is to have subscribers recruit new subscribers.

E-mail newsletters can contain graphics of all types along with other design elements that make them easier to read or more attractive for the reader, but those who create and manage listservs should take into consideration the download time for people with minimum broadband capacity. People resent e-mails that take too long to open. Voluminous materials may be better accessed by providing links within the e-mail, thus allowing the recipient to decide whether or not they want the additional information.

For the nonprofit, presenting its case, as well as soliciting new prospects (as potential volunteers, supporters, financial contributors), should be an ongoing activity, and some thought should be given to where the coalition might obtain lists of e-mail and postal addresses of prospects. Individual coalition organization members should be encouraged to share their basic data lists and to include a "subscribe" button in the listserv icon on the home pages of their websites. The whole purpose of the coalition is to take advantage of the numbers of the aggregate members.

Politicians who are supportive should be invited to write guest columns for the nonprofit's newsletter (e-mail or hardcopy) as this gives them exposure to the group's community, helps to solidify their support, and sends the message to the public and public officials that these politicians are on board with the group. It is particularly helpful if the guest-columnist politician is a centrist and not someone identified as to the far left or right of their party. Similarly, inviting potential stakeholder leaders to write a guest column may help to further their endorsement of the nonprofit's cause and may result in their allowing a nonprofit representative to write a guest column in *their* newsletter.

Blogs: Blogs (weblogs)—now firmly established political tools—are individual writer's personal thoughts and opinions distributed online (usually by means of a website by which people can access the blog) or sent to a listserv. Blogs play a role in an advocacy effort by expanding the reach of the nonprofit's message and promoting dialogue about the issues the nonprofit is trying to address. By personalizing opinions about the issues, they may avoid being boring.

As blogs run the spectrum of opinion it is safe to assume that they may end up being used both to support and to criticize the nonprofit coalition's position. While criticism cannot be always avoided or controlled, it is important to have tools to counter any attacks and promote the nonprofit's position. Blogs are good to encourage supporters to be proactive and to educate and inform the base (and a wider audience) as to facts. They can also effectively help to provide a counterpoint for the possibility of the external critical blog, as well as to expand trust and solidify support for the coalition's position.

Meetings and gatherings: Whether a meeting or other interactions are convened by the advocacy coalition, or the coalition is simply sending a representative to another group's meeting, person-to-person contact is an opportunity for it to spread its message and interest new people in working for its cause. Town hall meetings, regularly scheduled civic group gatherings (e.g., Rotary Club), and PTA meetings are all examples of the possible audiences the coalition might be able to identity and lobby. Gathering the largest bloc of support is part of the *making of the case.* Expanding on this initial bloc of support is part of the *presenting of the case.*

The coalition's meetings: It is impossible to schedule a time and date for any kind of gathering or meeting that will work for everyone. But the more notice the coalition's gives people, the greater the likelihood of the group reaching its minimum goals for attendance. The more important the meeting, the more formal should be the announcement, as the way in which people are notified may tend to influence the perception of the importance of the meeting. Meetings should be scheduled so as to be convenient in both time and place to the greatest number of invitees, and the selection of the location should take into consideration freeway access and parking. Building sites should be able to accommodate everyone. The meeting or gathering room should have comfortable seating, climate control, and other facilities, and provide whatever necessary A/V or other tools needed.

Meetings will attract more people if the agenda is known up front and the purpose of the meeting is made clear and perceived as relevant and necessary. Attendees should feel that they will walk away from the meeting feeling confident that their attendance was worth the time commitment.

Information presented at a meeting should be compiled in printed handouts wherever possible and presented in a clear, understandable manner. If possible, coffee or other beverages and lite snacks should be supplied as it makes people more comfortable. If funding is an issue, people can simply pay for their choices or everyone can contribute to a small petty-cash fund.

All-day meetings should have ample time for breaks and lunch, and experience shows that starting the meeting very early and running it until the end of the workday yields an audience that is inattentive and increasingly uninterested in the issues at hand. The tedium of an all-day meeting can be broken up somewhat by holding both plenary and subgroup breakout sessions, and by multiple presentations and speakers. Meetings that incorporate exchanges of information among the participants may work better than meetings that are essentially "talking heads."

People can be invited to meetings in multiple ways—from telephone calls to web postings, from faxes to formal printed invitations. The more formal the invitation, the more importance that may be attached to the meeting. Regularly scheduled periodic meetings obviously work best with smaller numbers of people.

Meetings can be in person or by telephone, and though it is a technology not yet widely used, through videoconferencing. Telephone meetings can be arranged by a central call-in number or one party (with the capacity to do it) initiating the call to all participants (and there are now many companies offering free telephone conference calling—at only minimal long-distance toll charges. Calls with over ten people can make inclusive dialogue more difficult as there is a tendency among a few people to dominate the conversation. A moderator is advisable in any teleconference. Calls may often be to simply transmit information, or the primary purpose may be to foster a discussion or set up a Q&A session.

Conferences and conventions are a separate meeting category and require extensive advanced planning and, more often than not, substantial funding. Event planning is an art, science, and business in itself and demands detailed planning and personnel resources. To the extent such skills and resources are not available in-house, and to the extent the budget allows, engagement of outside professional-event planners may be a wise option.

The way meetings are conducted should be given some thought by the planners. Too often, there is little consideration about what works and what doesn't. A case in point is the conference panel session where three to five experts sit at a long table and each rattles off prepared or off-the-cuff remarks, observations, and advice regarding his or her area of expertise. If any time remains for questions or an exchange with the audience members, it is usually taken up by one or two people who invariably never seem to get to a real question at all. This approach rarely transmits much useful information to the audience and almost never allows for any real interchange between the panel and the audience. Somehow, the device enjoys near-universal employment, and we never bother to rethink the whole approach. In advocacy situations, if the nonprofit is able to get people to a conference in the first place, it would be a huge mistake to bore, alienate, or otherwise squander their goodwill and potential help to the cause by mundane and pedestrian presentations and wastage of their time. The nonprofit must think outside the box for everything it does, including making conferences more exciting.

Other groups' meetings: Many groups, particularly those identified as stakeholder groups, will be sympathetic to the nonprofit's mission or open to its representative addressing their membership. The nonprofit must make a master list of such groups in its territory, then methodically proceed to call or write to each one and ask if there might be an opportunity to make a brief presentation on an important community issue to the stakeholder's members at one of their meetings (a call should be followed up with a letter, and vice versa). Many stakeholder groups will have different protocols and guidelines for processing these kinds of requests (including some with the requirement of a relatively long lead time, so the nonprofit should ask early); many others will be far more casual. Within the nonprofit's allotted time, it wants to make a compelling presentation about its objectives, including some minimal background for context; what the relationship of its objectives are to the people it is addressing; and, what kind of specific help they might provide.

The nonprofit should get right to the point and not waste time; it should summarize all issues, distribute literature, and allow for some Q&A time. Getting stakeholder groups to formally and officially support the nonprofit through the adoption of a board of directors' resolution or another proclamation of some kind can be a natural outgrowth of these kinds of presentations, but as many groups have formal procedures for requesting such action, and approval may be available only at certain meetings during certain times of the year (prior to their annual business meetings where the whole of the membership can adopt such actions), the nonprofit needs to plan long in advance for this method to be an option.

Announcements: If the content of the communication is short and simple, an announcement by e-mail, fax, telephone, website, letter, or postcard, or one made at a meeting can be the proper mechanism. Again, presentation impacts whether the message is seen, internalized, and remembered. Announcements to those unfamiliar with the issue (e.g., a new stakeholder audience, the general public), will need to be repeated—the number of times depends on the importance of having large numbers of target recipients internalize the message and react positively. Generally, the more the announcement is repeated, the better the chance that it will be heard. It is important to remember that one is bombarded on a daily basis with more information than one can possibly process. As a result, all communications, no matter how minor or mundane, benefit from being well thought through and transmitted in a creative way. It is better to get one single idea across and provide a way for targets to get more information than overload them with too much information that will not be processed. As the proverb advises: *the devil is in the details.*

MOLDING PUBLIC OPINION

Public attitudes are created by influencing how things are perceived. As in advertising, if a message is repeated often enough, over a long enough period of time, it takes on an air of truth. That's why advertising works. Nonprofits need to become better at marketing their ultimate products as valuable, not just engage in marketing efforts that increase the size of their audiences, funding bases, or constituent groups. Molding public opinion is not an easy task—the public can be suspicious, hesitant, and reluctant to move as various interests want. Moreover, the public is large, non-homogeneous, demographically and geographically diverse, preoccupied, slow to react, resistant to change, and generally apathetic politically. Making an issue resonate with the public as absolutely essential to their well-being—to the point of making it sacrosanct and beyond attack—is a major undertaking with only minimal chance of succeeding, but any degree of success will benefit the nonprofit enormously in its advocacy and/or lobbying efforts, and by and large, nonprofits start out such tasks with the advantage of an identifiably valuable product or service. The effort is worth it in the long run.

SUMMARY

In making the case for legislation (or sometimes for opposing it), it is incumbent on the advocacy group to consider every situation on which the legislation might have some positive or negative impact. Who benefits, who loses by passage of the legislation? Those who benefit in some way need to be recruited to the nonprofit's side. Those who will be hurt need to be placated or isolated and neutralized. The objective is to maximize the number of those who will benefit and minimize the opposition from those who will lose something so that the nonprofit can have minimal opposition and optimal support. Presentation of the nonprofit's case should be as methodical as possible and have as wide a distribution as can be managed. Effective presentations are *repetitive* over time.

GRASSROOTS MOBILIZATION

Grassroots mobilization is more than just recruiting volunteers and organizing an effort by them; it implies moving large numbers of different sectors of the public in support of the nonprofit's position or cause, mobilizing these people to be activists on its behalf.

FANNING THE FLAMES

Making the public aware of the nonprofit's issues is an obvious prerequisite to motivating them to take action on its behalf. Once the nonprofit has succeeded in bringing about widespread public awareness of its issue (no easy task), it needs to invoke a strategic approach to moving them to action. There are three key steps to persuading the public to take action:

1. **Instill a sense of urgency:** The nonprofit should convey the urgency of the task. Whether it accomplished public awareness of the issue by word of mouth, publicity, advertising, stakeholder assistance or otherwise, all of these techniques should be employed again to advise the public that it needs their help now (and it should be very specific in spelling out what they need to do). It should use whatever tactics work to move people to meet the deadline (i.e., sense of outrage, dire consequences attached to what is at stake being lost, etc.)

2. **Provide multiple opportunities to help the nonprofit:** The coalition must provide the public many opportunities to be supportive. It can ask for letters to legislators (people can be directed to the nonprofit's website and provided with tools that will help them write the letters), phone calls, e-mails, attendance at a rally, or even financial donations (the group should be specific as to how it will use the money raised—e.g., to fund an advertising campaign; petition circulation, etc.). The point is to give the public choices as to how to help.

3. **Educate the public about what is at stake:** Education of the public must be an *ongoing* effort. The nonprofit needs constant publicity that puts its issue before the public if it wants a true grassroots support effort. The task is to somehow get to the "tipping point" where a true groundswell of public action arises to support the nonprofit (or as close to this as it can get). Television and radio obviously have the greatest potential to reach the largest audience, but the nonprofit shouldn't underestimate the power of word of mouth and other communication mechanisms.

Like every other aspect of an advocacy and/or lobbying campaign, the attempt to secure a grassroots response requires strategic planning, forethought, and time on the part of personnel. There are instances where a real grassroots movement develops on its own initiative and quickly snowballs into a phenomenon all its own, but these are rare and cannot be easily manufactured. But momentum can be created and built on.

GRASSROOTS TRAINING

Ideally, grassroots volunteers can be organized on some kind of tier basis, with captains for each layer, thus allowing for both centralization and control, and decentralization and independent decision making. The captains can be trained to provide their groups with the knowledge, skills, and background to empower them to be effective lobbyists; to keep their teams all on the same page; and to train volunteers under their watch. If this kind of hierarchy is beyond the scope of the nonprofit's lobbying effort, then it will want to at least provide universal training to all volunteers. The best approach is an in-person seminar or tutorial held periodically in different locations so as to be convenient to the greatest number of people, but again, this may not be a viable option given constraints of time and funds. In the alternative, the nonprofit should prepare a brief and concise written manual (it need be only a few pages covering protocols of meetings, letter writing, and other communications with officials, as well as a summary of the campaign's messages) and use the web for online training. Several mechanisms that are commonly used are given below:

- **Talking points:** a simple sheet giving the major points of the nonprofit's message and reasons to support its position
- **FAQ sheet:** containing essentially the same information as a talking points sheet, but in a Q&A format
- **Lobbying do's and don'ts**
- **How to lobby**: a step-by-step list of ways to communicate the message

Whatever format the nonprofit selects, all training materials should be readily available to download from its website, and links to this training section should be provided on as many of the group's constituent base and stakeholder websites as possible. The nonprofit will increase its effectiveness if its representatives have even a rudimentary understanding of how the process works, and make themselves at least minimally familiar with the messages it wants them to convey. Training materials should be as user friendly as possible—simple to understand, easy to access, and minimally time-consuming so as to maximize the number of people who will avail themselves of the facility the group is providing. To the extent the nonprofit makes training an interesting and fun experience, an opportunity for people to network and interface with peers, the group increases the number of people willing to avail themselves of the option. The advantage of in-person training is that people can interact with one another, and this personal contact may help to build loyalty to the cause and widen the circle of potential supporters. Training should also be ongoing so as to allow for bringing new volunteers up to speed during the campaign.

CONSISTENCY

One hallmark of successful lobbying is consistency of effort over time. Passage of legislation during a single session takes months, and the path is almost always marked by twists and turns. Some legislation takes years to pass. Opportunities for major advances toward a specific goal sometimes arise without notice and as a result of exigent circumstances that no one could have foreseen, and nonprofit coalitions need to be in position to capitalize on these opportunities. Too many nonprofits lobby in bursts and spurts without any strategic approach to applying pressure and exerting whatever influence they can muster throughout a long campaign. This is so partly because it is difficult to always maintain grassroots support over a period of time. People who are asked to help, and then do, figure they've done their part. When they are asked again to do something else, a percentage of them will inevitably drop out. This situation can be improved somewhat by the nonprofit educating its membership and support base that the campaign must function over a time period, and that people will be asked to help at specific points along the time continuum. If people expect multiple "asks" they are less likely to ignore these requests. The problem can also be dealt with by paying attention to motivating the membership. If the base is large enough, it can be divided so that one sector is asked to take the lead for a part of the campaign, to be replaced by another sector, and so on. This approach has the advantages of healthy competition between sectors of the same group and of not having to ask people to do too much.

TIPS ON PRESENTATION

One of the most important assignments in *making the case* is to synthesize and summarize the most salient points into three to five one-sentence bullet items that are worded so as to stand out and be remembered. The entirety of the essence of the arguments for the nonprofit's position will be these few simple declarative sentences that summarize the value and benefit of whatever the nonprofit is seeking; and from these few sentences may come the slogan around which the whole campaign can rally. Thus, an arts advocacy coalition may have reams of evidence to support the proposition that arts organizations generate economic activity beneficial to the community, that the cultural sector creates jobs, draws tourists, increases the attraction of talent to local corporations, increases home values, and contributes substantially to the tax coffers of local government, but the bottom line is all that will be remembered is a simple declarative summary statement (with facts). For example, the arts economic benefit can be summed up quite succinctly:

> "The arts in California are a $5.5 billion economic engine, generating 400,000 jobs that add $300 million in tax revenue to local and state government; one out of every four tourism dollars is arts related - $17 billion a year; 68% of all Californians favor increased state public support for the arts." Moreover, students who have Arts education perform better academically, are more likely to graduate from college and less likely to be disruptive [in the classroom], join gangs or do drugs.
> —2004 Economic Impact Study; 2001 Public Opinion Survey

The nonprofit better have the facts to back up its declaration, but the declaration should only contain the message (even the above declaration may arguably still be too long, too detailed). If the declaration contains anything more, the nonprofit would be expecting people, including its targeted lawmakers and its core volunteers and supporters, to synthesize and remember too much. It is possible to take any one single point in the "message" and use it to target a narrow niche of the wider public who may only be interested in this part of the message. But the capacity to identify such "niches" may demand a level of sophistication unavailable to most advocacy coalitions. The nonprofit should make it simple for its volunteers and supporters to carry its message forth.

The case must be presented not only to the base constituency and supporters, so that they understand the message and everyone operates on the same page, but also to the media and the public, so as to increase the scope of support. The final step is, of course, to get the messages heard by the government decision makers the nonprofit wants to influence. The nonprofit shouldn't keep the best arguments in support of its position secret, and it should never forget that lobbying isn't an exercise confined to decision makers; this exercise must encompass a larger audience, for government decisions are now always political. The only way to level the playing field for nonprofits is to make sure that the decisions that impact them will have to be made in the light of ongoing media and public scrutiny.

DIRECT LOBBYING

PRESENTING THE CASE TO THE DECISION MAKERS

The most important message to convey to elected officials is that whatever the nonprofit wants from them is a very high priority to a substantial bloc of voters in the officials' districts. The only way it can send this message is through some kind of demonstrable show of support (that may take the form of letters, telephone calls, personal visits, rallies, petitions, editorials, and so forth, or best of all, a combination of all of the tools available).

Ways to Convey the Message to the Target Elected Officials

As elections are a politician's highest priority, communications from constituents in an officeholder's district (i.e., people who can vote for the official) are more important than communications from people outside the district. The point is to have diverse populations and interests repeat the message over and over again so as to demonstrate widespread support for the issue by people (voters) in the district. All of the tools available in making the case to the nonprofit's own base, to its stakeholder supporters, current and potential, and to the media and public will, hopefully, also help make the targeted officials aware of the issue. What follows in this section is a discussion of direct lobbying—attempts to convince specific officials to support the nonprofit's position.

THE BEST LOBBYISTS

Who makes the best lobbyist? People who have an elected/appointed official's ear, who have access to the official, and can get their message heard and considered are the best lobbyists. Those generally included in this classification are

- **Major contributors**: Most legislators and other elected officials will respond to the pleas of major contributors, at least to the extent of giving due consideration to what the major contributor wants. This doesn't mean everything a contributor wants is done. Far from it. But the access is important. Major contributors aren't generally ignored.

- **Close friends**: Elected officials are like everyone else—they have circles of long-time friends whom they like and trust, and these people have access and influence on the official.
- **Colleagues**: Legislators and others have peer groups composed of other legislators and officials, and these people have not only access and influence, but also the ability to trade their support in the interest of their own priorities. Politics and government are about compromise and trade-offs.
- **Moral conscience:** Everyone looks to other people who have the requisite perceived level of credibility and authority to legitimately act as conscience keepers of society, and these people may have influence on an elected official's actions.
- **Family**: Often overlooked, and nominally beyond the boundaries of permissible lobbying, an elected official's wife and children undoubtedly have influence on the official. It helps to know if the decision maker's family is already supportive or active in some way in the cause of the nonprofit.
- **Agents**: Agents are those who speak for definable, organized blocs of people, particularly within the district, and they command attention. Included in this category are business and worker groups (trade/employee associations and unions), the education community, local politicians, civic organizations, and others with organizational bases. Some may have direct relationships with an elected official, others may not.
- **Young people**: Younger people in high school and college, as a class, make excellent lobbyists and are invaluable as a volunteer group—they are energetic, passionate and committed, and idealistic. They often have time within their schedules that older people do not. They do not shy away from some of the useful activities that older people often shun, such as door-to-door canvassing.

People with access to the official and the power to influence him or her one way or another don't all necessarily live in the official's district, but, for the most part, those within the local district make the case better than those who do not.

The nonprofit should remember that even though an official does not agree to support it, or even takes the opposing position, it shouldn't assume the official is "a lost cause." They should work such officials—that's the point of lobbying. The most vociferous and entrenched opponents have changed their minds and converted. Enemies can become friends. Time constraints may prohibit lobbying of every member of a body, but if resources permit, every member should be targeted. The nonprofit never knows where or when it might gain or lose a vote. It shouldn't limit its potential for victory by excluding too large a class of possible supporters by categorizing them as "lost causes"—at least not too early in the process. It should remember that nonpartisanship is the goal.

NUTS AND BOLTS TOOLS

PERSONAL VISITS

Arguably the most effective communication is a personal visit. And, doubtless, a personal *site* visit involving the elected official coming to see one of the nonprofit's activities or events, which allows the official to see first-hand what the nonprofit's mission is all about, is ideal. There are probably many opportunities to invite a legislator, and nonprofits should schedule an event such that its timing increases the chances that an official will be able to accept the invitation and will perceive some benefit in doing so (media coverage, for example). As officials are busy with hectic schedules, it is incumbent on scheduling a meeting (whether a site visit by the legislator or a meeting on the legislator's turf) as long before the need arises as is possible. Even then, owing to last-minute obligations, it is common to have a scheduled meeting (and often a site visit) handled by staff and not the elected official. Site visits should be scheduled when the legislator's attendance is not likely to be required for government work (at a committee or other meeting, hearing, etc.). State legislators are usually in their home districts on Fridays and set aside time to meet with constituents. A home district meeting is less likely to be cancelled and easier to schedule, and it saves the time and expense of traveling to a state capitol. Congressional representatives also schedule regular visits to the home district as many are home every weekend. Local officials are, of course, easier to meet, and they do not travel out of the area in the discharge of their duties as an elected official.

When first contacting an official, the nonprofit's representative should tell the official's scheduler who is calling and whom the caller represents, and that the caller lives in the district and wants a meeting with the official to discuss an issue (whatever it is that the nonprofit is seeking support for). The representative should tell the scheduler about the persons who will accompany him or her to the meeting, and give their names.

Paul Minicucci advises *the Rule of Three*—meaning, an individual should take along two other people to a meeting with an elected official. Often, staffers will be present at the meeting, and having three people on the nonprofit's side ensures that it will not seem outnumbered. One of these people should be someone the legislator knows personally, on a first-name basis, preferably a long-time supporter and contributor. This will set the proper tone of receptivity for the meeting. The nonprofit's representative should be brief—everyone's time is valuable. The second person should be someone in the district who has a story to tell of how this person (and by implication the wider district citizenry) benefited (or will benefit) from the work of the nonprofit. It is important to personalize the work of the nonprofit, to give it a human face. Articulate young people or kids give excellent testimony, and are memorable and hard to ignore. Business people speak with a certain authority and make excellent storytellers. Media people bring an obvious cachet. The better the person's oratory skills are, the better able they are to tell their story inspirationally, the greater the chance the official will internalize the nonprofit's message. The nonprofit representative should make the basic argument—cite facts and figures and answer specific questions. The nonprofit should take every opportunity to set up a follow-up, face–to-face meeting—and if meeting on the official's turf, it should invite the official to one of its meetings, events, luncheons, or other gatherings.

The people accompanying the nonprofit's representative should be briefed before the meeting so they are knowledgeable about the basic facts and background, including the legislator's prior support (or lack of it), about the issue at hand. The nonprofit must determine who will speak and in what order, so that its representative can orchestrate the presentation to maximum effect. The nonprofit's team members don't want to step on each other as they present its case or respond to a legislator's questions, so they should determine up front who will guide their side of the meeting. It is a good idea to agree on some hand signal or another way to let those who accompany the nonprofit's representative know when to remain silent and when to jump in. The team should prepare a packet of materials to take with it and leave with the official (in all likelihood for his or her staff to review, if at all). The packet shouldn't be so large that it intimidates someone from looking through it; it is better to submit materials over time if there is too much to absorb.

Whenever possible, nonprofits should try to create a photo-opportunity event to which the legislator can be invited to attend. The promise of media coverage is enticing to elected officials, and the personal attendance allows the nonprofit to repeat the message personally. An experience that provides a positive outcome for the legislator is likely to create a more favorable impression of the cause of the nonprofit than might otherwise be the case. The nonprofit should remember that it is only human nature that elected officials might be more sympathetic and responsive to people who are likely to respond positively to a future request from the legislator (e.g., for campaign support). The "*I scratch your back, you scratch mine*" quid pro quo will always be a major part of our political system.

The nonprofit's representative should show up on time (or even a little early) and be appropriately dressed. While s/he should always be courteous, this doesn't mean s/he has to be supplicant. If the official has been supportive in the past, thank the official at the outset for this past support. The nonprofit's representative won't have too much time (frequently less than ten minutes), so he should keep the small talk to a minimum and cut to the chase quickly. If the representative doesn't know the legislator personally, he shouldn't be inappropriately chummy or personal. Although the elected official works for the nonprofit too, as the group is located in the official's district, the representative shouldn't be patronizing. People relate best to people they perceive as "good guys"—fair, honest, and above all friendly. It is important that when the nonprofit representative and others leave after the meeting, the legislator knows that the issue is of critical importance to the nonprofit and to a segment of the voters in the legislator's district. The nonprofit team members shouldn't beg and never threaten, but they should be forceful and should leave having created the impression that the nonprofit is serious about the issue, represents a large bloc in the district, and that it wants and expects support. It should also have made clear that support *for* the legislator is conditioned on the legislator's support for the group. (But the nonprofit should never make a direct threat, never make a quid pro quo offer, never even intimate that it will exchange campaign support for a pro vote. The message that this is of such high importance to the group and its constituents, that its support for the target is conditioned on the legislator's support, can and must be sent tactfully, and it should be inferred indirectly by the legislator). There is nothing wrong in sending this message—it is the essence of the political system. We vote for people because we believe their positions are in alignment with our positions. If they are not, we vote for someone else. The same is true of the support we provide during election cycles. Of course, if the nonprofit's representatives never voted for the target, never supported the person's campaign efforts, were never even involved in the campaigns of any candidates, this inference of reciprocity of support may seem like just talk and go unheeded. This is why it is important to have an ongoing, existent lobbying effort that includes a 501c(4) corporation and a PAC, so that decision makers can easily make the inference. And they will. And this is why many lobbying efforts involving campaign support make contributions to opposing candidates—though virtually all such efforts usually favor one candidate or one party more heavily than the other, depending on the favored party's history of support for the lobbying group and its issues. If the nonprofit has a bipartisan board of directors, there are likely to be people from each party who can be enlisted to help send the right message to the right target.

After establishing at the outset why the nonprofit wanted the meeting—in simple, direct language ("Senator, we're here to ask your support for Senate Bill No. 000")—its team should set the context of whatever it is the nonprofit is asking the legislator for, by providing a little background. It should then move immediately to a concise statement of why the nonprofit thinks what it has asked for is good for the people of the district the target represents; it should outline in three to five simple bullet points why the action it recommends is good for the people; why the legislator's support makes sense, particularly economically, in relation to budget matters. (A request for something that costs money, when there isn't any money available, must consider how it will pay for itself by generating new money, or where in the budget the money can come from) If the nonprofit doesn't address this part of the problem for the official, it starts out in a hole. The nonprofit must be prepared to argue why a new expenditure is justified as essential. It can, and should, anticipate opposition arguments and counter them, giving the official reasons why its position should prevail over the position of those who oppose it. It is always better to emphasize the positive outcomes. The nonprofit must share information about who supports it (stakeholder groups). It should present any package of materials it has prepared. The "friend" of the legislator accompanying the nonprofit's representative should chime in that the action the group seeks has widespread support, and that it is of the highest priority to him or her too. Finally, the storyteller should deliver the anecdotal message. The team should remember to invite the legislator to a specific future event, in the district, preferably one that will have a large audience and likely media coverage, before it leaves.

If there are questions, they should be answered honestly and directly. If the nonprofit's team lacks the information to answer them, it shouldn't try to bluff it, and should never provide inaccurate or speculative information. The team should tell the legislator it will get back with the answers, and then make sure it responds as quickly as possible. The team's job is to provide lawmakers with answers to questions they will likely be asked in supporting the nonprofit's position. Many times, potentially supportive officials need the nonprofit's help in deflecting criticism inherent in their taking its side. They look to the group to provide them cover and justification for taking a stand. This need is often paramount in controversial situations. No elected official is going to take the nonprofit's side if the political cost is too great, unless it can convince the official that the benefit outweighs the cost and provide him or her with solid, defensible justification for their support. It is important to always remember that no matter how convinced the nonprofit is of its value and worth of its mission, there are countless others who feel the same way about their organizations and their causes. From the perspective of the elected official, the choice isn't always, or even usually, between absolute good and bad, but rather between gradations—there are more good things that one would like to support than can be reasonably chosen. This is particularly applicable to anything that requires funding, as funds are limited. And the nonprofit should remember that there are also conflicting benefits and costs involved in most legislation—benefits to one segment are constantly being weighed against costs to another. Too often, nonprofits simply make their case and ask for support without any consideration of the political realities involved. The nonprofit should learn to think politically, realistically, so that the legislator knows it understands his or her problems and that the official and the group are both on the same page in trying to resolve complex and delicate issues. And the nonprofit should be prepared to accept less than what it seeks, as a general rule. Compromise is the hallmark of politics. Nonprofits should build on success.

The nonprofit should always follow up a meeting with a thank-you note and, within days, make a phone call to staff inquiring if they have reviewed the materials presented, if they have any questions, or if they need further evidence of any kind. The nonprofit should try to have one or more supporters who are close to the legislator telephone the official to convey and reinforce the message that people care about the issue in the home district. This process should be repeated by as many people in the district as can get meetings with the legislator throughout the period leading up to the date of the final decision or vote. It is a costly mistake to have a good meeting and conclude that nothing else need be done. One meeting is simply the beginning of a process.

Within two weeks of the meeting, the nonprofit should begin a concerted effort to secure the legislator's presence at some related event in the district. If it has a good product (meaning its cause is just, its programs or projects or services bring value to the community), there is no better way to demonstrate this value than having the target official see it with the his or her own eyes, firsthand. Getting the decision maker on the nonprofit's turf is immeasurably valuable and should be a priority. The nonprofit should arrange a media photo opportunity or present the official with an award for past support. Whatever works to get the official to join the nonprofit at its event, where the group can expand on the positives of its position, is of paramount importance. Once the official is at the nonprofit's event, the group should make sure there are many voters within the official's district in attendance who will "buttonhole" the lawmaker and engage in lobbying. The nonprofit shouldn't forget to add the official's and key-staff-member's names to its mailing list.

Public sentiment can be communicated to legislators in the following ways:

Letters: Ranking very closely to personal visits is the personal letter from a constituent who resides in the legislator's district or territory. Personal letters (as opposed to form letters) should be concise (never more than one page), and should always, at the outset, state the issue or exact piece of legislation involved (include the bill number if there is one) and the desired action by the legislator. In the following paragraphs the writer can share a perspective of the effect the legislation or other action/nonaction will have on the people in the district. What will be the benefit and the negative consequences? Why is the legislation important? How does it impact people? How does the likely benefit measure up to other priorities? Personal opinions can be forceful, but shouldn't be argumentative, threatening, or combative in tone.

There should be no attempt to try to overstate the power and influence of the supporters or those of the nonprofit itself. If the writer knows the legislator personally, the letter should say so at the outset, so that staffers reading the letter will know there is a personal relationship involved and thus accord the letter due priority. Even if there is no personal relationship, the letter should state at the outset that the writer is a resident voter in the legislator's district. Letters should be on letterhead stationery where possible, and handwritten letters are fine, as long as they are brief and legible. There should be a request for support (asking for a yes vote or another specific request) and for a reply from the legislator in the closing. Letters should always be limited to a single issue or piece of legislation. Attachments and enclosures of materials are fine, but they are not necessary, and if included, should be brief. Copies of local newspaper coverage should be included, as receipt of one or multiple copies of news reports serve as a powerful message.

Providing the nonprofit's constituent base with sample letters to guide them is a common practice, often demanded by volunteers, but fraught with the danger of increasing the chances that all the letters will be perceived as form letters, thus diminishing the impact of the personal communication. It is important to try to convince those the nonprofit asks to write letters that they express themselves *in their own words.* Many people are uncomfortable with such a form of expression, and they should be reassured that they need not be Hemingway, that they need to simply get their point across, and that direct language is the best. Letters from children can be effective as well.

As is the case with the personal meeting, those who write letters should know the issue and refrain from inaccuracies, bluffing, and adopting threatening postures. Care should be taken that the name of the person to whom the letter is addressed is spelled right *always*, without exception or excuse. People should be encouraged to proofread and spell-check their letters.

Letters from organizations, representing whole groups of people, obviously carry a certain weight, yet the quantity of communications is often a critical variable in creating the impression from the legislator's perspective that there is substantial public feeling about an issue, and therefore organizational letters *in lieu of* personal letters of the organization's membership should be discouraged in favor of organizational letters *in addition* to personal letters. Organizational letters must always be on letterhead stationery, and may come from the executive director, chair or board on behalf of the organization.

It can be helpful for the coordinating team if copies of letters sent are in hand so as to permit tracking of who has written and when, and the scale of the communications. It may be difficult enough to get people to write letters, let alone send copies, but this should be encouraged.

It is axiomatic that if people, when asked to write letters, don't do it almost immediately, they won't do it at all. Busy schedules and too many commitments tend to make people forget all of the things asked of them. Every effort should be made to encourage people to write immediately when requested, without browbeating them to the point of turning them off. One method of increasing the percentage of letter writers among the nonprofit's supporters is to hold letter-writing events when and wherever potential supporters can be gathered. An excellent opportunity is provided by previously scheduled events and meetings—it's easy to set aside ten minutes to have groups of people compose letters. A simple presentation can make it easy for them, and the organizers can collect and post the the letters, thus relieving the writers of this extra burden. Letter-writing parties—events organized for the specific task of writing letters—are another approach, though again, with busy schedules, these events aren't always easy to attract meaningful attendance.

If the legislator voted in favor of the nonprofit's position, even if this vote was cast for a losing cause, follow-up thank-you letters should be sent. Virtually no one does this, and it's a mistake. If the nonprofit generates five hundred support letters and the legislator voted its way, and then it generates four hundred follow-up thank-you letters, I guarantee the legislator will be more favorably disposed to the nonprofit and its organization in the future. Nonprofits must remember the first commandment of lobbying—that lobbying is all about relationships.

Ideally, letters should be the beginning of a dialogue between the constituent and the legislator—one letter does *not* constitute a dialogue. Two or three letters, over time, follow-up thank-yous, responses to the legislator's responses, telephone calls, meetings—together they constitute the dialogue and the beginning of a personal relationship. The task should be made as easy as possible, by providing the writer the name and address of the legislator to whom they should write (or make access to this information simple to get in the nonprofit's e-mails or on its website). It should outline the protocol of letter writing—the dos and don'ts. The nonprofit should give them background, some bullet-point arguments, and the timeline for posting the letters. The more of their questions the nonprofit can answer before these questions are asked, the higher percentage of positive response it will enjoy. Therefore, a brief, concise, letter-writing primer delineating all of the above and a FAQ sheet should be prominently displayed on the nonprofit's website and widely distributed to its supporters.

The nonprofit should remember that letters from friends of the legislator, major contributors, people in positions to influence public opinion, fellow colleagues, and party members are all more likely to actually cross the official's desk than other letters. Letters from kids and students play particularly well with the media, and legislators as well.

Because it is difficult to get people to write letters, caution should be exercised in not asking people to write too often for too many causes. Many advocacy efforts send out repeated alerts and pleas for people to write to their legislator and the mayor or governor, then to subcommittee and committee chairs and members, and then again to legislative body leadership and the media. There is very little chance that more than a minuscule percentage of people in the pool the nonprofit is tapping to write in support of its position will respond and write ten to fifteen or more letters on multiple occasions. In fact, the request may create a backlash and resentment. If the nonprofit can get the same person to write four letters—two on one ask, and two on a second ask—it is doing extremely well. The single most-important person for them to write to is the elected official representing them in their district (or in some cases, to the governor, mayor, or

President), asking their representative to speak with the mayor, committee chair or party leadership on their behalf. To maximize the response to its pleas to communicate with elected officials and to maintain its credibility, the nonprofit should pick and choose very carefully the occasions it wants people to write in its support and the issues it wants them to write about. It shouldn't ask for too much, or too often, and it should avoid words like "urgent" and "crisis" every time it asks for help. If it does, these words will soon lose their meaning and using them when the nonprofit really needs them will no longer be an option.

Faxes: Faxing letters or other materials is acceptable. However, it is inadvisable to transmit multiple pages of information as it takes too long and, particularly in the case where the information is unsolicited, may provoke resentment in the recipient. Faxing letters may be easier for people than printing out an envelope, affixing postage, and posting the letter, and is thus useful in increasing the number of people willing to write letters in the first place. But posted mail on stationery, with a printed return address on the envelope, may command more attention than a fax, and be perceived as a more important communication.

Those who fax copies of letters to officials should follow up by sending hard copies by post wherever possible. The nonprofit would be amazed at the volume of letters and faxes and materials that seem to get lost in the average elected official's offices, and thus a follow-up telephone call to ask if a letter or fax was received is always a good idea.

Use of faxes may be the only way to communicate in writing when a vote or committee meeting is scheduled and there isn't time to respond by post. Sometimes an avalanche of faxes to a legislator can clog the official's machines and systems, and while it is simply bad manners to do so, nonetheless it does attract the attention of legislator and staff and singles out the nonprofit's issue.

Telephone calls: While telephone calls lack the one-on-one personal and visual contact with the legislator that a meeting affords, if the callers get through, the calls are still personal. However, unless the elected official knows the caller personally, depends on and dearly values this person's support, or the person is in a position of importance, it will be problematic that the caller can get the official on the telephone. The person will, instead, most likely speak to a staff member. Still, persistence pays off. Speaking with a staff member is important, and the opportunity should never be passed up.

Callers should identify themselves at the outset (even before being asked) and ask to speak to the legislator about whatever the specific issue at hand may be. One can (and should) leave a message with the most-senior staff member who is available, either when one makes the call or at the callback one has requested. On the first call, the caller, when talking to anyone other than a senior staff member (as the legislator is unavailable), should ask for a personal callback. If the caller doesn't get a response within a few days, the person should call again, and be polite but very persistent. If the caller has the opportunity to make the case with a senior staffer, the opportunity should be taken, but the call should be ended with a renewed request for the official to return the call. The official works for the caller, and if caller is a voter in the district, the caller has a right to request to speak directly with the official. Often, if the caller has an ongoing relationship with a senior staffer, it can help sway this staffer to make the argument to the elected official, so staff shouldn't be dismissed, disrespected, or ignored. They have far more access to the official than other people.

When speaking to an elected official, out of respect, one should address the official by his or her title—"Senator Jones" or "Assemblywoman Smith." One should get to the point right away and avoid small talk. It is unnecessary and likely not appreciated anyway. At the outset, one should identify oneself and specify the organization one represents. One should also say that one is a resident of the official's district, and why the call is being made—"I'm calling to ask you to support increased funding in the budget for the environmental protection agency." If the caller is asking for support or opposition to a specific piece of legislation, the bill number should be identified, if possible. Two major reasons why the support sought is important to the caller (and the group or others in general) and of value to everyone in the district should be provided. The caller should be polite, but firm. If the legislator offers anything other than a firm commitment in the caller's favor, the caller should request the official to call back when a final determination has been made. The nonprofit's representative should volunteer to provide background materials and information in support of the group's position, ask for a personal meeting, and invite the official to the organization. One should be ready to answer questions from the official, but like in the personal meeting, if the caller can't answer a question, he or she should offer to get back to the official with an answer, and then do so as quickly as possible. The caller should always thank the official for the official's time, and follow up the call with some written communication, further conversation with a staffer, or a scheduled meeting. The follow-up to any communication with the official drives home the message and that the nonprofit is serious about the issue.

On issues that are important on their face or which garner substantial media coverage, legislators frequently keep a running tally sheet of calls they get for or against specific action by them. And every officeholder has some internal level of voter response below which the issue has no status as important. Thus it is to the advantage of the nonprofit that there are significant numbers of calls in support of its position, even if the objective of these calls is simply to leave a message:

> "Please tell the Senator I fully support SB bill #464 for increased health care for senior citizens and that I want to know if he (or she) can be counted on in support of that legislation? I would like to talk to the Senator personally and schedule a meeting. Please have him or her call me."

An effective telephone component of a lobbying effort requires calls to be made continuously and in significant volume over time. Nonprofits should remember that other groups are lobbying the legislator for support for their own positions, and even where desired outcomes of different constituent groups have nothing in common, there is a comparison of the scope of district and public sentiment, and the unavoidable contrast by the legislator between successful and seemingly pathetic campaigns to win his or her support. Thus one thousand telephone calls from teachers and parents on an educational issue is noteworthy, whereas twenty-five calls in support of an overhaul of the juvenile justice system is forgettable.

E-mails: Because people have so little time, and because e-mails have become so easy to send and their use is so widespread, people are increasingly using e-mail to barrage an elected official with information and requests for support. If the e-mails are personally drafted and very concise and to the point, there is nothing wrong with this approach, though it is still preferable to write letters. On more than one occasion, when a flood of e-mails pours into an official's offices, resulting in a virtual paralysis of their inboxes, I have witnessed these offices asking for the backers to "call it off." While this eventuality certainly assures that the official hears the message, it is unclear whether or not s/he is so annoyed as to hear, but not listen.

Petitions: Another way of using e-mail is to create an online petition that urges specific action on an issue or piece of legislation and circulate this petition for signatures. After the return of the petition with a predetermined number of signatures (one hundred, five hundred, one thousand, ten thousand, etc.), it is submitted by e-mail to the legislator. This is more impressive if there is some verification that the signatories are resident constituents of the legislator's home district. Friends and close contacts as well as people who wield influence in the community shouldn't get lost in a petition, but rather communicate to the legislator—individually and personally in the form of a meeting, letter or telephone call—otherwise the impact might be lost.

Stakeholder communication should follow the same principles as those for the base nonprofit group or coalition—meetings, telephone calls, letters, faxes, and e-mails, in this order. Certainly, stakeholder groups should be asked to directly contact the targeted official in writing, on letterhead, with an official endorsement of, and plea for support for, the nonprofit's position. To the extent the stakeholder group can solicit individual support from its membership, this support can add to the impression of widespread demand for the legislator to support the position. Most major organizations such as AARP, the PTA, the chamber of commerce, and others, will require submission of a formal request for endorsement by their board of directors in the form of a specific resolution, and this takes some prior planning, as the procedures and protocols for such approval must be calendared well in advance.

Rallies: There is one additional, time-honored mechanism to communicate sentiment to elected officials (usually entire chambers or government, in general, as opposed to trying to sway a single, individual, elected member or appointee of the chamber), and this is to hold one or more rallies, usually at or near the central site of the governing body (e.g., in front of city hall or at the state capitol). Rallies demonstrate that the issue is important to a lot of people. If large enough at a given level, they may command media attention, particularly, television coverage, which is otherwise hard to get. If they are of sufficient size to denote that an issue is important, rallies can help to lift the issue to a higher priority and elevate its importance in the pantheon of issues before a body or individual legislator. The involvement of civic and business leaders, spokespeople, and celebrities, elected officials—all can increase the likelihood of coverage and success. Attendance by schoolchildren is frequently the hook television needs to carry a story.

Rallies can attract media attention and motivate the rank and file of any lobbying effort. Large, successful rallies help to build awareness, identity, and a sense of community; invigorate the troops; facilitate dissemination of information; may make it easier to raise funds; and send a message to target government officials.

Yet successful rallies require time to plan and people to coordinate, and these resources are often in short supply. Moreover, rallies may require people to travel some distance to attend them, and this takes time from these people's lives. At best they are difficult to pull off even with a large, dedicated base of believers. For these reasons, planning and executing even one rally is a major endeavor. But, rallies are part of the American political landscape and can be very effective devices. Virtually every rally that can put even a minimum number of people in front of a government building can garner some kind of media coverage. Civic, business, political, and other leaders who speak at the rally give it legitimacy and credibility and establish the principle that the rally is representative of a larger bloc of people than just those in attendance. Celebrity spokespeople participation adds a certain sexiness that is attractive to the media and makes the average citizen take notice (though one would suppose, not always favorably).

Planning includes the appropriate-site selection, permits, long-range reservations, date selection (to ensure there are minimal competing events or known items that will dominate the news on the day of the event). It also includes a strategy to ensure as large an assembly as is possible, and the management of these people on rally day to ensure positive public impressions of the cause of the group. Cleanup, media involvement and coverage, and after-the-event awareness of targeted officials of the implications of the rally must be considered as well. This is a *job* that needs coordination and planning, with oversight. Deciding to stage a rally requires an up-front commitment of those whose participation will be necessary to ensure success.

Public hearings/testimony: There are frequent open hearings before committees and subcommittees charged with approving or disapproving specific legislation, at which the public can testify on a limited basis. It is important that the nonprofit always have knowledgeable people testifying before such committees when and wherever possible, as absence from these situations is conspicuous and creates the impression the issue is not important enough for the nonprofit's supporters to show up at the hearing. It is yet another opportunity to repeat the message, and every such opportunity is important. Some special and ad hoc committees' area of focus may dovetail with the coalition members' priority issues. Often, these committees are authorized to hold public hearings and the chair is looking for a good focus for such an event (and media coverage for himself or herself). If the nonprofit's issue may generate some goodwill among an important interest group for the legislator, this may be a reason for him or her to convene a hearing. It can't hurt to ask.

There is no reason why an organized nonprofit coalition can't sponsor and convene its own public hearing, town hall meeting, summit, or another gathering to draw attention to the issue. In such a case, it should invite the media and be sure to have prominent people attend, testify, or take a place on panels so as to maximize both attendance and community interest. The whole purpose of this kind of gathering is to have your "message" heard by a wider audience, so the coalition should use the opportunity to recruit new volunteers, involve stakeholders, and pique the interest of the media.

Rule 9: The media must be won over.

Rule 10: There must be continuous communication at all levels.

Rule 11: The public must be educated and motivated to support the objectives of the coalition.

Rule 12: Volunteers are the grassroots foot soldiers of lobbying battles; they must be trained and cherished.

SUPPORTING SPECIFIC CANDIDATES

INSIDER HARDBALL

The key to insider hardball lobbying lies in participation in the election and reelection campaigns of specific candidates. The avenues for such participation include endorsement, financial contributions, fund-raising, providing access to the nonprofit's networks and contacts, and direct involvement by the nonprofit's people. Playing the "money" card is what distinguishes lobbying in the private sector from lobbying in the nonprofit sector, and is at the root of the disparate influence the former has in comparison with the latter.

The private sector often confines its support to financial contributions, avoiding official endorsements. These financial contributions are often by way of attendance at fund- raising events and are in addition to direct payments to a campaign. Business campaign contributions may come from the corporation, its PAC, and/or the senior officers and their wives personally so as to maximize the total dollar amount allowable under current laws and regulations. Moreover, the private sector often contributes to both parties, although not usually in equal amounts. There are endless fund-raising events even in nonelection years. Often, lobbying firms will, in this way, contribute to scores of candidates (sometimes the number of candidates may constitute a very high percentage of total number of seats in a given legislative body). Masking contributions is one approach to playing the financial support card while trying to remain impartial and not burning any bridges.

An endorsement of a candidate by a group, including a nonprofit, that has a large, loyal base of supporters or followers can be a valuable asset to candidates, but boxes in the group that is making the endorsement, by its alignment with one candidate in preference to another. It is possible to endorse both candidates in a given contest, and this support would be more of a stamp of "acceptance" or approval than of taking sides. It is less valuable to the candidate, but still a commitment "chit" that can later be "cashed in." Helping to raise funds, beyond direct contributions or attendance at fund-raising events, escalates the level of support and commitment. The network and contacts of the nonprofit—within the organization and the wider community—may be of great value to people running for office to mine for potential contributions, endorsements, or other kinds of help, and these networks and contacts may be substantial. Just as private sector corporate leaders may be able to recruit other financial donors for the candidate, so too might nonprofit leaders help to expand the number of supporters the candidate can appeal to. Recruiting volunteers to help fill slots in a campaign in conjunction with the other means of support is full-blown involvement and puts the nonprofit in one camp or another, and therefore carries the greatest possible benefit and risk.

Whatever form of support may be offered or denied to candidates for office as part of a lobbying strategy, the approach taken by the nonprofit should be deliberately slow and cautious, characterized by discretion, and focused on the long term. It is part of a larger strategy, tied to relationship building and, as such, will take time and patience to develop intelligently. Efforts to unseat or defeat a specific candidate probably isn't a tactic to be employed by newer coalitions, but rather an alternative best reserved for savvy, long-term players with considerable experience. The possibility of such action, and the inference of both the capacity and the willingness to take on incumbent lawmakers should, however, loom as an unspoken option to the nonprofit, and the coalition should use this specter as a weapon and a reward.

PREPARING YOUR BASE FOR A SEA CHANGE IN APPROACH

While nonprofits are composed of a wide spectrum of people who share a mutual vision about the cause and agree on the mission statement, this doesn't mean there won't be disagreement on whether or not the group's advocacy and/or lobbying effort should or shouldn't include financial support to specific candidates. There may also be disagreement on whether or not the group should create a PAC and a 527 organization, and certainly which candidates should be supported, and which ones not. Some nonprofits will want to avoid the risks involved, others will see it as essential. This conundrum can be particularly acute where there is disagreement over which candidates to endorse, or more troubling, when those in the political party of the candidate that does not get the endorsement object to an organization to which they belong and support entering the political fray and supporting a candidate of the other party. Democrats may not like a nonprofit endorsing a Republican, and vice versa.

The nonprofit needs to prepare the organization for the idea of an expanded lobbying effort that involves candidate support. This represents a major shift in nonprofit policy and strategic thinking, and there will be doubters and detractors. The nonprofit can't build a foundation on resentment and disagreement, so each nonprofit coalition member needs to come to the umbrella organization as united as possible in support for the group effort.

There are only two central questions for any nonprofit and its members to consider in this area: (1) Should the organization include financial candidate support as a part of its overall lobbying effort because such a strategy will improve its efforts to influence target decision makers? and (2) Can the nonprofit make the only criteria for the organization's support of a specific candidate whether or not s/he is supportive of the organization's position and its mission? If the nonprofit can frame this issue so that the only objective standard is whether or not a candidate for a public office (or an incumbent) does or does not support the goals, objectives, positions, and mission of the nonprofit organization (or coalition), then it can avoid some of the protest against moving into this new arena. Support is not to identify the organization with one party or another; it isn't personal, and it is only political in the sense that the organization (coalition) needs legislative or executive support for its legislative agenda. The purpose is to align the organization with those who support its position.

Organized political action is nothing if it is not cunning in its ability to adapt and find new ways to channel funds to candidates to enhance their lobbying efforts. The aggregate of individual contributions, identified as coming from a specific interest group, enhances that group's power within the system and, reform aside, will doubtlessly be here for a long time. Those unable or unwilling to organize to play this game remain at a distinct disadvantage in the quest to exert influence on the process. Insider hardball tactics has to do with money and the exchange of favors—you play, you benefit.

FINANCIAL SUPPORT TO SPECIFIC CANDIDATES

Whatever forms are used to provide financial support to specific candidates, the basic questions are to whom to give that support (money and otherwise), when, and how much (up to the allowable ceiling amount).

Whom to Support

Nonprofits, particularly at the beginning of their participation in the campaigns of candidates as one platform in their overall lobbying activities, shouldn't rush into any commitments. If the nonprofit has engaged the services of a professional lobbyist, advice as to how to proceed should be sought from this source. Consideration should be given to supporting key, powerful leadership including committee chairs and those who have been most supportive. Some thought should be given to supporting the opponents of those who have been major obstructionists to the organization's goals. The nonprofit should reward its friends and punish its enemies. Unless the nonprofit's issue is inalterably partisan, it is a good idea to contribute something on both sides of the aisle. Spreading contributions over a wider number of candidates reduces the perception that any one candidate is receiving preferential treatment or being targeted. Candidates not receiving funding support will note those that are, and perhaps be persuaded to be more attentive to issues facing the nonprofit in the future. As the nonprofit becomes more familiar with how contributions can be maximized to its benefit, expansion of support can follow.

As most incumbent seats are relatively safe, so are contributions to these officeholders. There is little risk that the nonprofit will be supporting a losing candidate and exposing the organization to the enmity of a victor it has shunned (but as the 2006 election demonstrated this is not always the case). Even incumbents in safe districts are actively engaged in fund-raising, though their own seats are seemingly not at risk. There several reasons for this: (1) the official likely has future ambitions for which a growing war chest is an asset; (2) there is remarkably little restriction on the use of these funds, and politicians who are successful in raising more money than they need to finance their own campaigns often transfer some of those funds to their colleagues, particularly those in closer contests, and thus increase their power base within their parties and are owed something by those they help; (3) in some juris-dictions, officeholders, on leaving office, can actually convert remaining campaign funds to other uses, including their own retirement funds. Thus all officeholders are constantly "dialing for dollars," as it were, and this is why those who can contribute or refer the candidate to other potential contributors have greater advantages than those who can't. Betting on a "sure thing" at least means money is allocated to a win-ner, and even well-financed incumbents in safe districts are aware of who supports them and why. Officeholders come to rely on contributions made over time, and the implication that continuation of this kind of support is dependent on the official's support does not go unnoticed.

As term limits (in fifteen states) and turnover in the legislative ranks have lessened the importance of the seniority system, leadership changes more frequently than it once did. Savvy political operatives will have a good idea of who is in line to move into powerful leadership positions, and contributions to these officeholders can pay dividends later.

How Much to Give a Candidate
The amount to contribute depends on the total amount available to contribute to all candidates and on prescribed legal limits—both limits to individual candidates and to total contribution ceilings to all candidates. Contributions do not have to be large to be noticed or appreciated. A $500 or $1,000 contribution is a meaningful amount, even at the federal level. Contributions should never be made without thought as to how to make them stand out in the official's mind. Thus, attendance at a $1,000-a-plate dinner which five hundred people attend is less desirable as a way to make the contribution than that at a $1,000-a-plate lunch where there are only one hundred people. It is important not to get lost in too large a pond and squan-der some of the advantage of contributing in the first place. Attendance at ten $100-a-plate breakfasts over time may register the nonprofit's support more than attendance at one such event. These are all judgment calls. Making the contribution right after a meeting where the candidate professes sympathy to the nonprofit's needs, or makes a pledge, signals that his or her support spurred the contribution. A $1,000 contribution to someone running for city council obviously stands out more than the same dollar amount contributed to someone running for President of the United States. A large amount elevates the contributor to a higher echelon and smaller group of supporters.

When to Give
Access to elected officials is probably greatest when they are running for office. Most members of Houses or Assemblies stand for election every two years; chief executives every four years; and members of the Senate every six years, with a third

of the members running every two years. City council and board of supervisor members usually have four-year terms; the terms of members of various elected boards and commissions range from two to six years on average. Thus every two years there is an election. Term limits, where in place, have increased the frequency of turnover so that there are more new office seekers and officeholders elected than in places where incumbents can run without limit on their time in office. Once elected, incumbents are less likely to lose a reelection bid. Arguably, the best time to first contribute to a campaign is early during the first run of a candidate for a particular office. This is when the candidate is most in need of funds, endorsements, support, and friends, and relationships begun at the beginning of a politician's career have an advantage over those struck up later. Before the candidate wins the office for the first time, the candidate is more likely to make a firm commitment to the nonprofit's issue and remember they made this commitment. Getting a candidate to pledge support to the nonprofit's cause before an election is easier than trying to get this pledge after s/he is elected. There are benefits in making contributions early in the campaign (sometimes, perhaps, even prior to the candidate's formal announcement), as those who are on board early are regarded as real friends of the candidate and not as Johnnies-come-lately. In very close contests, there may be a benefit in waiting until later in the campaign, when the candidate needs a last-minute infusion of funds to make a final push for victory. For nonprofits, it may be advisable in some situations to let their professional lobbyist attend fund-raisers to express support on their behalf.

GETTING THE PLEDGE OF SUPPORT FROM THE CANDIDATE

While there are no guarantees that a candidate will support the nonprofit after the election, and seeking such a guarantee or quid pro quo for the group's support is probably inadvisable if not legally questionable, there are a number of ways to get a pledge of support from a candidate for public office prior to the election. First, the nonprofit should assess which candidates are likely to be more sympathetic to its needs and supportive of its positions. Second, it should inquire within its membership base if anyone knows the candidate personally, as access through the "personal" gate is probably the best. Third, the nonprofit should invite the candidates to meet with the group (and it is always advisable to invite all the major candidates so as not to show favoritism at too early a juncture). A meeting can be a two-way street—making the case to the candidate for support over time, and the candidate making a pitch for votes and support or expressing legitimate reservations as to the wisdom of what the nonprofit is asking for. A candidates' forum, where all the candidates are invited to make a presentation to the nonprofit's membership base, is a common tactic. It can be either to let the candidates make their pitch to the group's membership, or to seek the organization's formal endorsement. In seeking a pledge of support, some thought must be given to how the politician will later characterize the pledge. The nonprofit should remember that politicians are experts at deniability—never getting into situations they can't manipulate and keeping their commitments vague. The best time to try to lock politicians into support is at the beginning of their career in office, and the more specific the public statement of support the better (e.g., "I support more public funding for the arts," or "I support legislation to save the xyz river"). Public statements—written or oral—are better than private pledges because it is harder for the official to renege. The nonprofit should remember to always differentiate between a candidate who is on the campaign trail and seeking funds and an incumbent discharging official duties (and thus, offering a contribution at a meeting in legislators' offices is always inappropriate). Getting support is a small dance and a matter of finesse, and the nonprofit will know when it has support (or can pretty much assume it does and rely on this assumption).

In the case of incumbents, their voting histories and past support or opposition may provide a much clearer picture of whether or not the nonprofit wants to consider offering its support to them. For candidates seeking reelection, where there has been no prior pledge of support, the same strategies can apply. But the group should bear in mind that it will arguably be more difficult to lock down the incumbent to a firm, specific commitment unless s/he is in the midst of a close contest. Most lobbying interest groups support candidates who have supported them, or will likely, support them.

PARTISANSHIP

More often than not, partisanship is a complex issue across the country. Thus, education is by and large a nonpartisan issue, although strategies and approaches as to how to improve the education system in America have become somewhat partisan. The arts are more of a partisan issue—certainly nationally—now perceived as supported by Democrats and not supported by Republicans. But the exact reverse is true in some states where Republican majorities support the arts to a greater extent than do other states with Democrat pluralities. The difference may be less philosophical and based more on budgetary constraints and established priorities, on local custom, and individual sets of circumstances. Moreover, often, a Republican in the White House allows for greater arts support in Congress than if a Democrat is President. The environmental movement is likewise perceived as increasingly partisan in the support it has at various levels, though again it isn't absolutely fixed which party is supportive and which isn't, with crossover support along every junction. Partisanship—party loyalty to given precepts—is compromised with the relative importance of a given issue at the local level. Whether or not a nonprofit area is or isn't a partisan issue depends on the different and changing circumstances of the local district, further evidence of Tip O'Neil's famous maxim, *All politics is local.* Elected officials will break ranks with their party every time if it means that their chances of election or reelection will be enhanced. Party loyalty stops at the door of impending defeat, and the parties know and accept this reality. This fact is further evidence that mobilizing local public opinion is very important to nonprofit advocacy. Nonprofits should do everything in their power to avoid having their position or their issues categorized as partisan—irrespective of whether the label falls to the "left" or the "right" of the political spectrum. If the issue is already somewhat partisan, the nonprofit (coalition) must devise strategies to return the issue to nonpartisan status as soon as possible. This is crucially important.

Nonprofits cannot afford to be limited by a false perception that support for one candidate or one party over another at any given time will jeopardize their support within the other party, that they will be punished for taking a stand, and that the possible loss of what is at stake is simply too great to even risk it. They must make clear their support is itself bipartisan, and that can best be accomplished by making sure that there is at least the appearance of evenhandedness in their contributions to candidates. Elected officials will not necessarily assign the nonprofit the moniker of enemy, but rather will become aware that the nonprofit is a political player, and that the benefit or detriment is due to a given official's position on a given issue, not to their party affiliation. Nonprofits must send the message that they will support *whoever* supports them, and withhold support from *whoever* opposes them, without reference to party or political persuasion.

There may well be instances where this support flows to candidates of different parties in the same jurisdictional territory—if not in the same election cycle, then over time. This support or withholding of support is based not on party affiliation but the voting record of the elected official on the issues critical to the nonprofit. Unfortunately, there are issues representative of segments of the nonprofit community that have become partisan in the last two or three decades—or at least seemingly so on the surface. Where nonprofits find themselves in the unenviable position of having their support truly partisan, even where they may currently enjoy a majority situation, these nonprofits must work harder to return their missions to a bipartisan status in a given jurisdiction to avoid disaster when there is a switchover in the controlling party.

On occasion some specific interest groups will actually target an elected official and attempt to defeat this candidate. This is a whole different ballgame than offering support to those who are supportive, and simply not offering support to others. Targeting someone for defeat, of course, involves contributing to and working for this person's opponent, but the effort is often characterized by contributions that exceed normal support, and there is some public indication that the effort is not just to elect one person but to defeat another. This kind of political power play is risky for two reasons. First, if it fails, unabashed enmity will be created, and, depending on the power and position of the targeted individual, failure to unseat him or her will doubtless engender retribution. Second, it generates perceptions of partisanship by the targeted individual's party, which will likely close ranks in the individual's defense. Parties don't like one or more of their members targeted; it is a direct threat that has enormous negative ramifications for them, particularly if successful, but even if it is only an attempt, and they seek to quash those who would emulate the attempt by making an example of them. Still, for very powerful groups, it is an option to target unsupportive officials, one they may have little choice but to pursue. If the strategy is successful, this success may enhance their power even in the face of retribution by the party and engender fear in the hearts of all elected officials. This strategy is part of the American political scene and perfectly legitimate, but it may be inadvisable for all but the most savvy in the nonprofit sector (the NRA is an example of a group with the resources, power, and experience to successfully use this strategy). For most readers of this book, for most nonprofit coalitions, the better approach is probably the simple intimation that substantial financial contributions already being made over time to an individual will simply dry up and disappear without support from this individual. Loss of an ongoing stream of contributions is a serious enough threat when every dollar raised is essential to success in today's expensive campaigns.

ACCESS WITHOUT ANY COMMITMENT INVESTMENT

Politics can be a risky business with much at stake. Sometimes, risks may be worth taking, and thus there may be a case for the nonprofit to financially support a candidate who has not pledged commitment. Such may be the case with powerful, key officeholders, with those that are up and coming and likely to move into powerful positions, or those that the nonprofit believes will come to support them. Support for these candidates may be seen as an investment by the nonprofit in the future. A contribution to one of these candidates should be made part of a larger strategy to win this person over as a supporter.

ENDORSEMENTS

As alluded to above, an official endorsement of one candidate in preference to another aligns the nonprofit with this candidate and may alienate the candidate and party that was not endorsed. Such alienation may be acceptable if the endorsed candidate is victorious, but if the situation is the reverse, the endorsement may have negative consequences. Engaging in the endorsement process is a card played by entities that believe strongly in one candidate in preference to another, in situations where the endorsing group wants to cultivate the image that it will go further for those who support it, or where the opposition is intractable. There may be nothing to lose by supporting even a losing candidate if the other candidates are so opposed to the nonprofit coalition that nothing would change their minds anyway. Endorsement of some candidates isn't particularly risky, because of their likely victory at the polls.

WORKING FOR THE CANDIDATE

Working for a candidate, holding fund-raisers, and providing volunteers to manage the candidate's headquarters, phone banks, walk precincts, and the like are the maximum commitment an organization can make to a candidate. Such a commitment is generally made in the expectation that if this candidate is victorious there will be reciprocity of support, not as a formal quid pro quo, but as this candidate has already clearly expressed support for the nonprofit coalition's positions. Unions and industries associated with one party or the other and environmental nonprofits are examples of groups that make this type of commitment. While it is entirely possible to organize volunteers to canvass door-to-door, help get out the vote, solicit petition signatures, and add people to the rally "crowd," providing this kind of support is labor intensive and requires a great deal of organization. Coalition leadership should be careful not to promise a level of support it might not be able to deliver on. In large coalitions, it is likely that there are individuals who (as individuals) work for opposing candidates and parties, and these people should be encouraged to let the candidate know of their support for the coalition's positions.

BUILDING THE RELATIONSHIP

Contributing to a candidate's campaign war chest, particularly early in a politician's career, is an excellent mechanism to build a relationship with the person, who might be elected as an official in the future. Decision makers are like other people in that they tend to remember their friends, those who were with them early on. In terms of developing a meaningful relationship over time, it is arguably better to make smaller contributions during each election cycle than one huge contribution during one election.

BETRAYAL

There may be situations in which the nonprofit financially supports a candidate only to have this candidate withhold support that the nonprofit thought was at least highly likely, if not guaranteed. How does the nonprofit react to and handle betrayal? In the worst-case scenario, a candidate, who makes a clear, public commitment to the nonprofit, and whom the nonprofit fully supports, wins the election but reneges on the commitment. In such a case, the first step is to confront the official and seek a satisfactory explanation (I say satisfactory because politicians are adroit and skilled at rationalization, at coming up with seemingly valid reasons why they had to vote this way instead of that way). If the nonprofit feels that the betrayal was willful and that it was "suckered," then it can either walk away from the situation, call public attention to the betrayal, or target the offending person for defeat in the next election cycle. In the situation where the nonprofit targets the offender and succeeds in unseating the official, its cache will rise dramatically and other officeholders will be more reluctant to betray it in the future. If the nonprofit tries to unseat the person and fails, others may be encouraged to buck the nonprofit when it suits their purpose, seeing there will be little consequence. This situation isn't likely to arise very often, as people generally honor their commitments and are not so duplicitous as to reverse their public stand frequently. Those who do so, consciously tarnish their own reputations and often have reputations that precede them.

As relationship building is a pillar of effective lobbying, and as relationships are, by definition, personal interchange between people, betrayal is easily seen as "personal." The nonprofit's people shouldn't take any defeat or setback personally; doing so will cloud their judgment, interfere with sound strategic thinking, and take the group off track. Betrayal is disappointing and frustrating, but it is not completely uncommon in politics. The nonprofit should accept that this happens and react in ways that will maximize both its image and reputation, and its chances of success in the face of this setback. Its reaction may be to brand the perpetrator as an enemy and seek retribution at some point, or to give the culprit a second chance. Whatever the reaction, it should be based on what will maximize the nonprofit's effectiveness and increase its number of supporters—a decision to be made dispassionately. Lobbyists need the memories of elephants, but how they act on these memories is a matter of choice. They shouldn't let emotion cloud sound judgment.

SLATES OF CANDIDATES

Some interest groups will endorse a slate of candidates or a party ticket and urge their members to vote the slate or ticket. With the rise of voters self-identified as "independent," and the decline in the power of unions and others to control their members as solid voting blocs, this type of endorsement is less employed and of less value to both the candidate and to the organization behind the blanket endorsement. Rarely are such slates bipartisan and rarely do they include candidates from both parties.

PUTTING UP CANDIDATES FOR OFFICE

Although the idea is often mentioned, precious little has been done to advance the notion of people who come from the nonprofit arena running as candidates for public office. Most elected officials are lawyers and business people, with slightly increasing numbers of teachers and other interest areas represented here and there. One way that elected bodies and government in general will begin to truly appreciate the values and contributions to the civic body that "public-benefit corporations" (nonprofits) bring is to have in office people who come from the field. And why not? There is logic to the concept that people who have spent their career lives in direct involvement with the nonprofit world would make ideal elected officials—free in large measure from special interests based on profit, experienced in local communities, networked to large segments of those communities, and passionate about making society better. These appear to be very sound qualifications to this writer.

SUMMARY

To be competitive with private-sector special interests, nonprofit advocacy coalitions need to support specific candidates. Both the organization and organizational members, and the individuals comprising the support for the coalition—those who believe in its mission—need to peg their support for specific candidates on these candidates' past records and current stances in support of the mission of the nonprofit. The nonprofit's support for individual candidates needs to include financial contributions, and to make such contributions legal, its coalition must create the necessary structures that will allow it the widest latitude, adhere to the rules governing each structure, and mobilize the individuals comprising the coalition to act. This, in turn, creates the necessity of fund-raising for non-tax-deductible contributions to support the structures and activities of the coalition, including candidate support. Whom to support, when, and how are decisions to be made by each coalition in consideration of the specific facts and situation in which it is operating at any given point in time so as to maximize its influence and leverage (which is exactly what private-sector special interests do). Finally, a future in which people from the nonprofit universe are themselves victorious office seekers will be a much rosier future for the nonprofit world.

MAKING LOBBYING EFFECTIVE

All politics are local.
Tip O'Neill

Anyone can lobby. To paraphrase Tip O'Neill's maxim, "All politics are personal." People care, first and foremost, about what impacts them directly. If there is a murder in Moscow, who cares? If there is a murder in a city across the country from where you live, who cares? But if there is a murder on your block, you want something done immediately. Lobbyists should always remember that it is those that are directly impacted, positively or negatively, who care the most about an issue.

GENERAL CONSIDERATIONS

Effective lobbying requires that the lobbyist have some familiarity with how the system works—be it local (city councils, school boards, et al.), state or federal government—and a command of the issues involved. Some people are very knowledgeable, but just aren't that good with "people." Those with great people skills, those who are eminently likable, probably make better lobbyists than those who lack these skills even though the latter may know more about the process and the issues involved. Some people are less threatening than others, some are perceived as more powerful than others, some are seen as more friendly than others. If you were the official being lobbied, who would you relate to best? Effective lobbyists are articulate and know how to present arguments and materials. This said, nonprofits will benefit by providing materials and training to those who will lobby on their behalf. Such preparation can be minimal or can be in-depth, but should include some input on the value of interpersonal skills—it can make volunteers more confident, less intimidated by the process, arm them with cogent arguments, and acquaint them with the objectives and issues involved. Advocacy and lobbying can be taught.

To be sure, access to deep pockets, having powerful friends, commanding large armies of volunteers, and having the full complement of paid staffers are all advantageous in waging effective lobbying campaigns, and every nonprofit should strive to build an organization without peer. But the reality is that few nonprofits will be able to amass all of the resources that might constitute an unparalleled machine. So, nonprofits must make do with what they have at any given point, and build on this base for the future. If nonprofits refrained from the lobbying effort simply because they were at a comparative disadvantage in the tools they had at their disposal, they would never lobby. I argue throughout this work for a certain base level of capacity, but I would encourage any level of lobbying as preferable to no lobbying at all—at least until capacity can be built.

The key to effective lobbying is legwork and perseverance. The process of legislation or other government action is often tediously slow for much of the time, with final decisions and changes made at the very end of the process in a frenzied environment of compromise. Legislators and other elected government officials (and their staffers) are people with feelings, emotions, ambitions, fears, and needs—like everyone else. They should be treated with respect—not blind supplication and deference, but with courtesy; and the nonprofit should expect them to treat it the same. Politics and political issues can excite deep emotions in people. Those with causes are passionate. Nonprofits will have friends and enemies, but it is important to remember that alliances, positions, and players change, that compromise is the watchword of the political system, that we are a pluralistic model, and that dealing with one's enemies doesn't mean civility must be sacrificed.

Legislators must balance competing interests, operate in consideration of reelection, toe the party line to one degree or another, satisfy diverse constituencies, and juggle hectic schedules and personal lives. Everybody wants something from them. Smart lobbying bears all of this in mind, and tries, where possible, to offer something in return. Quid pro quo isn't always mandatory, but some reciprocity, more often than not, is appreciated and remembered.

Nonprofit advocates and supporters should have a healthy skepticism as to what they are told by elected and appointed officials. They should question all declarative statements that emanate from politicians, and look at the motives that may lie behind every position anyone takes. Politics can be a dirty game, and it is wise not to be naïve. Many hard lessons are learned by the experience of being "sandbagged" or blindsided. To avoid being snookered, a little cynicism and exercise of caution are advisable. The art of putting a "spin" on things has, unfortunately, made avoidance of giving truly responsive answers to questions endemic. The nonprofit should not rely on promises made to it.

Some officials who don't agree with the nonprofit's position are nonetheless good people and may be supportive on some future issue. The nonprofit shouldn't burn bridges. The nonprofit can never have too many friends, and it already has too many enemies. Lobbying isn't about personal life—lobbyists don't have to like all of the people they need to be on good terms with. As the old proverb states, "Politics makes strange bedfellows," and nonprofit representatives will occasionally need to work with people and groups they wouldn't be caught dead with in their personal life, people whose stances they might find odious. Unless working with them compromises one's ethics or the mission of one's organization to a great extent, one should suck it up, grin, and bear it. Some people, of course, are just plain difficult to relate to, and keeping distance is the only alternative. Experience suggests that everyone deserves to be cut a little slack at least once, but also that, as the old Chinese proverb warns, "Man burn your fingers once, shame on him. Man burn your fingers twice, shame on you." The point is simply that succeeding is difficult enough without the nonprofit making it more difficult itself.

Lobbying over time requires that the nonprofit thank and reward its supporters and friends, and that it exacts a price from those who oppose and thwart its efforts. Rewards can come in many forms—gratitude, campaign support and financial help, support for legislation near and dear to the legislator, access to networks, photo opportunities, and the like. Punishment is exacted in the form of withholding support, contributions, endorsements, photo opportunities, and other things of value to a legislator, and transferring those benefits to another official. It is not, and shouldn't, be characterized as personal, nor does it need to always sever a relationship.

Sometimes both sides must accept the past and move on to the future. If there is never any cost to a legislator for failing to be supportive, or for being outright oppositional, then there is little incentive for the legislator to be supportive the next time, and politics is a game where trade-offs are the norm and power is the currency. Withholding something of value previously provided is much more effective than the mere promise of something in the future; that's why lobbying is best as an ongoing activity.

Both rewarding and punishing supporters and detractors should come after the fact, with only the organization's image and past reputation indicating any potential action up front. Under no circumstances should direct promises or threats be made during any given contest for backing. The game should be played as the rules exist. To be certain, there is a falsehood here, and politics operates under certain pretensions and the illusion of certain niceties, but this is how it is. If the nonprofit is involved over time in the lobbying game, it is sometimes involved in legislation that has little to do with its agenda or needs. But the group's initiatives for or against legislation is calculated as an investment for acquiring, in the future, the ability to get what it wants (e.g., stakeholder support). Supporting other interest priorities is a delicate balance. Lobbying only when the nonprofit's interests are directly involved circumscribes its potential power and sphere of influence; spreading its support over too broad an area increases its vulnerability.

Finally, as officeholders at every level are elected by local voters, it is crucial to remember that the most effective lobbyists are resident voters of the officeholder's district—they are the ones who determine whether or not an officeholder can keep his or her job. Thus, all issues need to relate back to the benefit or loss at the local level. Legislation impacting the oil industry will be viewed differently by a legislator from Vermont than it will be by a legislator from Houston. Gun control may appeal to legislators from Hawaii, but not to those from North Dakota. Runaway film production might be an issue to the voters living in Hollywood, but the voters in East Los Angeles couldn't care less. Offshore oil drilling may upset voters in South Carolina, but it has little impact on voters from Nebraska. It doesn't matter that all of these issues are more complex than a cursory relation to self-interest, that what happens in one place affects all of us in some way; voters by and large do not get past the cursory level.

Professional Lobbying Firms
No matter who the client of a lobbyist is—a mega company or a foreign government, a modest social cause or a small nonprofit field—the client is an outsider to the inner world of government. Government, like other industries or spheres, is a private inner sanctum to which only those who toil within its walls really belong. It is, in many respects, a "club"—one is either a member or one is not. Lobbyists are part of this "world"—members of the club. They act on this stage; interests that hire them do not. This makes an enormous difference in the two areas—access and information—that are most important in leveraging influence on government action (or to put it another way, on those who make the decisions). Lobbyists are full-time actors on that stage—and interact with the other actors on multiple levels—business and social. If a lobbyist has a beer two or three times a week with senior staff members

from half a dozen legislators' offices, this person naturally has access and is likely to be privy to information that clients are not. Large lobbying firms may have scores of lobbyists who in the aggregate cover just about the whole senior staff of Congress. The reason why professional lobbyists are important, particularly at the national and state levels, is that they can navigate the system in ways that their clients cannot, and at a cost that is far less than that if these clients were to duplicate the service in-house. They have the ongoing *personal* relationships built over years that this book has so frequently held up as one of *the* critical factors in successful lobbying.

The nonprofit should remember that lobbying firms are businesses that depend on client billings to cover their expenses. As they grow and expand, their "nut" increases so that they must have minimal billings to cover fixed overhead. This overhead can be high. This means they must produce results for their clients or they are not likely to keep them nor attract new business. It is under these kinds of pressures that the whole system works. Money is the "grease" that keeps the system operating, and like any other such system, money tends to corrupt the process to one degree or another. This is not to say the whole process is corrupt, only that with so much at stake, there is a high level of intensity involved, and in the political game, where the stakes can be very high, and the money can be significant, all sorts of things happen—including, unfortunately, the clouding of people's judgments and ethics.

Lobbyists can be full-time professionals or part-time volunteers. Professionals arguably bring expertise, experience, and existent relationships to the table, but not every firm is right for every nonprofit. If hiring a firm is an option, then choosing the right firm requires research and legwork. Nonprofits that intend to hire a lobbying firm to manage and augment their in-house and grassroots efforts should inquire as to lobbyist's reputations and backgrounds, and interview at least three such firms before making any decision. Talk to other groups who have lobbyists, to get recommendations. Talk to clients of a firm the nonprofit is interested in to ascertain how satisfied they are or aren't. The nonprofit shouldn't select a firm solely because someone on its team likes the firm. It should dig deeper. A small firm or individual lobbyist may provide more personal attention but lack the power and network to be effective. Yet the nonprofit must be wary of getting lost in too large a client roster as well. It should be wary of the professional lobbyist who guarantees specific outcomes, and equally wary of the firm that refuses to promise specific actions.

If the nonprofit hires a large lobbying firm, it should be sure to meet the individual lobbyist within this firm who will handle and oversee the account. Lobbyists, as individuals, are like other professionals—some are very good, others are not. Some lobbyists are highly regarded by elected officials, others are held in little esteem. Some are smart, others average. The nonprofit wants someone who is astute, hard working, well respected, and savvy, and someone with whom it can get along, someone to whom it can relate. The chemistry between the nonprofit and the lobbyist is important. The nonprofit should trust its instincts, but it should exercise "due diligence" in investigating lobbyists. Because nonprofits should strive to make their issues nonpartisan, they may wish to avoid hiring lobbying firms that are associated too much with one party or the other.

Every government body, every agency, department, and legislative branch has its own culture built over time, and its own way of doing things, and familiarity with the nuances of these unwritten yet codified protocols and procedures can be very advantageous and save a great deal of time. The nonprofit should pick a firm with experience that seems well suited for what needs to be done for the nonprofit to succeed. But it shouldn't expect that hiring a lobbyist is the end of its involvement. It is important that nonprofits do not make the mistake of thinking that if they hire a lobbying firm their work is done and the professional firm will handle all aspects of their advocacy plank. First, this would be a very expensive buy, and second, lobbying firms are only as good as the effort behind them—good firms will tell the nonprofit this, up front. The nonprofit shouldn't make too long a commitment to a lobbyist up front—there should be periodic review of the firm's progress and analysis of benchmarks in their success on the nonprofit's behalf. The nonprofit shouldn't lock itself into a situation that may prove to have been ill-advised. Having a relationship over time with a lobbyist can breed friendship, but liking someone personally is not a justifiable reason by itself to retain the person's services—results should be the prime measurement. Finally, the nonprofit shouldn't pay retail. It should ask for a consideration as a nonprofit, and negotiate the fee.

Even if a professional lobbyist is hired, the nonprofit or coalition needs someone in-house to manage the overall effort. Effective lobbying requires orchestrating efforts on multiple fronts. Choosing one person to guide the campaign requires that the person can make a commitment to stay the course. Changing leadership in midstream can be very disruptive.

Volunteer or in-house managers of advocacy and/or lobbying efforts should be people who are experienced in and good at organizational management, who can delegate authority, and who can command the respect and dedication of others. Ideally, the volunteer overseer should have a basic knowledge of government operations, procedures and protocols, and some experience dealing with advocacy.

Key Legislative Champions

If passage of legislation is the objective, then a member of the target legislative body will need to introduce and sponsor the bill. Recruiting this official is an important first step in the process. Is this official powerful? Respected? Well liked in the legislature? On good terms with the Executive? Does s/he truly believe in the cause? Is s/he passionate? Is it a priority to him/her? What advantages does s/he bring to the battle? What committees is s/he on, which ones does s/he chair? Often, the choice among legislators who will act as the chief backer, spokesperson, and author of the legislation sought is small and the list short. The more choices the nonprofit has, the better choice it can make. Multiple champions help, and it is particularly helpful to recruit support from both parties of any given body so as to keep the issue nonpartisan, but one responsible person in the majority party, preferably on the key committee that will oversee the bill, one focal point as the key champion, is essential.

In state legislatures and Congress, the key legislators are the oversight committee and subcommittee chairs, the leaders of the House (or Assembly) and the Senate, and the governor or President. On the city council/board of supervisors or school board at the local level, all members are arguably important but the one who will sponsor the legislation is the key member. The mayor, superintendent, or other executive is likewise important, because it does little good to pass a bill that the Executive is likely to veto. This is not to say that there are no other important legislators at all these levels that can both help and hurt the chances of the legislation passing, but rather that without the key people the game may be over anyway.

Drafting Legislation

Drafting legislation is both a skill and an art form, yet it is not beyond the pale of smart people. The best-drafted legislation deals clearly and comprehensively with its subject matter, and is drafted so as to have the best chance of passage and approval; it must appeal to the majority party, be nonthreatening and inoffensive to the minority, and written so as to maximize Executive support and withstand judicial review. Staff members often draft the bills, with legislative counsel input at some point in the process. The initial draft may be quite vague and brief, both to meet a deadline for filing legislation, and also to keep the language open as the intent is to amend and provide final language at a later date. The nonprofit should seek to be included in the drafting process if this is possible, as this gives it a chance to ensure that the language meets the objectives of the nonprofit and that there are no surprises in the legislation introduced.

THE MEDIA

Media coverage of the issue at hand (funding, specific legislation, rules/regulations, etc.) is one of the dynamics of the lobbying function. Media coverage brings the issue to the public's attention and elevates its status and importance. Substantial media coverage, usually reserved for more controversial issues or issues that might have a salacious aspect that will pique public interest, may motivate the public to express their views and take positions. Conversely, the absence of any media coverage diminishes the importance of the issue and relegates it to a status that may or may not be important, but one that certainly does not command attention. Ideally for the nonprofit effort, media coverage is positive in its slant, substantial enough to facilitate the recruitment of grassroots activist support, and continuous enough over time to impact decision makers. Legislators' votes are often very different depending on whether these votes are subject to the spotlight.

Elected officials are, without question, keenly aware of media coverage of issues perceived to register with the public *in their districts*. They are far less concerned with all but the biggest issues of importance outside their voting constituent territory. Under the "go along, to get along" rule, legislators support what is important to other legislators, so that they will get the same consideration in return.

The nonprofit and its representatives should always remember that not everything they do is newsworthy. They shouldn't waste media outlets' time sending them press releases and information that have no news value or they risk cultivating a reputation as people to ignore and whose materials can routinely be filed in the trash can.

Radio: Radio talk shows may be ideally suited to cover a local issue for the nonprofit. Again, as with all media, the more there is some kind of "hook" that differentiates one story from another, with something likely to interest the public, the better the chance to get media coverage—particularly television and radio, where ratings are king. Often, talk radio in a given area will lean either left or right, and it is important to assess how the host regards the nonprofit issue. If the host has a positive attitude, then the nonprofit can usually only win from the situation. If the attitude is negative, the risk of mobilizing opposition through the show needs to be balanced against the reward of possible public support. The nonprofit's representative at the show should bear in mind that if the organization's position "waves the red flag" at the talk show host, an invitation to it to be a guest is likely to be a setup. The host intends to use the nonprofit's views to incite listeners and to discredit the nonprofit, make fun of it or increase the show's audience in other ways at the group's expense. These may be the host's intentions, but this doesn't necessarily mean the nonprofit shouldn't do the show, but that its representative should be prepared for an attempt to "roast" him or her. As radio talk show audiences tend to lean in one direction or another, the nonprofit's representative may or may not be either preaching to the choir (which may be a good reason to do the show) or talking to the wall (which is a reason for the person not to waste time in stirring up the opposition). The nonprofit shouldn't just automatically accept every invitation.

Television: As previously discussed, the farthest-reaching media is television, particularly when coverage is not limited to a one-time event. Combining vocals and pictures in a repetitive sequence is extraordinarily powerful in grabbing the attention of the most people. Because "ratings" are the bottom line, television tends to avoid "issues" that lack a dramatic visual. Nonprofit programming or funding, no matter how beneficial, no matter how valuable, is basically a talking head story that runs counter to the principle of strong visual imagery and brings disastrous television ratings. As previously discussed, there are numerous ways around this quandary. Celebrity spokespeople garner coverage. Rallies, picket lines, and demonstrations are tailor-made staples of television news coverage. Children included in the story are, often,, the hook necessary to attract television.

The nonprofit should accompany any pitch it makes to television stations with video they might use as background (called 'B' roll footage in industry parlance). It should remember that television stations have different crews for weekdays and weekends and late evening. The group should always include a phonetic pronunciation of names that might be hard to pronounce in any written submission to television (or radio). It might consider offering to provide the station with a list of names of "experts" who can be contacted for "talking head" shots. In short, it should do whatever it can to make it easier for the television station to carry its story.

Both television and radio *editorial* support should be not be overlooked. Approaching a station general manager is basically the same as approaching a newspaper editorial board—a telephone inquiry, probably followed up by a brief explanatory letter (with or without accompanying support materials), a scheduled meeting, and presentation asking for the editorial support (see below).

Newspapers: Newspaper coverage brings two principal types of benefit to a nonprofit lobbying effort: (a) straight news coverage—in either the front or metro sections (including human-interest story angles); and, (b) editorial support. Larger articles, frequent coverage, the inclusion of photographs—all help to make straight news coverage valuable in recruiting and mobilizing grassroots support, stoking motivation of the troops, and making the target decision maker aware of the issue. News coverage depends on the newspaper's perception of the nonprofits "story" as newsworthy.

Editorial support: Newspaper editorial endorsement and support for the nonprofit's positions and causes can be solicited and cultivated. Every nonprofit effort should schedule a meeting with the editorial board at every major newspaper in the non-profit's area. This is easy to do—a simple phone call or letter, explanation of the issue, and a request to meet with the board to make a brief presentation. Virtually every newspaper has an editorial board, composed of senior editors, writers, and columnists who determine what position the paper will take on issues. Almost all welcome community-based nonprofits to meet with them and make the case for their issue. Most are sympathetic. The nonprofit should call the newspaper and inquire about editorial board meetings and presentations. The call should be fol-lowed up with a brief explanatory letter stating the case for the paper editorializing in favor of the position adopted by the nonprofit. The letter (if requested) or the actual presentation before the editorial board should clearly state the issue, what action is needed by government and why, the timeline, why it is important to the community (how the people benefit, what they will lose if the government decides against the nonprofit), and perhaps one or two specific examples or stories of people who are involved in the nonprofit or are impacted and affected by the issue at hand. A concise summary of any research or facts, figures, data that support the position, and what the nonprofit hopes the paper will say in the editorial should also be given in the letter. Then, if the nonprofit has made its case in the letter, it should schedule a meeting time and date, and make a formal presentation at the meeting. A non-profit representative might take one or two people along to the meeting—ideally someone who knows someone on the editorial board (a major advertiser?) and some-one (a student?) who has a story to tell regarding the issue and the nonprofit. If the nonprofit is submitting a letter, it should be a brief summary of what it will present at a meeting in more detail. The nonprofit should follow up the meeting with a thank-you letter and any supporting materials either requested by the newspaper or those that will help it make the case. The nonprofit should keep in regular touch with its contact person after the meeting—whether or not it gets the editorial sup-port—and build this *relationship* for the future.

Op-ed: In addition to editorial endorsement or the newspaper taking the nonprofit's position, there are also mentions by columnists, endorsements, and op-ed pieces (opinion pieces from citizens). Most papers have op-ed guidelines (the number of words usually varies from four hundred to eight hundred) and print letters to the edi-tor or otherwise feature op-ed opinions on a very regular basis. Op-ed pieces may not be printed for one or two weeks after submission, so the nonprofit should make sure to consider its timeline when submitting a piece. A representative should call the edi-torial desk at the newspaper to get clarification on the paper's policies and to make personal contact with the people at the editorial desk. It isn't unusual for a newspaper to edit some opinions submitted, for purposes of space management, not to change opinions. (Newspapers may not necessarily be familiar with the nonprofit's issue and may thus edit op-ed pieces submitted to them in ways that sometimes might appear to the nonprofit that the "essence" of their point was cut out. In such case the non-profit should courteously point out their concerns in a follow-up letter. The nonprofit should include a brief cover letter with its submission and the writer's name and con-tact information (this is mandatory as most newspapers refuse to print anonymous op-ed submissions). The nonprofit should always send copies of op-ed and favorable editorial support printed in local newspapers to legislators and other decision makers and post them on its website.

Elected officials and other decision makers are aware of coverage of issues in their districts as well as coverage that transcends geography. They know when editorials urge them to move in one direction or the other—for example, to pass legislation or oppose it—and even if the editorials don't change their vote (and often they do), they remember them. Officials know full well that media coverage molds public opinion. It is one factor in their decision-making processes, and effective lobbying is acting on as many of thee factors as the nonprofit can identify and access.

Press kits: Media outlets receive countless press kits from an endless parade of peo-ple and organizations that seek coverage and support. People have become very cre-ative in designing these kits and presenting them, so as to distinguish their kits from all the others. Kits should frame the issue clearly and concisely, and this "summary" should be placed as the first thing someone will see when opening the kit. The objec-tive of the coalition should be framed so as to have news value.
Contents of the kit should include

- a press release announcing the lobbying effort or reaction to legislation introduced
- summarized research and evidence that supports the position taken
- testimonial support from people who have name or identity recognition
- reasons why the issue is important locally, particularly in the legislator's district
- any proclamations, petitions, manifestos, or endorsements that have been secured

All of the material should be presented as creatively as possible so as to warrant attention, but the creativity should never diminish the professional look or the simplicity and directness of the message. The nonprofit's first hurdle is to get some-one at the media outlet to *really* look at its kit and read its message. Something ought to distinguish the kit and increase the chances of a response. Packaging may help. A personal relationship with the recipient almost always helps. Having the kit delivered by a parade of high-profile people probably helps. Kits can be sent to a small, targeted list of media outlets or to the whole of the media community. Follow-up telephone calls to those to whom the kit was sent, a week or so after the mailing, to inquire if the recipient has any questions, can call attention to the kit and perhaps encourage someone to find it and take a look at it.

Press releases: A single press release (as opposed to a whole kit) should cover the who, what, where, when, and why of the subject matter, and should be newsworthy. It might include the launch of a lobbying campaign; introduction of, or reaction to, specific legislation; an event –(rallies or demonstrations); the release of impact studies; major meetings; stakeholder involvement or endorsement, and so on. Whatever the subject of the release it ought to be important enough to be construed as newsworthy. The nonprofit should assume that the reader knows nothing about its organization or issues.

Press releases should contain all the important information at the beginning of the release in order of importance. Often, editors will use the wording of the release, but cut and edit it to make it fit the available space. They will usually cut from the end of the release first. The nonprofit should make it easy for them to include something in the paper about its objective. Spelling and grammar, and facts and quotes, should be checked and double-checked for accuracy, and the active tense should be used to give statements in as few words as possible (no more than one page, front and reverse). The release should be proofread before it is sent out.

Standard 8½ × 11-inch letterhead or plain paper should be used, with the words "Press Release" centered at the top. Line spacing should be set for 1½ or double spacing. In the next line the date and the words "For Immediate Release" (or, if the information is not to be made public until a certain date, "Embargoed until. . . (insert date)") should be included. The name and telephone number/e-mail address of the person to contact should be given if the recipient requires this information. Quote marks should be used for all quotes, and the names of the people who made the remarks should be given and be correctly spelled. The figure "30" should be written at the bottom of the release, signifying the journalist's standard symbol for the end. One or two lines describing the organization and full contact information should be included at the bottom.

Media mailing list: The master media list should break media outlets into categories (i.e., newspapers, radio, television, etc.), by geography, and perhaps size and reach of the outlet (i.e., the number of subscribers, listeners, viewers, etc.). Software tools easily allow management of such a database.

Event Coverage
Information about where and when an event is staged, who the speakers are, which notable organizations are participating, and the purpose (if unusual) may all help to get local media to cover an event, particularly if the event has the potential to produce photo opportunities and, for television, good visuals. There are several proven types of events that can usually generate coverage:

- **The award event:** This is an event bestowing a major honor on an individual (with some community profile) for exemplary contributions to the nonprofit's cause, often over a lifetime. Unless the event is staged as a fund-raiser and there are cumbersome logistics and ticket sales to complicate the planning, an award event can be relatively simple to stage.
- **The rally**: Rallies, with well-known speakers, and a relatively good turnout, can garner coverage.
- **The demonstration**: The demonstration is similar to the rally in some ways. A political demonstration is a time-honored American tradition. It can be as simple as a dozen people carrying placards and marching in front of a government

building, or as large as thousands of people engaged in a "sit-in." The demonstration differs from the rally in that it is somewhat "confrontational" by definition; it is the exercise of a "political" right. Because of the difference in characterization, demonstrations seem to get press coverage in greater quantity and frequency than rallies do. In fact, very small protests, if staged right, can almost always garner media coverage, including, otherwise hard-to-get television coverage.

- **The fund-raiser**: Some fund-raising events, if they are unique, or feature prominent names (celebrities/elected officials), can garner indirect media coverage of the lobbying issues.
- **The press conference**: Only if there are major celebrities, including sports and/or film stars, or senior elected officials participating, and the issue is specific and "hot button," is a nonprofit likely to get a turnout for a press conference (hot-button issues might include anything controversial, public safety issues, or major, *immediate* economic-impact issues). Press conferences require considerable planning to effect media attendance—the site should be unusual or special in some way, the reason for the conference important and newsworthy (e.g., the release of a major public opinion survey or research study with significant results), and distinguished guests featured. The nonprofit might try holding a joint press conference with one or more other groups to increase its chances of securing greater coverage.
- **The dedication**: The dedication of a major new facility, particularly one with cultural or architectural significance, with hoopla, bands, and so on, should get coverage, and can be used to talk about the lobbying message.

One of the primary reasons for checking to see if there are any scheduled conflicting events *before* committing to a given date is to avoid potentially competing news events that might, for whatever reason, be more attractive to the media than the nonprofit's event. There are "slow" news days when there is a dearth of front-page or page-two types of news stories to cover, making it more likely for the nonprofit to get coverage (weekends are usually slower news days). Conversely, there are days when there are so many "A" list type events/news happening that the nonprofit's event has virtually no chance of coverage. The nonprofit should seek the slower news days and avoid the busy days to the extent possible.

The "Day of . . ." event: One special-event approach is to proclaim that a certain day is dedicated to observing the value and meaning of a certain specific cause, for example, Earth Day, Arts Day, or Save the River Day. Setting aside a special day to commemorate, celebrate, or otherwise call the attention of the whole community to a particular cause allows for multiple events to be organized and also for packaging the issue and highlighting it in ways that will make it more attractive for media coverage. Some kind of rally or crowd event as the centerpiece of the day, to which the public is invited, is the usual method employed to anchor the activities surrounding the "day." A "day" event can be an annual occurrence, which, after a while, grows in stature and becomes part of the social calendar of a territory, increasing media coverage and enhancing the image of the coalition. It is a device to increase both public awareness of, and support for, your cause.

Creation of such a "day" by a coalition is simply a matter of the group making an announcement. Getting a government body, be it the city council or the state legislature, or an official, be it the mayor or the governor, to officially proclaim the "day" is entirely possible as officials like to issue formal proclamations that indicate they appreciate and support a constituent group's interest without making any kind of real commitment. It allows elected officeholders to point to their support for the group during elections, even if such facilitation is not really much of a stretch for the politician.

There are numerous ways to call attention to a "Day of . . ." event. There should be a press release and a press kit to announce the day, information about the activities and events being held as part of the day's celebration and background materials why the particular cause is important and why a day is being set aside to mark the cause should be included.

Other ways to celebrate the day might include the following:

- **Contest:** The nonprofit could hold a poster contest among schoolchildren to help create the day's official poster, or a slogan contest with local radio station support.
- **Newspaper insert:** Sponsors can be gathered, and a package of facts, figures, photos, and the like presented to a newspaper for a special "insert" on the day's edition.
- **Awards event:** An event scheduled to present awards to people in the community or to elected officials who have been supportive in the past might garner coverage.
- **Parade or festival:** A parade or a festival centered on the issue can be held.
- **Rally:** The nonprofit can hold a rally.
- **Protest:** A protest against an injustice can be organized.
- **Public hearing/town hall meeting:** The nonprofit can hold a public hearing at which notable people offer testimony in support of the value of the cause, or an open town hall meeting to talk about the importance of the cause the community.
- **Dedication:** Dedication of a work of art, a memorial of some kind, a new building, an open space, or whatever the nonprofit can think of, with celebrities speaking, can be organized.
- **Special lecture:** A special lecture or presentation of a special speaker who will talk about the issue can be scheduled.
- **Kids celebration:** If the issue lends itself to some event that is centered on children, the media might be interested in covering it.
- **Retail tie-in:** The nonprofit could figure out some angle that will work as a local tie-in. If the issue isn't controversial, but something that the community by and large supports in concept (better education, public safety, art and culture, health care), the nonprofit might be able to talk a retail chain, mall, or major store to do some sort of advertising tie-in/display. This should be marketed as a win-win situation for everybody.

The nonprofit should identify existing events being held on the same day or near the day, and schedule its event to avoid conflicts. If there are events that complement the group's "day," such as performances scheduled on the date of an arts day, it should investigate possible tie-ins to these events and co-opt them as part of its celebration. The overarching objective in planning events is to involve the public as widely as possible. The setting aside a "day" for the nonprofit's cause is both a media and mobilization tool; as an annual occurrence it helps to build brand-name identity for the organization, greater awareness of the nonprofit's issue by the public, and solidarity within the nonprofit's support base. Any time a nonprofit can gather a crowd, it can pitch this audience to help it by becoming supporters, volunteers, or contributors.

ADVERTISING

Very few nonprofits or even coalitions of nonprofits can raise sufficient funds to launch any kind of meaningful advertising campaign as part of a lobbying effort. Advertising—whether television, radio, print, billboard, or other media—is expensive and normally requires repetition over time to be effective. There are a few ways to emulate advertising:

Public service announcements (PSAs) on radio: Radio spots—of ten-, thirty-, and sixty seconds—are not unreasonably expensive to produce. The nonprofit needs a studio, the right voice, and a memorable concept and copy. Some of these may be obtained by donation. Home studios are common now. The cost of duplication of tapes or CDs and their distribution to target stations, including postage (tape and CD mailing boxes/envelopes are available at larger stationery stores), is likewise not very high. Stations are required to run a percentage of PSAs over given time periods, and each station has a policy as for submission and selection. The nonprofit shouldn't expect to have a PSA run during times of the day that are premium advertising slots (such as morning drive time), but any runs can be helpful. A press kit or other short pitch as to why the PSA fits the station's citizenship aspirations is necessary, and any other way the station can be personally "lobbied" may also help. At the least the nonprofit should contact stations, then make follow-up telephone calls after mailing the CD and press kit. A listing of radio stations in the nonprofit's area (city, region, state, nation), with contact information, can be obtained from any library or the web.

Television PSAs: Television spots of ten, fifteen, thirty or sixty seconds are more expensive to produce and distribute, and it is difficult to get them aired. They must be professionally made and must meet certain broadcast standards. Obviously, the visual angle is the critical factor, with memorable content a close second. Celebrity participation is a good hook. Animation works too. There may be a film school at a college near the nonprofit, and it may be able to enlist the help of students in the production of a spot. Otherwise, the approach is similar to radio spots. The nonprofit can contact its local Ad Council chapter or a regional office and inquire as to how to submit a plan for a full-service campaign—but remember that these ventures take long-term planning. Many local cable stations offer options commercial stations may not. Access to local coverage cable stations may be much easier.

Print: Print advertisements can also qualify as PSAs when part of a larger campaign with a sponsor such as the Ad Council. Otherwise, print ads are generally relatively expensive depending on the circulation of the newspaper or magazine (not to produce, but to buy the space for) and are a less viable possibility, as newspapers are less inclined to provide pro bono space. Most newspapers are, however, willing to offer discounts to nonprofit groups (but may decline that courtesy if the advertisement content is too blatantly political).

For the lobbying coalition that can afford to buy advertising on the media outlets discussed and engage an agency to professionally create the advertisements, the game is the same as it is for Procter & Gamble and General Motors—create memorable, lasting impressions that accomplish the objective: selling soap or cars, or moving people to specific lobbying action on behalf of the nonprofits. All of these traditional advertising tools may be employed by the nonprofit on its own or other websites, and increasingly there are audiences for these messages.

QUASI ADVERTISING TOOLS

There are ways in which nonprofits can send their messages to their own bases and stakeholder groups and even some segments of the public, and these methods cannot be technically classified as advertising:

Speakers' bureaus: Volunteers can be trained to make effective presentations to a wide variety of groups—civic clubs, businesses, trade associations, schools, senior groups, and municipal government (including city councils, boards of supervisors, school boards, and the like). The volunteers must be recruited, trained, given materials, and then booked into appropriate venues of willing audiences. This takes time and people to arrange. It is a potentially effective means to spread word of the message and to educate and inform segments of the public that might otherwise be totally unfamiliar with the issues. Speakers' bureaus also present opportunities to widen the nonprofit's stakeholder support. Presentations can be simple talks, augmented or not by power point or other media presentations. Printed materials can be distributed, or people can be referred to websites. Each presentation can also be used as grassroots volunteer solicitation and even fund-raising device. Speakers' bureaus may be a very good long-term strategy.

Video: With the advent of relatively sophisticated camcorders and software editing programs, more nonprofits will be able to make a video presentation of what they do, or even specifically, make the case for the lobbying position. Once made, these videos can be used in conjunction with speakers' bureau presentations, or segments can be edited out of the work to serve as visual PSAs for television distribution. Copies can be burned into DVDs and widely distributed for use by each organization within the coalition and by stakeholders. The content of these videos and DVDs should be included in materials available on the nonprofit's website. The video can be a powerful support tool for garnering media attention and can be used to educate and inform the very decision makers the lobbying effort is trying to influence. These videos can also find airtime on local access shows and even other locally based television stations, serve as effective calling cards and as a powerful part of the press kit, and be shown at the meetings of the coalition's members to maintain high morale and commitment of the rank and file.

Power-point presentations: Today, anyone can create a professional-looking power-point presentation that can be used in numerous situations to *make the case* to potential funders/contributors, supporters, backers, stakeholders, and the ultimate decision makers. Presentations accompanied by visuals usually make a stronger impression. These too should be a part of the nonprofit's website.

Legislative orientation meeting: The nonprofit should schedule an orientation meeting for legislators and their staff to acquaint them with the issues facing your organization and to *make the case* to the public for the value of what the nonprofit is doing and its positions. Such orientations can be tied to specific pending legislation or scheduled earlier in the legislative session, prior to the deadline for introducing bills, as a way to acquaint legislators with issues that may need redressing via legislation. It will be difficult for the nonprofit to attract many legislators, but the nonprofit might be able to get staff to attend the orientation, particularly if the group is creative in planning the event. Providing lunch or some refreshments is often a good hook; celebrity attendance helps, and personal calls to legislators or their staff, from people they know, inviting them, is often a successful strategy. The nonprofit might hold an orientation meeting just for new, "freshmen" legislators or for a specific caucus.

The nonprofit should keep the orientation brief, make attendance easy and convenient for those it invites, and have materials (not too much) available for distribution. The group could use a power point or other means of making its presentation visual, as visuals are more likely to stick in the minds of those attending the presentation. It should keep up the pace of the program, which shouldn't get too technical. The nonprofit should always follow up an orientation (or any other meeting) with thank-you notes, phone calls, and the offer to provide more information or materials. The group should always try to schedule a further face-to-face opportunity (it should remember that its goal is to develop ongoing *relationships* with legislators and their staffs). Orientations for state or federal legislators will obviously need to be held in the Capitol, and thus travel for the orientation team is a factor to consider.

Making-the-case print materials: Depending on the data and other relevant materials available, assembly of a binder or portfolio of all the documents, studies, and materials that make the case for the adopted position on the issue can take time and the result can be voluminous. Nobody will likely read the entire package. Thus it is necessary to prepare an executive summary that highlights the evidence assembled in a clear, organized, easy-to-navigate manner. The nonprofit should include summaries of arguments, with facts and data and examples to back up and illustrate points (besides charts and tables where possible, as they are easier to read and digest). Not every subargument need be included, just the major bulleted points. Some people might be more interested in one part of the argument than another, and this section can be pulled out in its entirety or summarized alone.

It is probably a good idea to create at least two documents from the larger packet.

- **Short-form brochure**: This is basically a two-page document including only the major points, with easy-to-read headings. The layout should be attractive and easy on the eye, and should draw the reader to the points the nonprofit wants to make. This brochure can be the basic calling card for the whole lobbying effort.
- **Executive summary:** The longer summary provides more detail, more data/charts/graphs, illustrations of the real-world impact, but it too is relatively short (eight to ten pages) with a layout that leaves a lot of empty space between major points so as to highlight them.

The appearance of printed materials is important, and thus if the budget permits, printed materials will benefit from professional graphic artist layout and design. The nonprofit shouldn't think that because it has distributed copies to every legislator or decision maker holding power over the issue at hand that each of them will read it. Very few, if any, will read even the shortest summary. Many will lose them. The nonprofit will probably have to provide them with copies more than once or twice. It will have to provide staff with copies, and figure out how to make the points in the summaries in other ways as well—at meetings, in letters, via the media, in person, and via surrogates. Again, all materials in whatever form—audio, video, CD, DVD, power point, and print—should be put on the website for easy access and wider distribution.

As an exercise, the nonprofit should be able to immediately state the five major points in its argument for the decision maker's support, and be able to back up each point with the most important facts and figures and personal stories, if and when asked. The message must be even simpler than this presentation in five points, and the base message must be repeated over and over again to drive it home. The nonprofit should strive to stay on message at all times. But it should also be prepared to back up the message, whenever asked, with at least the next level of expansion of the argument—each level becomes more specific and detailed.

Here's an example of a message about the arts striving for more funding (arguing in favor of something):

The arts are good for the health of the state

- Good for the *economy*—jobs, as an economic engine, tax revenue
- Good for *education* of kids—provides job skills, kids perform better, more go to college, helps reduce disruptive classroom behavior
- Good for the *tourism industry*—results in longer stays and increased spending by tourists, and accounts for a large percentage of all tourist spending
- Good for *businesses*—attracts talent pool, increases real-estate values, prepares workforce
- Good for *diversity*—promotes tolerance, builds community bridges, and enhances the reputation of the area

And here's an example of a message about the environmental movement to ban off-shore drilling (arguing in opposition to something):

Offshore drilling endangers the state and isn't likely to net that much oil

1. A ban protects the coastline and beaches—essential to the tourism industry.
2. The likely amount of oil produced in ten years would satisfy California's needs for less than three weeks [or whatever the numbers are].
3. A ban protects endangered species from possible oil spills, including ecosystems important to the fishing industry.
4. The legislation permitting drilling, as proposed, is poorly written [a classic argument that can almost always be made about a piece of legislation one opposes, as a high percentage of legislation *is* poorly drafted and often creates as many problems as it purports to solve. In this case, one might point out the lack of monitoring of the activity, or lack of funds for monitoring, to ensure compliance with safeguards.]
   Note: If the nonprofit's major points can be reduced to four, or even three, key messages, then this is the right number. Five should be the maximum bullet points.

OTHER TOOLS

There are several factors to consider before deciding what other kinds of printed materials (or other means) to use to push the nonprofit's message, and they include

- **Cost:** What is the cost compared with other options?
- **Reach:** How many people will be exposed to the message and are these people a target group for one or more of the priorities of the communications strategy?
- **Shelf life:** How long will the specific item be kept by a recipient before being disposed of? (For example, a calendar is more likely to be kept by someone than is a flyer, and thus the calendar will create multiple impressions because the message will be seen repeatedly over time, by many individuals. Some items have a longer "shelf life" because they are passed on by one individual to another.)
- **Time/ease of production:** Will design and production of the item take a lot or a little amount of personnel time?
- **Distribution:** Will it be easy to ship or bulky and hard to handle? How will it be distributed? (The nonprofit wants to avoid using channels of distribution where the item will end up in a closet or on a floor somewhere and never reach its ultimately intended target audience.)

Possibilities might include

Postcards: Postcards that repeat the campaign's message and are expertly designed to attract the recipient's attention can be widely distributed by all of the coalition's members (and in turn to their member bases) and can build awareness. Computers make design within the reach of everyone, and printing can be done at any copy shop. And if postage expense is prohibitive for mass mailings, the cost can be shared by all the coalition members, the postcards distributed at events, meetings, and the like at no cost, or the message even sent by e-mail.

Flyers: Computer software now makes design, printing, and even distribution of flyers easy. Professional-looking, multicolor, eye-catching flyers can now be easily and simply designed and produced, and multiple flyers can be placed on a website for widespread circulation by downloading. Templates of flyers can be made available for any number of purposes—from soliciting volunteers and announcing meetings and rallies to urging specific action such as contacting legislators and fund-raising. Individual organizational members of a coalition can customize these templates to their needs and the profiles of their memberships. Flyers can be distributed at meetings and other events, posted in local retail establishments, and distributed in other imaginative ways.

Posters: A poster designed specifically for the lobbying purpose or campaign (particularly if it includes some kind of logo or other branding artwork) further helps to build identity and awareness of the issue and the campaign. Posters should include slogans, symbols, logos, and messages. Posters are not cheap to print, but the cost might be underwritten by a sponsor (given credit on the poster by placement of the sponsor's name or logo) or by a generous individual "angel" recruited to cover the costs, or the posters can be sold for a nominal fee. The budget may permit the expense, at times. Posters may be placed in retail store windows, in public places, and distributed in other ways; widespread placement helps to further build desirable public awareness and grassroots support. The nonprofit should think outside the box by considering contacting local-bus transit districts for fixing posters on the sides of buses; taxi companies for inclusion on the triangle signs atop cabs; and airports and train stations and other high traffic areas, where a poster might be seen by a lot of people. Holding a poster contest and inviting submissions can eliminate the costs of hiring a professional design outfit and garner publicity for the poster (and indirectly to the nonprofit's cause). Limiting the contest to schoolchildren is a good media hook and often produces wonderful posters. And posters can be converted to "yard" signs of the type commonly seen endorsing candidates during elections and distributed to supporters who then place the signs in their yards.

Bookmarks: Bookmarks are very cheap to produce, can have a long "shelf life," and are easy to distribute and inexpensive to ship.

Calendars: If a campaign is ongoing or very long term, calendars (pocket, desk, or wall) can be effective communication devices as they are more likely to remain in view over the period than other printed materials. Calendars designed specifically for elected officials, with space for the types of committee meetings, hearings, caucus gatherings, and the like might appeal to lawmakers and thus the nonprofit's message might stay in front of them for a prolonged period of time. As lawmakers are often statutorily prohibited from accepting gifts over a certain dollar amount, the nonprofit should check to see if the cost of a calendar qualifies under the applicable regulations.

Merchandising: Merchandising can both create awareness and identity and be used as a means to raise funds. If the campaign has a logo or one- to four-word "slogan," merchandising items can repeat this message. Merchandising items can grab the attention of specific target audiences such as the media and young people. Baseball caps, T-shirts, buttons, bumper stickers, banners, mugs, desk items, and calendars are but a few of the possibilities. These items can be given to legislators or staff members, but again the dollar limitations on gifts to legislators operative in the nonprofit's state (most states have a ceiling of $10 for any gift to a legislator) must be checked.

Tool kits: A tool kit for staff, volunteers, and stakeholder groups could combine arguments, facts and figures, research, resources, volunteer information, sample letters, contact information, important deadlines, flyers, logo, postcards, calendar (with dates of meetings/fundraising events); lobbying dos and don'ts; FAQs; talking points; website navigation guides; and protocols. A tool kit should contain whatever the nonprofit can produce that might be of help to its volunteers and supporters to better understand how to be effective lobbyists and ambassadors, to deal with the press, to help solicit donations and recruit other supporters, and to feel empowered, competent, and motivated. But the kit shouldn't contain so much material as to discourage its use.

Board of director resolutions: Resolutions by the board of directors of any organization (from organizational members of the coalition to stakeholder organizations or other supportive groups), officially adopted, urging support for the coalition's position on any given issue can demonstrate support of the community and that of the elected official's district constituent. Obviously, the larger and more powerful the organization, the more weight that will be accorded to an official act by its board. The aggregate total number of organizations issuing such resolutions may also carry weight. Resolutions by prestigious boards may also help to convince other boards to follow suit, thus promoting unity and the sense of community. As this is one of many "simple" devices that can take a protracted period of time to finalize, it is best to begin obtaining resolutions, proclamations, signed petitions, and so on, as soon as is reasonably possible during a given campaign, and these deadlines are yet another reason why initial strategic planning is so important at the outset. Often, the nonprofit has very little time to complete its tasks, particularly during a specific legislative campaign.

Proclamations: Proclamations are like manifestos but are generally issued by official government bodies or the boards of directors of single institutions/organizations. Generally they begin with one or more "Whereas . . . ," which are declarative statements about a situation or the benefits of a nonprofit mission, program, services, and so on, followed by a "Now, therefore . . . ," which is a declarative endorsement or call to action, followed by the authorizing signature of the body. Proclamations from city councils can influence state legislatures and other bodies. Proclamations are potentially good media hooks and help to motivate the coalition field by demonstrating official support.

Petitions: Nothing is more a part of civic action in America than the citizen petition seeking action or redress from the government. Petitions are very basic: "We the undersigned request/demand that . . . (<u>fill in the blank</u>)." They can be this simple or they can add a list of items wanted. The opening statement should be printed at the top of each page, and pages should be numbered. Space should be provided for the printed name and signature line, address, city/zip (telephone numbers or e-mail addresses are optional, but requirement of their inclusion may discourage some potential signatories). Petitions created to influence one particular legislator should include only names and signatures of people residing in the official's district.

Petitions can be circulated for signatures at events, meetings, rallies, retail outlets, and door to door, depending on the availability of volunteers. Volunteers should be trained so that they can answer questions and provide background materials, and this training will likely increase the percentage of valid signatures. Volunteers need to be polite, nonaggressive (but not shy), dressed neatly and be clean and smile a lot. This is a job for people who generally like people and have no problem with approaching strangers.

E-mail petitions obviously have the advantage of wider possible participation and do not need volunteers to collect the signatures, but there is also a larger percentage of invalid names, and it is harder to ensure that signatories are within defined districts (should this be an objective). Otherwise the protocol is essentially the same: the opening statement followed by entry of the individual's name and other information. People are asked to forward the petition to others, and when the signatures reach a predetermined arbitrary number—hypothetically fifty or one hundred—the individual who has made the last entry is asked to forward the petition back to a central e-mail for collection, tallying, and so on. Petitions can be posted on a large number of websites, and word can be spread in any number of ways—from flyers, to newsletters, to announcements, and so on. Finished petitions are forwarded to target decision makers both electronically and in printed, hard copies. E-mail petitions may not be regarded highly by politicians who may perceive them as less valid than traditional petitions, but this may change over time.

Manifestos: Manifestos are like petitions, but they are designed to launch a campaign by stating the central beliefs and tenets of the coalition regarding the issue, followed by a declaration of support for certain principles or specific calls to action. The manifesto is subscribed to and endorsed and signed by as many organizational coalition members and stakeholder groups as possible. Printing the manifesto on quality paper with a fancy border and font adds to its cachet. The manifesto can be sent to decision makers, posted on websites, and distributed to media as an angle of a news story about the lobbying effort. It can also be used to recruit additional supporters who can adopt or endorse the original manifesto.

Blue Ribbon Commissions: It is easy enough for the nonprofit to create its own Blue Ribbon Commission to study the issue at hand and come up with recommendations favoring its position. The nonprofit can use the goodwill and networks of its coalition members to recruit people with name recognition and in prominent positions within the community to serve on the body, and those whose credentials add expertise and thus credibility to the commission. The addition of a celebrity, if the nonprofit can identify and recruit one, increases the chances of media coverage. The nonprofit could invite a politician to chair or cochair the effort, and hold one or more public meetings and try to muster a good audience turnout. It should notify the press and arrange for a variety of people to testify about the various ways the coalition's position benefits the community. It can publish the commission report at the end of its proceedings, and stage a press conference or other media event to solicit media coverage. The nonprofit could distribute the findings through its website and by hardcopies to community leaders, elected officials, the media, and others.

Candidate questionnaires: Asking candidates their positions on issues of relevance to the nonprofit during election years can be valuable in assessing what needs to be done in a lobbying effort to secure individual officeholder's support and to get candidates to focus on the needs of the nonprofit. If the nonprofit is seeking to choose between candidates for its endorsement and support, this mechanism can help persuade candidates to consider the nonprofit's viewpoint. Nonprofits are required to treat all candidates for office equally, without favoritism, and thus identical questionnaires should be sent to all candidates for a given office. Likewise, if one candidate is invited to make a presentation to the nonprofit, then all the candidates should be invited. Endorsement must comply with legal restrictions (see discussion on 501c(3) legal questions).

Voting histories/legislator report cards: Compiling the voting histories on legislation affecting a nonprofit field can identify who has and who hasn't been supportive, and this, in turn, can help to assess who needs to be targeted and who needs to be thanked. The full voting records on all the issues important to a given field (e.g., the arts, the environment, seniors, education) can be compared against each other or some external criteria and "grades" can be given (numerical or letter) to indicate the rating (and perhaps ranking) of a given legislator's support of the nonprofit. A common means of doing this is to take a legislator's votes over the course of a complete legislative session in the period being used for the grading. Again, there may be legal rules governing how the nonprofit goes about compiling the report cards to ensure fairness in the process.

Candidate forums: Inviting all candidates for an office to appear at a forum to field questions or discuss various issues of relevance to the nonprofit or its field can yield increased support by the candidates and activity by the membership (as individuals) in support of, or opposition to, a candidate. If some candidates attend and some refuse the invitation, this alone can tell much about the candidate's support or lack thereof. All candidates must be invited to comply with governing rules in this area.

Note: Candidate questionnaires, forums, and report cards are all permissible lobbying tools, but there are governing rules requiring 501 nonprofits to treat all candidates equally. Thus, for example, it may be necessary to send questionnaires to *all* candidates. The nonprofit should check the regulations before employing these devices.

CHAPTER 8

POSTMORTEM

When a specific legislative or another advocacy and/or lobby campaign is over, whether or not the objective was achieved, it is wise, after a brief period to gain perspective (two weeks to a month, not longer), to look back and do an evaluation/analysis of what worked and what didn't, where were the strengths, where were the weaknesses, where were the missed opportunities, and how the organization/coalition can capitalize on these opportunities in the future. Losses and defeats should be analyzed with a resolve to succeed next time (there will always be a next time). Lobbying is a process employed over time.

Evaluation sheets should be distributed among the various component parts of the advocacy and/or lobbying efforts, including team captains, volunteers, board members, staff, paid lobbyists, public relations and other firms (if applicable), and the contact people in the supporting stakeholder groups. Interviewing the specific elected officials the coalition was tying to influence, particularly if the effort was unsuccessful, so as to learn from them why they think it failed, can be very enlightening. The feedback should be tallied and then an open meeting held to analyze the results and to make strategic recommendations as to improvement in the future. The final conclusions and report should be distributed to the entire organization, and whatever steps might be taken to improve the capacity of the organization/coalition to be better lobbyists should be implemented as soon as possible.

Victories should be celebrated with formal mechanisms to thank supporters—internal and external. Supporters can be presented with framed certificates of commendation or appreciation at an awards lunch or dinner, or at some other kind of event. Even in defeat, the team should be thanked, perhaps more profusely than if the team was celebrating a victory. If the effort was particularly long and difficult, and it strained relationships, these "fences" need to be mended as quickly as possible. Acrimony cannot be allowed to fester, and recriminations should not be allowed to develop. The best way to deal with problems is to recognize them at once—out in the open—and resolve to address their root causes.

This process is important in retaining involvement in the effort once a specific objective has been realized or lost. It is exponentially more work to recreate the apparatus from the ground up each time a new challenge arises. Improvement is easier if the core group continues to operate between major battles. After a major campaign it is normal for a percentage of the nonprofit team members to drop out, and they must be replaced sooner rather than later. Ongoing growth and expansion help to keep people motivated, involved, optimistic, and committed, and make it easier to raise funds. Finally, the constancy of the effort helps to change the culture of the organization/field and prepare it to embrace the function of lobbying for the long haul. The nonprofit will be surprised how things improve and change, and how the power of its organization is increased when the culture changes and adapts to accept the function of advocacy as part of day-to-day business operations.

The more nonprofits can learn about how to be effective, the more effective they can become. Advocacy and/or lobbying is an ongoing, never-ending function, and the successful players are those who hone their skills, expand their networks, learn from their mistakes, and exploit their strengths—they will reap the rewards in comparison with those who do not, and they will be better able to defend themselves when necessary and get the support they seek when they need it.

DEALING WITH DEFEAT

No matter how strong the nonprofit, how deep its pockets, how righteous its cause, how substantive its public support, the group will not win every victory despite its very best efforts. It must remember that a governmental affairs effort needs to have a long-term perspective. Important campaigns are better addressed if an advocacy and/or lobbying strategy has long been established. Thus, when the nonprofit loses a campaign, it must put this loss in perspective and ensure that its reactions to one defeat do not set it up for other defeats. Specifically, the nonprofit

- must not personalize the defeat to elected officials, particularly ones whose support it has had in the past or will need in the future
- must ensure that the defeat does not cause irreparable harm to its grassroots/ volunteer effort by the defeat negatively impacting morale and motivation of the group's base
- must ensure that the defeat is not perceived as anything more than a setback in one battle in a long war, so as to not damage its fund-raising ability or public image
- must assess why it lost, and what it can do to improve its ability to win, as discussed above

Attention to these details by anticipating the effects of a political defeat will help the nonprofit to prepare its base for this eventuality and ensure that its structure is not unnecessarily damaged. If the structure is damaged, the nonprofit must take whatever steps are required for immediate repair, so that the group is ready for the next encounter.

EVALUATION

Post-mortem evaluation should include a survey instrument focusing on the various component functions of the lobbying machinery: administration, organization, fund-raising, communications, research, volunteer/grassroots organization, media relations, the lobbying effort, and the intangibles of motivation, image, and leadership. The evaluation should be done as soon as possible after the end of a specific campaign or election, when memories are fresh.

Survey instruments should be easy to complete so as to maximize the responses. Using some sort of rankings or ratings scale, asking people to evaluate the effectiveness or smooth operation of various functions, or employing "yes/no" questions so people can "check" boxes, will increase people's willingness to respond. The nonprofit should always leave room on a form for people to register their thoughts and provide more substantive answers—Did the campaign work? How can it be improved, and what are ideas for its improvement? Where was it inadequate? Why didn't it work?

Surveys, in hard copy, can be distributed through the hierarchy of the organization (a smaller font should be used and the number of pages kept to a minimum, as a multipage survey will be perceived as too much work to complete). Putting the evaluation forms on the nonprofit's website or sending them by e-mail (directly to a sample group, using one of the inexpensive and very good online survey providers such as Survey Monkey) *is the preferable mode* as it simplifies the task for the respondents and organizes the data for the nonprofit. Directors, managers, captains, and other titular heads of various functions of the effort should help in supervising the evaluation process and in urging response participation, and should provide their own summary impressions and thoughts on their specific areas of oversight.

Focus groups of those involved on different levels of the advocacy campaign are another approach to learning from the experience. If feasible, the nonprofit should bring together the focus groups to facilitate a deeper discussion; but if this isn't possible, an interaction between these groups can be convened online or through a telephone conference. Focus groups should be composed of randomly selected individuals from a pool representing a cross-section of all of the areas of the lobbying machine, with eight to ten participants per group. The pool should include age, gender, multicultural, geographical, and other categories of participant profiles, approximating the composition of the whole group. An average focus group session will last between one and two hours. The purpose is to draw out of the participants specific impressions of what was right and what was wrong with the structure and organization of the effort, the strategy and tactics employed, the management of the people, the making of the case, the communications, and any other factor that might provide insight into what can be improved. It is important to note that there may be very little that gets classified as "wrong" or that might have been done differently—some contests are virtually impossible to win.

One-on-one interviews with key legislators (if they are willing), principals of retained outside firms, media people, and others will provide context and deeper insights after the fact. These interviews should normally be shared with the wider rank and file so as to both establish operational principles and involve the field in shaping the organization over time.

Public-opinion sampling, if money is available, may be educational and of value to ascertain the general public's familiarity with the issues of the nonprofit's campaign and its coalition's efforts. The nonprofit can do this itself using the online services of firms such as Survey Monkey, or by organizing its own focus groups, but this involves time-consuming legwork in getting the public to participate. Lastly, those most directly involved in running the campaign—the key staff—should gather together to offer their own insights into what went right, what went wrong, and how the coalition should proceed with its mission?

Finally, the nonprofit should remember the adage, "If ain't broke, don't fix it." If the advocacy coalition has established a solid foundation, and each of the key area functions is working, it shouldn't tinker too much with the coalition's machinery. The most important goal is to keep the machinery working; refinement comes over time and in small ways. If the nonprofit can make any aspect of the effort better, it should do so, but the group should wait until it has given due thought to what it wants to do, if there is no glaring problem or crisis. If the nonprofit has established a solid foundation, it will have the luxury of adapting to the changing circumstances in the ongoing refinement of the apparatus. The group should change what it can for the better, as soon as it can; but it shouldn't expect to implement wholesale changes overnight. And whatever it does, *it shouldn't quit!*

BIBLIOGRAPHY

NOTE: INTERNET LINKS

As of the date of publication, there are some fairly comprehensive bibliographies for nonprofit advocacy and lobbying issues on the Urban Institute website (www.urban.org/advocacyresearch) and on a site maintained by John McNutt (www.policymagic.org/general). The Nonprofit Advocacy Project of the Alliance for Justice has an outstanding one-stop website with resources for nonprofit advocacy (www.afg.org/nonprofit), and monitors and updates the legal requirements for nonprofit advocacy and lobbying on a frequent basis. The Charity Lobbying in the Public Interest website is also a good source of advocacy and lobbying information (www.clpi.org). And the opensecrets.org website (www.opensecrets.org) is a treasure trove of data on who contributes, how much, and to which candidates.

In the future, a search for "advocacy/lobbying—bibliography and resources" is likely to turn up many useful and relevant sites.

The following list of works relevant to the topic is but a sampling, and is by no means comprehensive or exhaustive.

Alderson, George, and Everett Sentman. *How You Can Influence Congress: The Complete Handbook for the Citizen Lobbyist.* New York: E. P. Dutton, 1979.

Alinsky, Saul. *Reveille for Radicals.* Chicago: University of Chicago Press, 1946.

Avner, Marcia. *The Lobbying & Advocacy Handbook for Nonprofit Organizations.* Wilder Publishing Center, Saint Paul, Minnesota, 2002.

Cigler, Allan J., and Burdett A. Loomis. *Interest Group Politics.* 4th ed. Washington, D.C.: Congressional Quarterly Press, 1995.

Domhoff, G. William. *Who Rules America: Power & Politics.* McGraw Hill, 2002.

Domhoff, G. William, and Thomas R. *Power Elites and Organizations.* Newbury Park, Beverly Hills, London, New Delhi: Sage Publications, 1987.

Drew, Elizabeth. *Politics and Money: The New Road to Corruption.* New York: Macmillan, 1983.

———. *Whatever It Takes: The Real Struggle for Political Power in America.* New York: Viking, 1997.

Etzioni, Amitai. *New Communitarian Thinking: Persons, Virtues, Institutions and Communities.* Charlottesville: University of Virginia Press, 1995.

Guyer, Robert. *Guide to State Legislative Lobbying.* Rev. ed. Engineering the Law, Inc., 2003. www.lobbyschool.com

Hopkins, Bruce. *Law of Tax Exempt Organizations.* Indianapolis, IN: Wiley, 2006.

Kingsley, Elizabeth, Gail Harmon, John Pomeranz, and Kay Guinane. *E-Advocacy for Nonprofits: The Law of Lobbying and Election-Related Activity on the Net.* Washington, D.C.: Alliance for Justice, 2000.

Lees-Marshment, J. "Marketing Good Works: New Trends in How Interest Groups Recruit Supporters." *Journal of Public Affairs*, 3, no. 4 (2003): 358–369.

Nownes, Anthony J., and Allan J. Cigler. "Public Interest Groups and the Road to Survival." *Policy*, 27, no. 3 (Spring 1995): 379–404.

Sabato, Larry and Glenn R. Simpson. *Dirty Little Secrets: The Persistence of Corruption in American Politics*. New York: Times Books, 1996.

Salamon, Lester M. *The State of Nonprofit America*. Baltimore: Urban Institute Press, 2003.

Sen, Rinku. *Stir It Up: Lessons in Community Organizing and Advocacy*. Indianapolis, IN: Wiley, 2003.

Smucker, Bob. *Nonprofit Lobbying Guide: Advocating Your Cause and Getting Results*. San Francisco, CA: Jossey-Bass, 1991.

———. *The Non Profit Lobbying Guide*. Washington, D.C.: Independent Sector, 1999.

Wildavsky, Aaron, and Naomi Caiden. *The New Politics of the Budgetary Process*. 5th ed. New York: Longman Classics Series, 2003.

Wolpe, Bruce C., and Bertram J. Levine. *Lobbying Congress: How the System Works*. 2nd ed. Washington, D.C.: Congressional Quarterly Press, 1996.

INDEX

CPSIA information can be obtained at www.ICGtesting.com
Printed in the USA
LVOW072152040613

337010LV00012B/270/P